AUSTRALIAN
POLTERGEIST

TONY HEALY & PAUL CROPPER

AUSTRALIAN POLTERGEIST

Strange Nation
Sydney, Australia

First published in 2014 by Strange Nation

ISBN 978-1-921134-35-7 (digital)
ISBN 978-1-921134-34-0 (print)

All rights reserved. Without limiting the rights under copyright below, no part of this publication shall be reproduced, stored in or introduced into a retrieval system, or transmitted in any form or by any means (electronic, mechanical, photocopying, recording or otherwise), without the prior permission of the copyright holders.

The moral rights of the authors have been asserted.

Copyright © Tony Healy and Paul Cropper 2014

Cataloguing-in-publication data is available from the National Library of Australia

Text and cover design, and typesetting by Xou Creative, www.xoucreative.com.au

This book is dedicated to veteran investigator
of the unexplained, Guy Lyon Playfair, to the late
Colin Wilson, and to all the other men and women who
have, throughout the centuries, wrestled with
the maddening mystery of the poltergeist.

The authors wish to advise indigenous readers that the book contains
the names and images of some deceased Aboriginal people.

BY THE SAME AUTHORS

Out of the Shadows: Mystery Animals of Australia
Pan Macmillan/Ironbark, 1994

The Yowie: In Search of Australia's Bigfoot
Anomalist Books, 2006

CONTENTS

Introduction 1

Chapter One: Weird Territory: The Humpty Doo Poltergeist 9
Chapter Two: A serial pest: The Mayanup Poltergeist 56
Chapter Three: A Ghost in the Machine 89
Chapter Four: "Caressa": Sex and the Supernatural 101
Chapter Five: The Vengeful Spook of Cannibal Creek 108
Chapter Six: The San Remo Polt 113
Chapter Seven: "Ghostly Missiles": The Cooyal Case 123
Chapter Eight: The Gordon Street Polt 128
Chapter Nine: "The Nice Old Man" of Alice Springs 132
Chapter Ten: "The Guyra Ghost" 136
Chapter Eleven: Spookiest of all: The Coalbaggie Bogey 158
Chapter Twelve: A Catalogue of Cases, 1845–1998 167
Chapter Thirteen: Rapping it up 255

Appendix A: Three Asian Fire Polts 261
Appendix B: Wild talents 277
Appendix C: Wild ideas 280

Bibliography 293
Index 295

INTRODUCTION

"It really *is* happening"

A sudden, sharp clatter, like a flurry of hail on the corrugated iron roof, caused Paul, in the kitchen below, to glance upwards. As he did so, a dozen grey pebbles cascaded onto the linoleum at his feet. It was as if they'd passed straight through both roof and ceiling without leaving a mark. Kirsty and Jill, standing just in front of him, looked up, laughed wearily and exclaimed, "Well – here we go again!"

For the next five days we dodged pebbles, knives, chunks of broken glass and a variety of other objects that seemed to appear out of nowhere, dropping or flying horizontally, banging into walls and floors both inside and outside the weirdly beleaguered dwelling.

One day Frank Robson, a *Sydney Morning Herald* journalist who witnessed many of those seemingly inexplicable events, turned to us and said, "I just hope that when I write about this I have the guts to tell the truth". Turning in his hand an object that had fallen, seemingly out of thin air, a few minutes earlier, he spoke again: "It really *is* happening, isn't it?"

It certainly was: the notorious Humpty Doo poltergeist episode of 1998 was in full swing.

What is a poltergeist?

"Poltergeist" is an old German term meaning "noisy spirit", and poltergeist episodes are those in which certain locations, families or individuals are said to be plagued by invisible forces that hurl furniture, crockery and other articles around, produce wall-shaking thumps and drop showers of stones both indoors and out. The inexplicable disappearance and reappearance of objects is frequently mentioned, and, in the modern era, electrical appliances are said to malfunction.

Less commonly, pockets of frigid air, nasty, scrawled messages, sudden outbreaks of fire and inexplicable oozings of fluid are reported. Although there is often a distinctly mischievous – and sometimes downright sinister – flavour to the proceedings, it is frequently noted that no matter how many dangerous objects are hurled around, people are rarely struck, and serious injury is extremely rare. It is often remarked that polts seem resistant to exorcism and that religious ritual aggravates rather than moderates their behaviour.

The episodes usually last from a couple of weeks to a couple of months.

An age-old story

Poltergeist events have been reported in virtually every part of the world for hundreds of years. In *The Story of the Poltergeist down the Centuries* (1953), Hereward Carrington and Nandor Fodor presented 375 cases dating from 355 A.D. to 1949. The range of weird phenomena detailed in those accounts is strikingly similar to what has been observed during apparent poltergeist episodes in Australia.

The following story, which Carrington and Fodor found in the *Life of St. Godric* by Herbert Thurston, the first Norman abbot of Glastonbury, is a good example. Dating from about 1170, it contains three ingredients – showers of stones, levitation of household objects and supernatural harassment of a hapless human – that have cropped up time and again in this country:

His hermitage was bombarded with showers of stones, and the Poltergeist threw at him the box in which he kept his alter beads; [it] took the horn which contained the wine he needed for Mass and poured it over his head; and ended by pelting him with almost every movable thing that his poor cell contained.

A spirited debate

There has been disagreement as to whether poltergeist episodes are different from "ordinary" ghostly events. In an effort to keep things in some kind of order, some psychical researchers reserve the term "haunting" for episodes that feature "normal" ghostly phenomena – apparitions, footsteps, disembodied voices, etc. – and which don't involve physical phenomena, such as showers of stones, levitation of furniture and the shattering of crockery.

There are several apparent differences between ghostly hauntings and polt episodes:

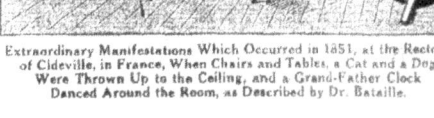

Extraordinary Manifestations Which Occurred in 1851, at the Rectory of Cideville, in France, When Chairs and Tables, a Cat and a Dog Were Thrown Up to the Ceiling, and a Grand-Father Clock Danced Around the Room, as Described by Dr. Bataille.

- Hauntings sometimes endure for decades or even centuries, whereas polt events rarely last for more than two years; usually, in fact, they persist for no longer than two or three months.
- Apparitions of people (and sometimes animals) are frequently seen during hauntings.
- While "ordinary" ghosts often seem oblivious, or at least indifferent to, the presence of mere mortals, poltergeists seem to delight in annoying us.
- Hauntings are normally linked to a particular building or to a location, such as a particular stretch of road, whereas polts are usually focused on a particular person or family. As we will show, some Australian polts, having latched onto an individual or family, have followed them from place to place. Our most persistent polt, which began its activities near Mayanup, WA, in 1956, followed people to three other locations many kilometres from the original site.

But as the late, great, psychical investigator Colin Wilson pointed out, some apparent polt cases contain details normally associated with "ordinary" ghostly hauntings, and some "ordinary" hauntings include poltergeist characteristics. He documented several cases that began as, apparently, classic polt cases but which changed over time to become almost entirely "normal" ghostly hauntings – and vice-versa. This has occurred in a few of our Australian cases.

So the line that divides poltergeist episodes and "ordinary" ghostly hauntings seems to be, at times, rather thin.

Are the meanies genies?

For most of recorded history, virtually everyone who experienced or chronicled poltergeist events believed that hobgoblins, demons, the devil himself or the restless spirits of recently deceased persons were causing the apparently supernatural mayhem. In many parts of Africa and Asia virtually all polt activity is still explained that way. Throughout the Muslim world, from the Middle East and North Africa to Afghanistan, Pakistan, Malaysia and Indonesia, the phenomena is commonly attributed to invisible entities known as *djinn* (*djinn* is the plural form, the singular is *djinni* – or genie). For more about *djinn* lore, see Appendix A.

Even in the "enlightened", secular, "western" world of today, nearly all residents of polt-plagued dwellings initially assume they are being pestered by the disembodied spirit of a recently-deceased relative or former resident.

Troubled teens – or slippery spooks?

It has been noted time and again that polt episodes usually involve a particular family and their residence and that the phenomena seems focused on one person, often an adolescent, and usually a girl. The child is often said to be unhappy and stressed, sometimes because of the recent death of a loved one, because she has been forced to live with a relative or employer she doesn't like, or for other reasons.

Some researchers suggest that the poltergeist phenomenon doesn't involve disembodied spirits of any kind. It is, they say, the result of psychokinesis ("mind over matter") generated unconsciously by the angst-ridden adolescents at the centre of the action. Because the effect is produced intermittently and unwittingly, it is referred to as recurrent spontaneous psychokinesis, or RSPK.

Others suggest that while a highly stressed adolescent (or in some cases adult) is usually involved, and that the individual may have some latent psychic ability, the phenomena is indeed produced by disembodied spirits. They suggest that spirits need to "feed off" psychic energy produced by the adolescents' angst to perform their paranormal tricks. Opinions differ as to whether the hypothetical disembodied spirits are the ghosts of deceased mortals or something else – something, perhaps, from another dimension or astral plane.

As we will show, a significant number of Australian polt episodes *have* occurred soon after someone's (usually premature) death, and on some occasions the pattern of activity strongly suggests the polt is the spirit of that person. Many other cases, however, contain no reference at all to recent deaths, premature or otherwise, and one or two cases seem to involve an invisible, mischievous force that "inhabits" a particular spot in the forest or countryside (e.g. Cases 11 and 26).

Guy Lyon Playfair, long-time member of the Society for Psychical Research and author of books on a wide range of strange phenomena, cheerfully admits that after several decades of investigating poltergeist episodes, he is still a long way from understanding exactly how or why they occur. He remains open to any reasonable theory, including the possibility that once an opening has been created to (for want of a better term) "the Other Side" by an anguished adolescent or by some other means, any number of different denizens of the spirit world, mischievous, benign, or merely curious, might "queue up" to take advantage of it.

While it is interesting – and fun – to bounce that, and other, ideas around, the more we learn about the strange field of poltergeistery, where uncertainty is the name of the game, the less inclined we are to engrave any one theory in stone. Greater minds than ours have wrestled with the problem and failed to pin down the slippery spooks, so in this volume we'll confine ourselves, by and large, to chronicling every known Australian polt episode and to pointing out unusual details that might shine new light on the mystery.

Regardless of how the phenomena are produced, to be the focus of a poltergeist's attention can be extremely frightening. Several people in our Australian files were severely traumatised by the experience. One of the few good things about polts, however, is that they very rarely cause physical injury. That may not be out of the goodness of their twisted little hearts, but it is nevertheless true.

The upside

There is, from our perspective at least, another good thing about polts: they are the most accessible of spooks, in that they're occasionally willing to turn on displays of their strange powers for the entertainment of all and sundry. So it is sometimes possible for researchers to go to a polt-infested building and actually see objects fly, not only at night but also in broad daylight. That's great, but as we and many other investigators have been frustrated to discover, there's a catch: the objects polts throw, though easy enough to *see*, are almost bloody impossible to photograph in flight!

A plethora of polts

Another "upside" is that poltergeist episodes seem to be by far the most common type of paranormal event. In *Beyond The Occult* Colin Wilson went so far as to suggest that "… at any given moment there are probably thousands of them going on all over the world and there is likely to be one going on within a dozen miles of where you are now reading this book."[1]

While some readers might find that notion difficult to accept, the number of Australian cases we've discovered and the plethora of foreign cases that come to us through the internet suggest that Wilson wasn't all that far off the mark.

---

1   Colin Wilson, *Beyond The Occult*, p. 235.

Folklore and flakelore

Folklorists and sociologists tend to treat the poltergeist phenomenon as myth or as some kind of social construct with nothing real at its centre. Those who "explain away" the mystery in that manner are, we believe, either ignorant of the facts or simply too frightened to stick their necks out and admit there might be something genuinely supernatural involved.

That being said, we *have* noted folkloric elements in a few of our older Australian cases and (particularly) in medieval European episodes, where people attempted to categorise and deal with the frightening events in accordance with the religious and folk beliefs of the time. Folkloric and religious elements still feature prominently in reportage of contemporary Middle Eastern, African and Asian polt episodes.

But while a few of our Australian cases do contain folkloric elements, our own experience suggests there is a great deal at the centre of the poltergeist phenomenon that simply cannot be written off as myth. After reading just a few of our collected cases most open minded readers will, we hope, be inclined to agree with us.

Sceptics

When told of a poltergeist event in a particular locality a common jocular response by people unfamiliar with the phenomenon is that "there must be some pretty strong grog up that way". To which we usually reply that if polt episodes were merely the result of excessive alcohol consumption, every second house in Australia would have one – and the Northern Territory would be world poltergeist HQ!

Dictionaries contain many different definitions of "scepticism", but one that would probably satisfy most people is as follows: "A critical attitude toward any theory, statement, experiment or phenomenon, doubting the certainty of all things until adequate proof has been produced". Open-minded scepticism is a very good thing; it is a vital part of the scientific method and the world would be in a terrible mess without it.

But scepticism needs to be not only open-minded, but also *informed*. We believe that most people who express scepticism about poltergeists are simply ignorant of the facts. Others, because of a deeply ingrained materialist world view, simply *cannot* believe in such things. To them the suggestion that invisible forces could throw physical objects around is just too silly for words – so they won't deign to even glance at the data. We are quite sure that there are yet others, including scientists, who suspect – or in some cases know damn well – that some polt phenomena is genuine but who, fearing ridicule or damage to their careers, avoid the subject like the plague.

Sceptical about skeptics

In recent years there has emerged a breed of very outspoken sceptics who, concerned that western society is in danger of sliding back into the Dark Ages, frequently take the offensive against creationism, astrology, water divining and anything else they consider a product of credulous, anti-scientific thinking. To distinguish themselves from less militant, home-and-garden sceptics, they have adopted the American spelling of the word – "skeptics" with a K.

It is frustrating but, we suppose, inevitable that journalists, in an effort to add balance to their occasional articles about poltergeists, frequently seek out such confirmed sceptics (who have usually never set foot in a polt-plagued building) and quote their ill-considered remarks.

While we understand – and, in fact, share – many of their concerns about anti-scientific thinking, we think that some of the more vocal skeptics don't, themselves, behave in a particularly scientific way. To us, the worst of them seem nothing more than loud-mouthed debunkers. Having decided long ago that certain things, like poltergeists, couldn't possibly exist, they don't attempt to really explain them; instead, they merely "explain them away".

Immediately after our on-the-spot investigation of the Humpty Doo poltergeist episode we contacted the Sydney branch of Australian Skeptics, offering to speak at one of their gatherings. They weren't in the least interested. Liz Fleming, who was the focus of an amazing range of polt phenomena during the "Caressa" case of the 1990s, received a similar rebuff from Canberra Skeptics.

In 35 years of research in several different countries and in every Australian state and territory, during which we have published two books and numerous articles about strange phenomena, and spoken frequently on radio and television, we have *never once* been contacted by a professed sceptic wishing to discuss any aspect of the unexplained.

We are, therefore, rather sceptical about militant skeptics. To paraphrase one of Jack Nicholson's most memorable lines: "The truth? They can't *handle* the truth!"

In fact, we like to think that we approach each case of supposed paranormal activity with at least a degree of healthy scepticism. We have identified quite a few Australian cases as probable hoaxes and several others as definitely bogus. In fairness to mildly sceptical readers – and to the militant skeptics – we have included all of those possible or proven hoaxes in our Catalogue of Cases (Chapter Twelve).

The rating system we use throughout the book begins at zero for apparent or proven hoaxes and ranges from half a star – for questionable or very poorly documented cases – through to five stars for our very best case, the Mayanup episode of 1955–57. With only two exceptions, we have reserved the four and five-star rating for very well documented cases where we were able to interview the eyewitnesses or in which we had some other personal involvement. Readers will make up their own minds, but we believe that many of the episodes outlined in the following pages involved genuine polt activity.

The great majority of eyewitnesses we've interviewed, including those who were apparently the focus of polt episodes, impressed us as being very sincere. Many found their experiences extremely stressful; none seemed interested in publicity or financial gain. It was clear they simply appreciated the opportunity of talking to someone who was prepared to listen.

The aim of this book

Having gathered the following material, often from very obscure sources, over the course of many years, our primary aim is to ensure that it doesn't become scattered and lost to posterity.

Several collections of Australian ghost stories have been published but this is the first book devoted entirely to Australian poltergeists. While we believe it will become a useful resource for ghost hunters, social scientists, folklorists and psychologists, we hope that it will also be of interest to a wide range of other people. Who, after all, doesn't enjoy a mystery – particularly one that's a little scary?

No extraordinary evidence

Although we present some interesting infra-red photographs that constitute strong evidence for the reality of the phenomenon, most of the data in this book consists of testimonial evidence: the statements of eyewitnesses. But such testimony, fascinating as it may be, falls short of proving poltergeists exist.

Extraordinary claims, as the saying goes, require extraordinary evidence, so although we present a huge amount of material that strongly suggests the polt phenomenon really does occur, we certainly don't claim to have *proven* that it does. We hope, rather, to simply persuade the reader that the subject is worthy of serious attention.

We believe that most people will be struck by the remarkable uniformity of reported polt activity from region to region over the course of 150 years and by the many ways in which Australian cases closely resemble obscure foreign cases dating back several centuries.

We're confident that any intelligent, fair-minded person who reads through our material, case by case, will admit that, at the very least, the poltergeist phenomenon can't be dismissed out of hand. And – who knows – even some card-carrying members of Australian Skeptics, supposing they design to actually open the book, may find the scales slowly falling from their eyes.

Anyone who thinks the poltergeist phenomenon is just a joke is ignorant of the facts – it's as simple as that.

These are the facts as we know them.

CHAPTER ONE

Weird Territory: The Humpty Doo Poltergeist

Northern Territory, 1998. Rating: ★★★★½

It was a dark and stormy night. Rain was holding off for the moment, but huge, black clouds were rolling and a dramatic lightning display was filling the steamy tropic sky with sound and fury. The residents of 90 McMinns Drive, Humpty Doo, sat on their patio, chilled beers at hand, enjoying the show. There were two young couples, Andrew and Kirsty Agius, Dave Clark, his partner Jill Summerville, plus their mate Doug Murphy. All five were in their late twenties to early thirties. Inside the house, fast asleep, was Kirsty and Andrew's 10-month-old daughter Jasmine.

As Nature's magnificent light show crashed and flashed in the sky above, strange, decidedly *unnatural* things started to happen.

When small pebbles began flicking out of the shadows and landing in their midst the group assumed that someone had sneaked onto their rented two-hectare (five acre) property to play a silly joke. But when the prankster failed to respond to their shouts and was not discovered in repeated searches of the grounds, they tired of the situation and moved inside – *only to have the pebbles follow them.*

90 McMinns Drive. (Healy/Cropper)

In classic poltergeist style, showers of the centimetre-wide stones – all apparently lifted from their 70-metre-long gravel driveway – landed on floors, tables, beds and heads after apparently materialising just under the ceiling. Though the ground outside was saturated, all the pebbles that fell indoors were bone-dry and distinctly warm to the touch. Hardly believing their senses, and being practical people, one of the first things the housemates did was to fetch a ladder to check if there was something amiss in the loft. As soon as they opened the ceiling manhole, however, a brisk shower of stones fell upon their upturned faces. Later that night, to their increasing dismay, knives, small batteries, spanners, shards of broken glass and other objects began to drop or to hurtle across rooms.

Over the next couple of days the polt – they soon realised that's what it had to be – cranked up the level of its vandalism, causing serious damage; a CD player was thrown to the floor and destroyed, windows and glass cabinet doors were smashed by ashtrays and other flying objects.

Things came to a head one Saturday night when it seemed their persecutor meant to actually drive them from the house: littering the floor with a blizzard of stones, wrenching appliances from shelves, upturning mattresses and – creepiest of all – making sinister scraping noises *inside* the internal walls. The events of that long night were almost too much for Jill and Kirsty. "It completely freaked us out; it was like something was actually inside the walls right next to us. We couldn't sleep; we were crying. We would have left the house but we had nowhere else to go."

Although the residents weren't particularly religious they were now willing to try anything to get rid of the paranormal pest. So – when you've got a polt problem, who ya gonna call?

Left: Kirsty, Andrew and Jasmine. Right: Kirsty, Jill, Murph and friend. (Healy/Cropper)

Three gutsy priests

The first thing Father Stephen de Souza of Darwin's St Mary's Cathedral did when he arrived was to look through the entire house. In the kitchen he "… noticed a microwave with a steak knife on top. As I walked away, one of [the residents] called 'Father!'"

Turning, he saw the knife flying straight at him. There was nobody in a position to have thrown it.[2] There was no time to jump out of the way but when it was about half a metre from his chest it stopped, "just as though it had hit something" and fell at his feet.

The Jesuit was unfazed. He had seen it all before. In his native India he'd been called upon to deal with several similar infestations. His "take" on the situation was that a restless spirit may have been drawn to the house, possibly because one of the occupants was, without being aware of it, a natural medium. Using age-old Catholic ritual he attempted to "bind" the spirit and reassured the tenants that it was very unlikely to physically injure anyone. He admitted, however, that in his experience prayer rarely caused a poltergeist to cease its activities. The imp would go away when it was good and ready, or, if its nasty tricks were indeed linked to someone in the house who was an unconscious medium, it might follow that person when they moved to a new residence.

Father Stephen's prayers gave the household a brief respite; the polt kept its nasty little head down for three days but then, just as the residents were hoping it was all over, the craziness started again.

Next to try popping the polt was Humpty Doo's parish priest, Father Tom English. During the first of four visits he saw several objects flying in ways that seemed to defy explanation. The polt, he said, "doesn't follow the laws of physics".[3] A pistol cartridge fell from nowhere to land at his feet, and other things "… crashed against walls … they'd

---

2   Frank Robson, "Humpty Boo!", *Sydney Morning Herald, Good Weekend*, 13 June 1998.
3   *Litchfield Times*, 2 April 1998.

"Everything went berserk": Father Tom. (Max Anderson)

just fly out of a room that nobody [was] in, for instance. Outside, things came crashing down near us"[4] Although inexperienced in such matters he gamely blessed the place and doused it with holy water.

This time the polt, far from being mollified or skulking off into the Twilight Zone, went ape: "… everything went berserk … things were flying around … when I was leaving [a medicine bottle] came flying out of the bathroom." Having done what he could, the priest departed, leaving a crucifix and bible with the anxious residents.

As night fell the polt continued its mayhem, smashing another couple of windows, hurling Father Tom's crucifix and bible around, smashing a container of holy water against a wall, banging and scraping and keeping the occupants awake for hours.

Next up was a Greek Orthodox priest, who went the Full Monty, setting up an altar on the kitchen table, blessing each room separately and reading arcane passages from a large black book. As the shell-shocked residents looked on, he was assaulted by an invisible force that tried repeatedly to wrench the book from his grasp and to twist his right arm behind his back. Ashen-faced, he finally sat down, bathed in sweat, declaring his adversary tougher than anything he'd encountered before.

The pest continued its mind-boggling antics for the next couple of months. Sometimes polt-peltings occurred every minute or so for about 20 minutes, followed by an hour or

---

4   Frank Robson, *Sydney Morning Herald*, 13 June 1998 and "Today Tonight" videotapes, April 1998.

two of peace; sometimes objects flew only once or twice a day. Occasionally a couple of days would pass without incident.

The phenomenon was spooky, to say the least, but the housemates, very tough, hard-working young men and women, soon noticed that although potentially lethal objects such as sharp knives and broken glass often passed uncomfortably close, no one was ever hurt. When they also noticed that young Jasmine's room was always left undisturbed they decided the situation was bearable – and resolved to stay on at the property. As Dave put it: "We don't want to move out, it's a nice place, we like it and we were here first [i.e. before the poltergeist]".[5]

Sinister messages

Once they got used to it, in fact, they found the weirdness quite interesting and even amusing for a while. But when sinister words and symbols began to appear on the walls and floor they became nervous again.

The words were scrawled with marker pens, spelt out in scrabble tiles and – strangest of all – formed extremely neatly on the floor using scores of pebbles, each of which had been carefully placed so that only a flat surface faced outwards. The most unsettling aspect of the first series of words: "FIRE", "SKIN", "CAR", "HELP" and "TROY" was that they clearly referred to their good mate Trouy Raddatz, who had been incinerated in a terrible road accident on the Stuart Highway, just a couple of kilometres from their property in January,

Andrew and "CAR" formed from gravel.
(*Northern Territory News*, 4 April 1998)

---

5   *Litchfield Times*, 2 April 1998.

shortly before the first stone fall. On March 20, a large cross and a trident – both constructed of hundreds of pebbles – also appeared on the floor.

A local schoolteacher, Annette Taylor, and her partner Lloyd Green happened to be visiting when the cross appeared. Lloyd testified later that the formation, which was "so neat and perfect … it would have taken me hours to make with a straight-edge, a square and a rule", had been constructed impossibly quickly on a section of the hallway floor that people were repeatedly walking across that evening. More weirdness was to follow: "As soon as [Dave] touched the gravel, it just flew everywhere. It pelted down the passageway. It was so loud hitting the walls, the baby woke and started crying. Then the tools started flying around …"[6]

An eavesdropping imp

During the course of that afternoon and evening the polt seemed to be intent on freaking Annette out. After being showered with gravel, she was narrowly missed by several other objects that moved through the air, sometimes very quickly, sometimes slowly, sometimes changing course in mid air, and sometimes simply hovering.

One of her experiences was particularly interesting because it seems to confirm the tenants' suspicion that the polt eavesdropped on their conversations. It underlines the contrary nature of the imp and is a very rare instance of a person being hurt by a polt-propelled object.

It happened as Annette, who is Maori, was telling her friends about the way poltergeists are viewed in her people's culture. Just as she mentioned the belief that polts didn't hurt people a pair of vice-grip pliers appeared in mid-air and began to move towards her young son Zeke, who was sitting beside her. "I reached up to grab them and they hit me hard on the wrist … my arm was swollen and purple afterwards."[7]

The media swoops

The residents weren't looking for publicity and for the first seven weeks only close friends and the three priests were aware of their problem. Eventually, however, the local *Litchfield Times* got wind of the affair. On March 27 the editor, Jack Ellis, and two reporters visited the house and were duly showered with stones. "I had all the [residents] in full view", said Mr. Ellis, "when I heard a rattle from the ceiling fan above my head and the shower of gravel just descended". Another shower followed soon afterwards. "You can't ignore it … something is happening in that house that I can't explain … [everyone who's been there]

---

6   Frank Robson, *Sydney Morning Herald*, 13 June 1998.
7   Frank Robson, *Sydney Morning Herald*, 13 June 1998.

tells the same story."⁸

In no time the story went ballistic: journalists from far and wide swooped on it like seagulls onto the proverbial sick prawn. The sleep-deprived housemates were soon fielding calls from radio stations and newspapers from as far away as Scandinavia. Unfortunately, as the *Litchfield Times* is a weekly newspaper, Jack's story appeared on April 2, causing many casual readers to suspect it was an April Fools Day joke. The haunting had, in fact, begun in late January.

Jack Ellis. (Healy/Cropper)

A brief radio interview with Father Tom English, recorded by a Darwin-based ABC journalist, was broadcast throughout Australia. That interview, which led directly to our own involvement in the Humpty Doo saga, formed part of a coincidence that was remarkable but at the same time, strange to say, not particularly surprising.

Most Fortuitous

During our many years of researching the unexplained we have noticed that when we are delving deeply into, and preparing to write about, a particular mystery, Lady Luck or – our favourite term – the "Cosmic Prankster", sometimes decides to lend a hand by producing, just at the right moment, a new and fascinating case of just the type needed. Many of our fellow researchers have noticed the same happy phenomenon.

In early 1998, Bob Rickard, editor of the British journal of strange phenomena, *Fortean Times*, asked us to write an article about a couple of classic Australian poltergeist cases. By March of that year our desks – Paul's in Sydney and Tony's in Canberra – were stacked high with material relating to the "Guyra Ghost" incident of 1921, the "Mayanup Poltergeist" episode of the 1950s, several nineteenth-century cases and numerous books about the world-wide nature of the polt phenomenon.

One day in early April, while we were still elbow-deep in those weird and wonderful stories and swapping ideas over the phone, Tony heard Father Tom being interviewed on ABC radio. The priest was clearly very excited and most adamant that some inexplicable force had hurled his crucifix and other objects around the Humpty Doo residence.

It was too good an opportunity to miss: within a couple of hours Paul had spoken by

---

8 "Today Tonight" tapes, April 1998.

phone to Andrew Agius, who said it would be ok for us to visit his polt-plagued residence, and within a couple of days we were booking flights to Darwin.

We flew to the Northern Territory on April 25th. There was little point in arriving earlier because Andrew told us that he and his housemates had signed a contract granting exclusive rights to the story for six days to Sydney-based Channel Seven. Although the promised $2000 would be useful, they signed mainly to get a break from the avalanche of enquiries from other media organisations and in the hope that video evidence would validate their story.

"Today Tonight", morning, noon and night

Greg Quail, of Channel Seven's "Today Tonight" program was given the assignment and on the 4th of April he arrived in the Northern Territory, accompanied by a four-man camera crew. Along for the ride was Max Anderson, a young Sydney-based freelance journalist.

Greg Quail. (Courtesy "Today Tonight")

Fortuitously for Anderson, he had recently researched an article about Stephen Bishop, a self-described ghost-busting psychic who runs the Chiara College of Metaphysics in Sydney. On hearing of the Humpty Doo episode, he sensed an opportunity. Phoning Greg Quail at Channel Seven, he did some quick horse-trading: "he could have my ghost buster if he'd take both of us to Humpty Doo; I, of course, being free to scoop my own story."[9]

Quail agreed, but when the party landed in the Territory he insisted that for the first few days Stephen Bishop remain in Darwin, well away from the supposedly haunted house. Although Quail assumed the polt activity was being faked, he wasn't taking any chances. If it proved to be the real thing – and if Bishop's ghost busting skills were genuine – he didn't want to risk having the spook exorcised before he'd captured some of its shenanigans on film.

To further improve his chances of getting good video evidence, Quail beefed-up his crew by recruiting two Darwin-based cameramen, Danny Sim and his assistant Jarrod Suttee. Then the whole party proceeded to Humpty Doo, where they were greeted by the shell-shocked residents and by the polt – which obliged by throwing all kinds of objects in and around the house during the entire time they were there.

---

9   "Ghost Writer" by Max Anderson, *The Australian Magazine*, 9–10 May 1998.

Although amazed and baffled, Quail and his men tried to remain sceptical, and for five days and nights looked high and low for evidence of hoaxing. They could find nothing suspicious about the building's structure, nothing odd in the loft and no holes in either the roof or the ceiling. With their seven cameras and eight pairs of eyes they kept all the residents under pretty constant surveillance – but saw nothing that could account for the many objects that dropped and flew all around them.

"We rolled up sceptics", said Quail later, "we're not leaving sceptics. We'd only been there for two hours and we realised it was all on. I thought we'd come here and uncover a hoax [but] we've … endured an onslaught of flying scissors, stones, knives, broken glass and, yes, three live bullets. Not once did any of us see even a suggestion that any of the five residents … was trying to pull a swiftie."[10]

Stones, he said, had materialised out of thin air and slammed onto a table while broken glass crashed into walls around him. "All five members of the Channel Seven team", he insisted, "have seen things we just can't explain … objects have appeared, seemingly out of nowhere, being thrown at or near us."[11]

On one occasion Danny Sim was on a ladder next to the open manhole when "… I heard this bloody piece of glass, or something similar, hit the [tin] roof just next to my ear … I was looking up at the ceiling, so I had an excellent view … and the next moment I saw it in mid air [below the ceiling] and land [on the floor below him]. It appears the glass went through the roof and ceiling simultaneously … all I heard from the boys below was, 'Oh shit!'"

Later, with Kirsty and the other residents nowhere near, Danny witnessed stones falling inside the garage and was startled by a spanner landing on the roof with a "tremendous noise". Then he became the only person other than Annette Taylor to be hurt by the Humpty Doo polt as an AA battery gave him a nasty blow on the side of his head. Interestingly, although his head ached badly for some time afterwards, there was no bleeding, no lump, and no bruising.[12]

Within half an hour of arriving, Max Anderson heard a smart 'Crack!' on a lounge room cabinet and saw an AA battery land right beside him. No-one was in a position to have thrown it. He then saw the seemingly inexplicable fall of a knife, broken glass and other objects. Outside, two cameramen were baffled by another knife that struck their hire car while they were stowing their gear.[13]

One phenomenon – the one the tenants found most maddening of all – occurred repeatedly during the next few days: often, just after beds had been made and bedrooms tidied, mattresses were found to have been upturned, dragged off beds and shoved against walls.

So Quail and his crew quickly became polt believers – but they also became extremely frustrated as the mischievous entity played hide-and-seek with their cameras. Operators

---

10 *Sunday Territorian,* 19 April 1998 and *Litchfield Times,* 16 April 1998.
11 *Northern Territory News,* 20 April 1998 and "Today Tonight" tapes, April 1998.
12 Ken Llewelyn, interview with Danny Sim, November 1998.
13 Max Anderson, *The Australian Magazine,* 9–10 May 1998.

with hand-held equipment were invariably facing the wrong way as objects landed right next to them. Their fixed cameras managed to record only two not-very-dramatic instances of objects in motion: a baby's bottle inexplicably falling from the top of a microwave and a pistol cartridge falling a few feet and bouncing off furniture.

Although the two short film clips would do nothing to convince a sceptic, there was, nevertheless, something decidedly odd about one of them. The baby bottle sequence was taken by a camera set up to cover the kitchen/family room. Throughout one hundred hours of filming the bottle was the only object in frame that moved. But, during the exact split second in which it left the top of the microwave, it was screened from view by Dave Clark's leg, as he walked past the camera. So all that was caught on film was the bottle in mid air, heading for the floor.

While thoroughly exasperated, Greg Quail saw no way the incident could have been hoaxed: "The bottle fell off in the millisecond – *two frames* – when [Dave] walked in front of the camera. You can't engineer that humanly … Dave could not have thrown anything at the bottle – he was six metres away". Max Anderson, too, saw it as further evidence the spook could run rings around them: "The [polt's] timing is not just excellent; it's genius!"[14]

Less than a minute after the bottle fell, cameraman Gavin Davidson had a curious experience while changing the tape on one of the cameras: a little sliver of glass fell right beside him, seemingly out of thin air. The timing, he said, was typical: "That seems to be when it happens: when the cameras are off. I can't explain how things just fly around the place …"[15]

Danny Sim witnessed something even stranger: As he was looking directly at a kitchen cupboard, a spanner hit it with considerable force: "It looked like it came out of the lounge room, but there was no one there … no one was in a position to have thrown it with such force." Even more weirdly, *neither of the cameras covering the space it must have traversed to get to the cabinet registered the spanner in flight.*

At the peak of the team's involvement, they had seven cameras set up in and around the house, running pretty well continuously. Their purpose, apart from, hopefully, filming objects in flight, was to keep a very close eye on the residents. But although the housemates were surreptitiously filmed everywhere indoors (apart from the bathroom, toilet and bedrooms) and at the outdoor bar, not the slightest hint of hoaxing was recorded, despite all manner of strange phenomena occurring day and night.

---

14 Paul Cropper, interview with Greg Quail, 2 Sept 2011 and Max Anderson, *Australian*, 9–10 May 1998.
15 "Today Tonight" tapes.

Max Anderson. (Max Anderson)

A cunning plan

Greg Quail came up with another tactic: for a couple of days, after her housemates left for work, he persuaded Kirsty to stay outside with her baby, either on the patio or at a friend's place, and instructed the crew to set five cameras rolling inside the house, go outside, and lock all the doors. No prizes for guessing what happened next: for hour after hour the cameras recorded a whole lot of nothing until the battery-expired signals went off. Then, as the duty cameraman walked to the house with new batteries, his exasperated but amused mates, sitting on the patio, would hear a tattoo of whacks as objects careened around the interior. Messages: "NO CAMERAS", "NO TV" and "PIG CAMERA" appeared on walls and floors to taunt them.

With the cameras indoors the polt intensified its activity outside. One day Father Tom dropped by for a visit. As he walked towards the patio where the crew was sitting around a large steel table, a .44 magnum cartridge appeared from nowhere and crashed onto the table. At around the same time, Danny Sim saw "a butcher's knife thumping on the table and stopping as though it was blocked. If you threw it with the same force it would bounce and ricochet."[16]

Later that afternoon two of the cameramen were sitting at the same table when, after a longer-than-usual lull, one of them yelled out in frustration: "Come *on*!" The challenge had hardly left his lips when a shower of stones hit the table, right in front of them, with

---

16   Ken Llewelyn, interview with Danny Sim, November 1998.

some force. Both men were shocked; there was no one else around.[17]

Trying hard to remain objective, Max Anderson decided that it would be imprecise for him describe the apparently polt-propelled objects as being "thrown" or "flying around": "No, our objects had appeared in our peripheral vision; we saw them upon or after impact, followed by any movement on the rebound which gave us any clues to the trajectory."

He had, however, seen so many objects bouncing around that remaining sceptical was becoming increasingly difficult. Some of the objects might conceivably have been thrown by the tenants but some really appeared to come out of nowhere: "I couldn't account for the steak knife, which bounced off the floor at Kirsty's feet. Or the heavy glass lid that fell into view while Kirsty was looking in the fridge." Outside again, he saw another bullet fall, scissors suddenly appear in the swimming pool and a coin land on the roof.

In a thought-provoking and entertaining article, "Ghost Writer", published a month later in *The Australian*, Max ably conveyed the difficulty of remaining calm and objective while experiencing "the rush of adrenalin ... the excitement of seeing something utterly, inexplicably fantastic" as objects crashed all around.

Murph. (Healy/Cropper)

He also dealt compassionately with the anxiety, frustration and fatigue the tenants were so obviously suffering. They were "at the end of their rope" after two months of almost incessant weirdness, "utterly frustrated and upset to the point of fury that Humpty Doo, Darwin and soon, possibly, the rest of Australia thought they were liars, druggies or mentally unstable ... they were getting no understanding and no sympathy while shit rained down all around them." Murph, a volatile biker who'd been the late Trouy Raddatz's best mate, seemed particularly desperate for the madness to end. Told that the crew – who he initially dismissed as "youse f***in' vultures" – had a ghost buster on standby, he snapped "Well, where is he? And when can he come? I'm sick of the f***in' thing."[18]

By April 6, although Max was "95% convinced" the polt was genuine, part of his mind was still denying what his eyes were telling him: he was "plagued with sensory denial", holding grimly to the thought that if anyone was hoaxing, it virtually had to be Kirsty.

His "sceptic bubble" finally burst one morning as he walked through the house with Kirsty (the other tenants were at work). The young mother had Jasmine in the crook of her left arm and a cigarette in her right hand. "I passed Murph's bedroom ... on my right

---

17 Paul Cropper, interview with Brendan Gowdie, 20 September 2011.
18 Max Anderson, *Australian*, 9–10 May 1998.

with Kirsty on my left. I [spontaneously] opened the door, saw it was empty and undisturbed, began to close it and heard a sudden 'Bang!' Confused, I heard Kirsty say 'That came from in there.' We opened the door again to see a piece of broken glass against the far wall … she could not have thrown that glass."

Ghost buster bested

Pondering the polt: Steve Bishop. (Max Anderson)

On April 7 Greg Quail finally let Steve Bishop off his leash, but when the psychic arrived at the house his sponsor, Max Anderson, was mildly embarrassed to hear him utter, in front of the cameras, a series of rather predictable "New Agey" statements. "My energy is being disturbed," he said, "… this is the most extreme case I've ever come across … The land's dead, lost its soul." Unsurprisingly, he found the house "oppressive". Moving around the property, eyes closed, taking deep breaths, he claimed to detect a "residual", like grey slime, in some of the rooms.

While Bishop's comments didn't greatly impress anyone else, Dave Clark thought his visit had a positive effect. As Anderson put it, Dave "professed to feel it strongly as Steve mentally cleaned and reset each room. The entity was squeezed using 'psychic seals' into one room, where Steve, in faith healer's voice, suggested it was going away … all would be right."

Although Bishop left himself with an "out" – saying that because the polt seemed to be "connected with the energy of the [local] earth and the land", his efforts to banish it might fail – and although the polt did not, in fact, moderate its activities at all after his visit – Max Anderson felt that the psychic was acting in good faith and that his efforts "seemed to give some of the residents strength."

Hot little hands

While the ghost buster didn't achieve much, another one of Greg Quail's polt-hunting tactics produced some very interesting evidence. He arranged for Brendan Gowdie, a Brisbane-based building maintenance expert, to fly up and join his team. Mr. Gowdie's

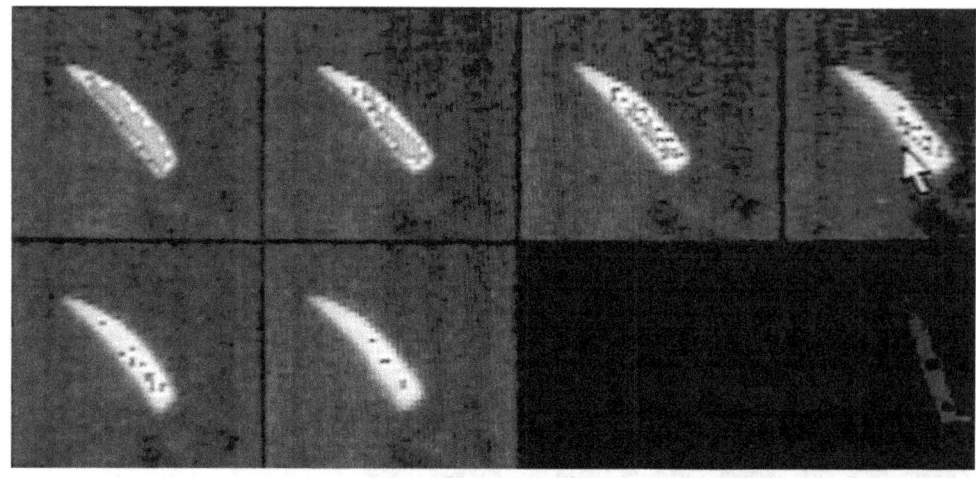
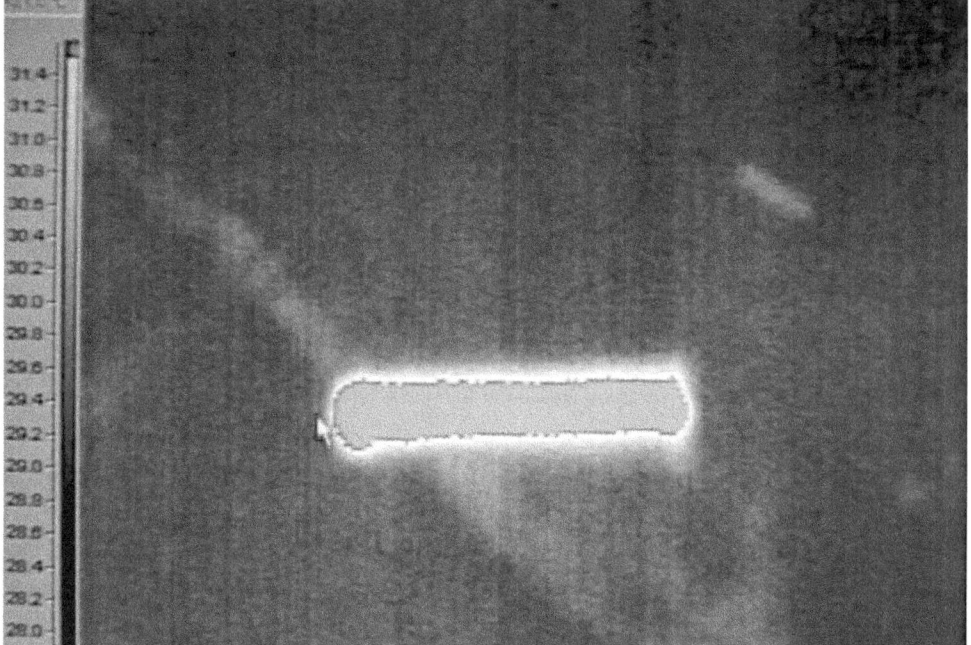

Brendan Gowdie's thermal images of glass shard and pistol cartridge. (Courtesy "Today Tonight")

task was to use his sophisticated thermal imaging camera to film as many of the flying objects as he could, as soon as possible after they'd landed.

Gowdie's primary mission was, as Quail put it, "to catch out humans", and preliminary experiments showed that if a person picked up and threw an object the camera usually revealed warm spots corresponding to fingerprints on its surface. But Gowdie's shots of the apparently polt-propelled objects revealed something completely different: *they were uniformly warm all over.*

As the residents were not told what kind of camera he was wielding, and what evidence it was designed to detect, Gowdie thinks it highly unlikely they could have faked the unusual thermal traces. To do so they would have had to warm the objects in a microwave and handle them with tongs.

Like most of the other investigators, Gowdie thought that if any of the phenomena was being faked, the hoaxer virtually *had* to be Kirsty, as she was the only one of the housemates who was at home most of the time. It is therefore interesting that he insists "things were happening when she wasn't even there."

On one occasion, for instance, he was *alone* in the house when a pistol bullet fell, right before his eyes, in the family room/kitchen. Film from two fixed video cameras shows the object falling from the vicinity of the ceiling before bouncing off furniture and onto the carpet. Gowdie's excited exclamations can be heard on the sound track, and his infrared photographs, taken just seconds after the bullet came to rest, show that it was markedly warm and that the warmth was uniform along its entire length. "There were no thermal fingerprints on it, nothing that [indicated] human contact."

So Mr. Gowdie, who'd arrived as a sceptic, left the site a reluctant believer: "From a scientific point of view I have no explanation. I was baffled … nothing about the place added up … there's some sort of poltergeist attached to that house."[19]

On 9 April, after four 24-hour work days and great inconvenience to the housemates – particularly to Kirsty – Greg Quail and his crew packed up and left Humpty Doo, having done all they could, given limited time and the uncanny ability of the polt (or hoaxers) to avoid being filmed in action.

Sceptics rule – OK?

On arrival back in Sydney the men were interviewed separately by Chief Editor Jimmy Hamilton, who found all of them to be "spooked, rattled, unsettled". Clearly, they all believed they'd witnessed something truly uncanny. As one excited cameraman put it, "We've entered the next dimension!"

Greg Quail was as excited as all the others. Handing the editor 20 hours of raw footage, he exclaimed, "We got it!"

But after spending the entire weekend looking through the footage, Mr. Hamilton had to inform Quail that he could find nothing that constituted proof of the polt's reality: sceptics would simply say the bottle had been toppled off the microwave by vibration and that all the flying objects could have been tossed from out of shot.

Fair enough: but we're a little surprised that Brendan Gowdie's infrared photography didn't cut any ice with the Chief Editor or the show's producers.

But sceptical as the bosses may have been, they nevertheless used the story to great advantage, beginning their coverage of it on 20 April and achieving very high ratings. As Jimmy Hamilton put it, because of Humpty Doo, the show "rated its arse off."[20]

---

19   Frank Robson, *Sydney Morning Herald*, 13 June 1998 and "Today Tonight" tapes, April 1998.
20   Paul Cropper, interview with Jimmy Hamilton, 22 September 2011.

Meanwhile, back in Humpty Doo, the haunted housemates were fairly pleased with the first instalment, which treated them and their dilemma reasonably sympathetically and which included interviews with father Tom and others who testified to the reality of the phenomenon. Their euphoria, however, was not destined to last.

Shortly after the first episode went to air additional footage arrived at the "Today Tonight" studio. It had been sent by the Darwin-based cameramen, Danny Sim and Jarrod Suttee, who'd stayed on at the house for a couple of days after the Sydney crew departed. The sequence, which was shot by Suttee, was quite exciting but also very contentious, and it would change everything.

Many objects had flown that evening, so Suttee had his camera set up in the family room, running fairly constantly. It was simple good luck, he believes, that he had it pointing in the right direction at the right time.

At the crucial moment he was standing behind the camera with Kirsty behind him and to his right, ironing clothes. In frame was a tall wooden cabinet, a short section of corridor and, opening onto the corridor, two doors – one open, one closed. Reflections of both the cameraman and Kirsty can be seen in the cabinet's glass doors.

Suddenly, a small white object (a plastic pot lid) flies from right to left across the field of view, hits the closed door with a whack, then ricochets off a short section of wall and onto the floor. Instantly, Suttee exclaims "Got that!" and, as Jill steps out of the open door to ask what happened, their reflections show Suttee and Kirsty moving towards the point of impact.

Greg Quail thought the footage interesting, but because the pot lid had not been scanned by the infrared camera he didn't consider it as important as the clip featuring the .44 magnum cartridge.

Then, while examining the film, a "Today Tonight" editor noticed Kirsty's reflection in the glass door of the cabinet and, on slowing the film, found that she appeared to rise up slightly, apparently just as the lid began its flight. He thought this proved she'd thrown it over Suttee's head, and quickly informed the "Today Tonight" executives, who immediately cried "Hoax!"

The unexpected turn of events threw Greg Quail, who'd been happy with the positive tone of the first episode, into a tail-spin. He was called into his boss's office and hauled over the coals. As his friend Max Anderson observed, "TV management doesn't believe in ghosts". "The story's a turd," said one insider, "and you can't polish a turd."[21]

So Greg Quail, polt believer, was told to do a rapid 180 degree-turn and become a hoax buster. Whereas his crew had previously interviewed 18 eyewitnesses – all of whom testified to the reality of the phenomenon – he now quickly interviewed a spokesman for Australian Skeptics and made a barrage of phone calls to Kirsty, demanding that she confess to the hoax. According to him, she finally did just that. According to her she did no such thing.

---

21   Max Anderson, *Australian*, 9–10 May 1998.

Nevertheless, at 6.30 pm on April 24, "Today Tonight" swung the axe: Kirsty was dismissed as a clumsy trickster, her housemates as simple-minded dupes, and the whole episode as a waste of time.

A premature burial

But while the "Today Tonight" bosses may have declared it dead and buried, the polt seemed to consider the obituary premature: it continued its pesky pranks while the residents, feeling used, abused and betrayed – and still waiting for the balance of their money – vowed to disembowel any other "f***ing media vultures" who dared to darken their door.

At that auspicious moment, Healy and Cropper walked hesitantly down the long, gravel driveway …

Welcome to our nightmare

We were received by two very tough-looking, unsmiling characters. Shaven-headed Andrew was polite but guarded; heavily-tattooed biker "Murph" didn't bother hiding his disdain for "youse media bastards". Rather than taking us into the house they led us to the small, roofed outdoor bar.

It was a tricky situation. Murph was the angriest-looking man either of us had met in a long, long time, and his body language suggested that if we said the wrong thing at that moment we would end up in intensive care. The guys were obviously right at the end of their tether – they'd "had a gut-full". After three months of frights, interrupted sleep and ridicule they were emotionally drained.

One recent development, in particular, was infuriating them: thanks to "Today Tonight's" hatchet job, Simon Potter, a Darwin-based spokesman for Australian Skeptics – who hadn't been anywhere near their property – was now crowing loudly that he'd been right all along.

Fortunately, we'd thought to bring along our entire Australian poltergeist file. The men started to glance through it, then began to scan the pages eagerly, exclaiming frequently over the many similarities between the nineteenth-century and early twentieth-century cases and their own experience. "This is exactly what's been happening here", said Andrew, "just what we've been trying to tell those bastards!"

Reassured that we were genuinely interested, they began to lower the barriers. After Dave and Jill, both quiet and easy-going, arrived home from work, and Kirsty emerged from the house with baby Jasmine, things became even more relaxed. Far from being a bunch of drunken layabouts as some of the media had tried to suggest, the residents were all decent, hard-working Territorians. Andrew was a driller, Dave a mechanic, Murph a commercial fisherman and Jill a shop assistant. Kirsty, with baby Jasmine to look after, was the only one not in paid employment. They struck us as being strong-minded, competent people. It was clear that above all else they simply wanted to be believed – and *very* clear that they were all righteously pissed off with "Today Tonight".

Lies and videotape

Greg Quail's claims about her supposed confession were, Kirsty insisted, completely bogus: "He wasn't after the truth because he'd already made up his mind."

Throughout his repeated, hectoring phone calls she could remember saying only one thing that he might have construed as a confession. During his final call at midnight on April 21, she'd shouted something like "Look – say what you bloody well like – 'I did it' – is that what you want me to say? Just leave me alone!"

One would expect that if Kirsty really had confessed she would have hastened to inform her housemates of the fact, but she didn't – and none of them believed for a moment that she'd hoaxed anything.

A moment of reflection: Kirsty and the cabinet. (Healy/Cropper)

As for the contentious film clip, Kirsty didn't dispute that Jarrod Suttee had his back to her at the critical moment. But what the camera had captured, she said, was just the reflection of her shaking Jasmin's clothes before folding them. She'd looked up from her work just as the object flew.

Before travelling to Humpty Doo we'd taped the "Today Tonight" episode containing the supposedly incriminating footage and viewed it many times. The quality of our tape, however, was so poor that, although the flying lid was discernible towards the end of its flight, we couldn't make out its entire "flight path". And while Kirsty, to judge from her dim reflection, did appear to rise slightly just as the object flew, we could see no hand movement or anything else to suggest she'd thrown it. Because of that, and because of our low opinion of tabloid television shows like "Today Tonight", we were very much inclined to accept her version of events.

One other factor influenced our attitude: we knew that Greg Quail, despite his insistence that Kirsty had hoaxed the pot lid incident, still believed that most of the phenomena he and his crew had experienced at Humpty Doo were genuinely paranormal. (More about the contentious "pot lid film" and alleged confession later).

Mysterious visitors

We were, of course, very keen to witness some of the polt's pranks, but to our dismay the housemates told us it had suspended all activity four days earlier. It was the longest interlude of calm they'd yet experienced and they were hoping it presaged the end of the whole horrible affair. Well, that was fine for them and we wished them well, but having just flown 3000 kilometres to view the phenomenon, we weren't so pleased that the polt had seemingly waltzed off into the ether. Was the Cosmic Prankster, we wondered, having a good old laugh at our expense?

The polt's departure might have been triggered by an odd incident that happened on April 21st. On that day, while only she and Jasmine were at home, Kirsty had gone outside and found two very dark or – as she put it – "bush Aborigines", crouched under a mango tree right next to the house, digging with their hands. When challenged, their reaction was strange: without so much as glancing at her, they walked silently away, up the long gravel driveway, climbed into a small orange-coloured car and drove away. Since then there hadn't been so much as a peep out of the polt.

We examined the site in question. Leaves had been cleared in a 6 foot by 2 foot (grave-size?) patch around a bowl-shaped hole. The hole, about eight inches deep and a foot in diameter (20x30cm), was towards the top end of the cleared patch. Given the rather spooky nature of the incident, an odd thought crossed our minds: the spot where the hole was situated in the cleared patch was – had a body been in the "grave" – about where the centre of its chest would have been.

Tony at the dig site. (Healy/Cropper)

Although we hadn't yet seen any polt activity, our research had persuaded us that such phenomena did occur from time to time, and that what was allegedly happening at Humpty Doo seemed to fit the pattern. Given that we were now embedded in a situation where uncertainty was the name of the game, we reasoned that everything connected to the events, no matter how tenuously, should be taken into account.

Could it be then, that the Humpty Doo haunting was the result of an Aboriginal curse? If so, had the two "bush Aborigines" been attempting to lift the curse – or had they been interrupted while trying to intensify it? Later that evening, Andrew took us aside and told us a few things, some of which did suggest an Aboriginal connection.

A series of slightly odd events had occurred a few years earlier, when he and Kirsty were living at Batchelor, about 65 kilometres to the south. The intensity of that episode was nothing compared to what was happening at Humpty Doo, and a supernatural explanation hadn't entered his mind at the time. But he now suspected that those events, too, were the work of a poltergeist.

The Batchelor episode consisted entirely of stones flying with great power and accuracy through their (open) front door. There was no screen door. The stones would hurtle down the hallway and crash against an internal wall without ever hitting anyone and without – he thought this a little strange – causing any discernible damage. This always occurred at night.

He frankly admitted that he was no great fan of the indigenous people, and at the time he suspected the stoning was the work of local Aboriginal teenagers, perhaps using catapults. They may have decided to target him after overhearing remarks he'd uttered over a beer or two at the local pub.

But if Aboriginal kids were responsible for the pelting, they were uncannily clever about it: Although he tried dressing in black and crouching for hours behind bushes in the front yard, he never saw where the stones came from.

After leaving Batchelor, the couple did a stint on a construction project near Gosford on the New South Wales central coast, where Andrew operated a drill and Kirsty was employed as camp cook. Again, decidedly strange things began to happen. On several occasions every single coffee mug vanished from the mess hall, only to be discovered standing upright on the roofs of surrounding huts or on top of tall posts. Weirdly, some mugs were found to be filled to the very top with dry instant coffee crystals. This time the couple attributed the incidents to the work of a sly practical joker, albeit a somewhat sick one: in addition to the wayward coffee mugs, a couple of large knives went missing. One of them was found in the (locked) cool room – stabbed into the hanging carcase of a pig.

Regardless of whether or not the odd episodes at Batchelor and in NSW were the result of an Aboriginal hex aimed at him, Andrew was pretty sure that the Humpty Doo events were focused not on him, but on his wife. Because she had to look after young Jasmine, Kirsty was of course, much more confined to the house than the other adults. Even allowing for that, Jill, Dave and Murph agreed with Andrew that the uncanny action intensified when she was present.

So we watched Kirsty rather more closely than the others, not only because if anyone was hoaxing it virtually had to be her, but also because if she *wasn't* hoaxing she may well have been an unconscious medium – one of those mildly psychic, sometimes slightly troubled individuals who, in the opinion of many psychic investigators, unwittingly facilitate poltergeist phenomena. With that in mind, we observed her, trying to see what might have attracted the polt's interest.

Like most young people who gravitate to the Territory, Kirsty was not afraid of hard work and unusual challenges. As well as doing stints as a chef, she'd worked at various other jobs, including truck driving. She was tall, dark, slim, quite good-looking, competent and self contained. Although she was hospitable and not at all unfriendly, we noticed that she rarely smiled or laughed. Perhaps, considering what she'd been through in the preceding three months that was only to be expected.

There was just one thing in her manner that struck us as being slightly unusual. It was something that in a normal situation would have gone unremarked – but this wasn't a normal situation and we were looking for anything that seemed out of the ordinary. It was a minor quirk: a steady, penetrating, mildly unsettling look she gave one from time to time. No doubt the young mother was tired, perhaps her mind was miles away, maybe she was thinking, "Why don't these idiots piss off and leave me alone?" But to us, that look called to mind something that was said about another poltergeist medium – Minnie Bowen, of the 1921 "Guyra Ghost" episode – who was "tall, thin and dark, with peculiar dark, introspective eyes … she never smiles and seems to look beyond or through you …". (See Chapter Ten).

There was no suggestion that any of her housemates suspected Kirsty was faking the events. They pointed out that although nearly all of the phenomena occurred when she was somewhere in the house, stones and other objects occasionally flew when she was away from home. (Even Greg Quail of "Today Tonight" noted that objects flew when Kirsty was not present: "There were times", he said, "when the crew was alone in the house and things happened.")[22]

Her housemates were adamant, in any case, that neither Kirsty nor anyone else could

---

22   *Northern Territory News*, 23 April 1998.

possibly have faked the hundreds of remarkable events without being caught in the act. They also insisted that none of them had any motive for disrupting the harmonious household. Indeed, considering all they had gone through in the preceding three months, we were impressed by how well they all seemed to get along.

They were a stubborn lot. In addition to coping with the polt, they'd recently had to deal with an attempt by their landlords, Kosta and Angela Boubaris, to have them thrown out. Mr. and Mrs. Boubaris claimed that, on returning from an extended holiday in mid-April, they were shocked to find that the house was being trashed, and immediately lodged an application for an eviction.

As we will show later, it seems the landlords should have been aware, well before April 1998, of strange events occurring in the house. Be that as it may, their application was heard by Magistrate Greg Cavanagh on 16 April.

Magistrate Cavanagh, predictably enough, told the tenants that he didn't believe in ghosts and that any significant damage done to the house while they were occupying it might be sufficient grounds for their eviction. He did, however, take heed as the housemates pointed out that nearly all of the damage had been inflicted on their own possessions. Damage to the house itself – mainly smashed windows and holed fly screens – was relatively minor, and had already been repaired at their own expense. When even the landlords' lawyers admitted the house was in good condition the eviction notice was overturned.

After all their trials and tribulations with the polt and the media the housemates were very pleased with their victory, but still fuming at the injustice of the landlords' action. As Andrew put it: "Why should we move? Bugger them. We pay our rent; we look after the place; *we* didn't break any of the windows and anyway – the place suits us perfectly".

Perhaps the move to get rid of Andrew and friends was an attempt by the landlords to remove the stigma of "haunted house" from their valuable property.

A very nice set-up

As the polt had apparently decided to take a few days off, we were free to explore the house and grounds without interruption. The well-kept, lightly-treed five-acre (1.85 hectare) property was almost, but not quite level: it sloped down very gradually from McMinns Drive, about 70 metres from the house. It was surrounded by a high man-proof fence; the only access being through the driveway gate, which was usually left open. The dwelling was a simple single-storey, four-bedroom, rectangular, fibro bungalow, painted eggshell-blue and elevated about 75 centimetres (2.5 feet) off the ground. A section of the iron roof projected outwards on one side, linking the house to a small laundry and providing cover for a patio and barbecue area. There were two out-buildings: the small, roofed bar, plus a large open-fronted garage that could accommodate up to four vehicles. Best of all, just beyond the patio was a generous-sized swimming pool. It was a very nice set-up. We could fully understand why Andrew and company were determined to stay despite a pesky polt and unreasonable landlord.

Jill with polt graffiti. (Healy/Cropper)

Although the rest of the house was clean and tidy, the group had (for the benefit of people such as us) left a couple of examples of polt graffiti in place on internal doors. The messages were evidently written with a marker pen, in a weak and wavering scrawl. Both had appeared while the television crew was at the house. One, "PIG CAMERA", wasn't particularly disturbing. The other, "TONIGHT DIE", seemed pretty scary, but as Jill suggested, was probably a reference to the program "Today Tonight" rather than a death threat directed at anyone in particular. Although the messages looked nice and creepy and we dutifully photographed them, they didn't, of course, prove anything one way or the other about the reality of the polt.

Despite all the references to his terrible death – "FIRE", "SKIN", "CAR" "TROY" and "HELP" – the residents strongly rejected the notion that their mate Trouy was haunting them. They hadn't failed to notice that whatever arranged the pebbles and tiles to spell out the words had misspelled his name. And it hadn't taken them long, either, to realise that the sly, mischievous entity sometimes attempted to play on their

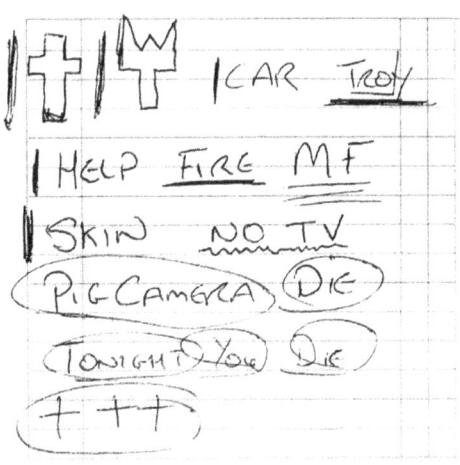

Andrew's record of the polt graffiti.

fears and concerns – after apparently eavesdropping on their conversations. Researchers in other parts of the world have documented many instances of poltergeists playing similar malicious mind-games.

So the friends decided to throw a challenge right back in the polt's nasty little face: walking through the house, they shouted several non-Vatican-approved invocations such as "You're not Trouy, you piss-weak bastard. Why don't you just F*** OFF!" Thereafter, all references to Trouy ceased and the residents, emboldened by their success, took to occasionally doing other things that seemed to annoy the spook. Andrew, for instance, found that he could sometimes stir it up by reading psalms from Father Tom's bible.

Frequent flyers

Andrew with spark plug. (Healy/Cropper)

Andrew told us that while a great variety of objects had hurtled through the house during the past few weeks there were some items the polt seemed to particularly enjoy chucking around. He showed us several of those "frequent flyers". One, a home-made bottle opener with a welded-on spark plug for a handle, often disappeared from the outdoor bar and dropped elsewhere on the property. Interestingly, when it reappeared it always seemed much less tarnished than it had been before the flight.

Other "frequent flyers" included various spanners, a small silver skull (broken off a Harley Davidson ornament), four live .44 magnum cartridges and several big knives. The polt's favourite toy, however, was the crucifix left by Father Tom English. Almost every day – and often several times a day – it would disappear from the top of a small bureau just inside the back door and, either immediately or somewhat later, drop or crash into a wall or floor.

The crucifix seemed undamaged, but Father Tom's bible looked distinctly worse for wear, after repeatedly colliding with various walls.

As nothing seemed to be happening at McMinns Road, we drove back to our rented cabin at Howard Springs, dropping into the *Litchfield Times* office on the way. There, Jack Ellis, the paper's friendly, laid-back editor, reiterated his belief in the poltergeist. He had weathered two stone showers at the house and could think of no earthly explanation

Frequent Flyers. (Healy/Cropper)

for the events. Neither could a young lady reporter, who'd also visited the site a couple of times. We envied their certainty, because it was starting to look like we might have to leave the NT without having had any first-hand spook experience.

Let there be a light

We needn't have worried. As we headed towards McMinns Drive at about 9 o'clock the following morning, Paul's mobile rang. It was Andrew. "Get down here quick", he said, "It's happening again – now!"

We arrived at the house, eyes wide and cameras ready. Stepping onto the rear patio, we took a pace or two towards Andrew and Murph who were sitting several metres away. Immediately, something struck the surface slightly behind us and to the right with a distinct "Tink". As the guys shouted "There it goes again!" we swung around to witness a large light bulb coming to rest on the concrete about two metres away. One step backwards was all it took to check there was no hoaxer lurking around the corner of the house.

We were pretty impressed. The corner of the house had been in plain view as we stepped past it onto the patio. A hoaxer would have had to run around the building at tremendous speed – noiselessly – to reach a place to throw the bulb – and would have had to retrace his steps – again noiselessly – at a similarly impossible speed to evade being seen as we stepped back. The only other possibility was that someone had been lurking

Light fantastic. (Healy/Cropper)

under the corner of the house, and had reached through a narrow gap above two horizontal steel slats to toss the object. Again, this seemed next to impossible: the crawl-space under the house was only about 75 centimetres (2.5 feet) high. Reaching between the slats and the floor to toss the object would have been awkward, risky and obvious, if not to us, then to Andrew and Murph, whose reactions seemed spontaneous and natural. We could, furthermore, see beyond the slats into the crawl-space – anyone crouching there would have been easy to spot. But what impressed us most was that the bulb, wherever it came from, would have had to be airborne for at least two metres before landing on the concrete – yet it had not broken.

The bulb was quite distinctive. Although the size of a normal household bulb, it was yellow-tinted. Whereas most of the things that flew around the place were familiar objects from the house or garage, this bulb was part of a minority that may have come from somewhere else. "I suppose it could have been in the back of the shed somewhere", said Andrew, 'but I dunno – I've never seen it before." Murph agreed.

A few minutes later, as Paul was chatting with Kirsty and Jill in the kitchen/family room, a sudden, sharp clatter, like a flurry of hail on the corrugated iron roof, caused him to glance upwards. A split second later a dozen grey pebbles cascaded onto the lino at his feet. It was as if they'd passed straight through both roof and ceiling without leaving a mark. Kirsty and Jill, standing just in front of him, laughed wearily and exclaimed, "Well – here we go again!"

Pretty exciting, to say the least – but we tried not to get carried away. Retreating to a quiet corner, we quizzed each other. Had Tony, who'd been outside, heard the clatter on the roof? He hadn't, but that may not have been particularly significant. Could Paul be certain that Kirsty or Jill hadn't thrown the pebbles? Absolutely: they'd both been standing right in front of him. There'd been no one else in the room.

During the next half hour or so a few other things happened, some decidedly weird, some less so. A small battery (AA size) flew or fell. Paul, standing a couple of metres away, heard it land and turned to see it on the linoleum. A second gravel fall occurred, this time on the carpeted lounge room floor. On that occasion it was not impossible that someone had thrown it – although if anyone did he or she was at great risk of being caught in the act: Paul could have glanced in that direction at any time.

Shortly thereafter, Tony, talking to Kirsty in the kitchen, heard a sharp sound. Glancing around, Kirsty noticed a plastic clothes peg on a bench-top. It had, she said, not been there previously.

With that feeble parting shot the polt must have decided to step into another dimension for a spot of tea, because things then returned to normal until the following morning.

That evening, perhaps because we shouted them pizza and beer for dinner, but more likely because we'd been alongside them through a minor polt-pelting, the housemates invited us to stay overnight.

During daylight hours we'd found the polt events exciting and amusing rather than scary, but that night, as we lay on the carpeted floor of the darkened lounge room, sheets up to chins, eyes probing the shifting shadows, ears scanning the creaking, scratching, scurrying sounds of the tropic night, the situation seemed less of a giggle. We may even have been slightly nervous. Paul seemed to think Tony was particularly jumpy: in the morning he regaled our amused housemates with the story, surely slightly exaggerated, of how, after one particularly loud, staccato cry from a gecko, he'd had to carefully peel his ghost-busting buddy from the ceiling.

As the night had been so uneventful, we wondered if the phenomena we'd witnessed the day before had been the polt's last hurrah. We hoped not, as we still hadn't seen enough to dispel all doubt about possible hoaxing.

"It's started again!"

Again, we needn't have worried. At about 11 am, as Tony was driving back to McMinns Road after a quick trip to Howard Springs, he was met by Andrew and Paul coming the other way. "It's started again", they yelled. "Big time!"

Half an hour earlier, since the polt had shown no inclination to get started, Andrew had volunteered to "stir it up". Taking Father Tom's bible, he'd gone to one of the back bedrooms – a rather pokey, low-ceilinged room that seemed to have more of a spooky feel about it than the rest of the house – and read aloud from *The Book of Psalms*. The tactic seemed to work: within a couple of minutes a couple of gravel falls occurred in the kitchen/family room – one shower fell right on Paul's head when Kirsty and Andrew were a couple of metres away, in clear view.

The much-travelled crucifix then shot across the room. Paul didn't see it fly – just heard it hit the wall with a resounding *whack* and fall to the floor. Seemingly, nobody in the room could have launched it on the trajectory it followed. A couple of minutes later a D-cell battery did the same thing – again with no one in position to have thrown it.

All this occurred with Andrew, Kirsty and little Jasmine in the room. Murph was also in plain sight, a couple of metres away on a sofa, trying to make up for the sleep he missed while out on his fishing boat the previous night. Completely out to it, he didn't stir even when pebbles fell right next to the couch.

As Tony entered the room a four-inch-long shard of glass struck the kitchen table, broke, and fell in pieces to the floor. Neither of us saw the glass in flight and although it *might* have been possible for Kirsty or Andrew to have tossed it, we thought that very unlikely. To do so would have put them at very grave risk of detection. Also, while armchair-based sceptics might think it plausible that young parents would, for some unknown reason, deliberately strew broken glass around their own barefoot toddler, we, who were on the spot and who were now getting to know the couple, thought it inconceivable.

As they cleaned up the debris, they stressed again that if they thought the child was in danger they would have baled out of the house months ago. As it was, no matter how close the objects came to her, she had never been so much as touched by one. Kirsty remarked that the only objects of concern were the ubiquitous centimetre-wide pebbles, which she had to constantly sweep up as they constituted a choking hazard for the child,

By now, we novice polt-busters, while attempting to remain properly sceptical, were strongly inclined to believe the phenomenon was genuine. We were also, in fact, excited, amused and thoroughly enjoying the show. Gratified by our open-mindedness, Andrew again attempted to "stir the polt". Accompanied by Tony, he took the bible to the "spooky" back room and again read psalms aloud. As Tony began to photograph him, excited shouts came from the kitchen/family room: more gravel plus one of the "frequent flyers" – a .44 magnum cartridge – had fallen/flown.

Stirring the polt. (Healy/Cropper)

Shortly thereafter something hit the kitchen wall with a resounding *whack* and Tony, who happened to be looking that way, saw a shiny projectile ricochet at great speed across the room at knee height, pass between Kirsty and little Jasmine who were standing about three feet apart, bounce off a cabinet and come to rest on the floor. It proved to be a rather nasty-looking object: the heavy, jagged base of a broken shot glass. As with many of the other flying objects, it was clear that nobody in the room (only Paul, Tony, Kirsty, Andrew and the child) had been in position to launch the glass on the trajectory it followed.

The glass was distinctly warm. This was of some interest because we knew that during many other poltergeist episodes people had remarked on how warm, even hot, some flying objects were. The phenomenon was noted right from the start at Humpty Doo and, as mentioned previously, the single most useful thing done by the Channel Seven crew during their time there was to employ Brendan Gowdie, whose thermal imaging camera had revealed that the surfaces of apparently polt-propelled objects were uniformly warm, whereas objects thrown by people displayed an uneven pattern of heat.

Although we believe Mr. Gowdie's photographs strongly indicate that paranormal activity was occurring, they don't constitute irrefutable proof of such activity and, in fairness to sceptical readers, we should mention that at the moment the warm, broken shot glass flew across the room Kirsty was engaged in washing dishes – in warm water. (Although Tony had, as mentioned, been facing her at the time, and had seen the glass flying *towards* her).

Immediately after that we did a quick tour of the house and found that Jill and Dave's mattress had been dragged halfway off their bed and scattered with pebbles. This, as previously mentioned, was one of the polt's most annoying tricks, which it played constantly, sometimes several times a day.

Unmaking the beds. (Healy/Cropper)

A pistol-packin' pest

Then the action came thick and fast. Back in the kitchen, as we sat facing Andrew and Kirsty across the small, round, dining table, a .44 magnum cartridge fell onto Paul's knee, and onto the floor. Andrew, sitting directly opposite, exclaimed that he'd actually seen it appear just a couple of feet above Paul's shoulder. Paul remarked that the weighty little object had hit him very lightly and that if it had fallen from any higher than a couple of feet he would have expected a much heavier impact. It had definitely fallen vertically. As with several of the other falling/flying objects, there seemed no way that Andrew or Kirsty could have launched it on the trajectory it took.

There were now two cartridges in the kitchen. Earlier, the housemates had shown us how, every now and then, sometimes a couple of times a day, they would gather any objects that had landed inside the house, take them outside and place them in a drawer

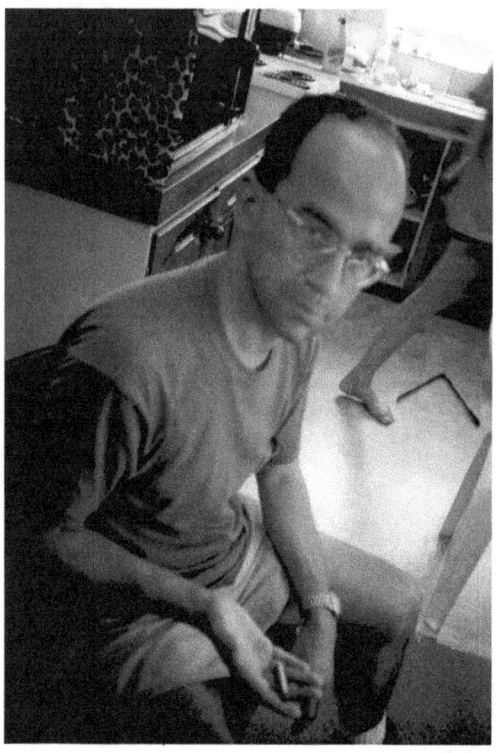

Targeted: Paul and the bullet. (Healy/Cropper)

next to the barbeque. Among the "frequent flyers" commonly stored in the drawer were four .44 magnum cartridges. As two of those cartridges were now indoors, we went outside to check on the others. They were there – but not for long: soon afterwards there were more thumps and bumps around the kitchen: the other two bullets had arrived, along with another couple of "frequent flyers" – the little silver skull and a small brass plug.

By this stage, although we were very inclined to believe the polt was genuine, we were still attempting to stay alert for anything that suggested hoaxing. We could think of no way several of the incidents could have been faked, but were still open to suggestions.

A lame-brained theory

As mentioned earlier, Simon Potter of the NT Skeptics Association had angered the tenants by repeatedly declaring, on television and in newspaper interviews, his belief that the whole thing was a hoax. So we looked through back copies of the *Northern Territory News* to see if he'd said anything that shone any light on the matter.

Although we were hoping for something a bit more substantial, we weren't entirely surprised to find that his recorded statements were ill-informed and that the theory he'd come up with to account for the flying objects was utterly implausible.

"It is quite simple", he said, "All you need is to get an object, such as a steak knife, and stick it to the top of one of the blades [of a ceiling fan], turn the fan on and sure enough the object is going to fly off ... And it can be done so the object will fly off moments, or even after a long period of time after the fan has been turned on. Even some stones mixed in mud on top of the blades would fly off and make it appear as if the gravel came from the roof or was thrown."[23]

In fact, the fans were the very first thing we'd looked at. As the house had no air conditioning, the fans were running almost continuously. In all the time we were there,

---

23   *Northern Territory News*, 25 April 1998.

in fact, we never saw them turned off, except when we did so to examine them. We saw no sign of glue, tape, Blue-tack or other adhesive.

During his first visit, Jack Ellis of the *Litchfield Times* had also thought to switch off the fans – and had then – with the blades completely stationary – been comprehensively showered with stones. He also experimented with his own ceiling fans at home and found that "The trajectory of the rocks was totally different – they were just flung against the wall."[24]

Potter's suggestion that stones could have been mixed with mud to make them stick to the blades of the fans was not only lame-brained but also ill-informed: the pebbles that fell were invariably clean and nobody had ever been sprinkled with dried mud. Besides, traces of such mud would have been very easy to find on top of the blades.

In any case, as we had seen, stones and other objects fell vertically in sections of the room well away from the fans; objects flew knee-high across the kitchen and family room, other objects flew and fell in the corridor and outside the house, where there were no fans.

Even if it were plausible that objects taped to ceiling fans could hurtle violently across a room in the manner we had seen (and we are certain it was not) why would anyone deliberately catapult dangerous objects, including broken glass and sharp knives, on scores of occasions over many weeks, through their living area at the risk of blinding, cutting or killing themselves, members of the press and public – and an eleven-month-old child?

Potter had infuriated the housemates quite early on, when, shortly after the media became aware of the story, he'd appeared on television to smugly declare the whole thing a hoax. When journalists told the housemates what he'd said and asked what they'd do if he turned up at the property, they reacted as one would expect: they said they'd knock his bloody head off. But three weeks later he was still claiming to be puzzled at being barred. "I don't know", he complained to the *Northern Territory News* on April 23, "why we [NT Skeptics Association] haven't been allowed anywhere near the place".

A blade and a battery

At one stage, hoping that the spook might deign to reply, Paul went into the bathroom and spelt out a word or two on the floor using scrabble tiles. Tony watched him for a while and then began to follow Kirsty back to the family room. After a couple of paces he spun around, intending to say something else to Paul, and as he did so a knife flew past about 20 centimetres from his right ear, coming down at a sharp angle and hitting the carpet a couple of metres in front of him.

That was pretty exciting but we tried to remain sceptical. Kirsty had been only two or three paces ahead of Tony when he reversed direction. Could she have thrown the knife?

---

24   Ken Llewelyn, *Caressa, From Call Girl to God's Child*, p. 126.

A near-miss. (Healy/Cropper)

But Tony's change of direction had been very sudden: he'd no sooner turned on his heel when the thing flew past his ear. Kirsty had been walking away with her back to him and, furthermore, would have had difficulty concealing the blade: she was barefoot, dressed only in brief cotton shorts and T-shirt and was carrying young Jasmine in her arms.

A few minutes later, as Tony sat in the family room, an object hit the wall in front of him with a resounding *whack*, narrowly missing young Jasmine, who was actually leaning on the wall at the time, and ricocheting onto the floor. The toddler was startled and for a moment looked distinctly puzzled.

Although she wasn't injured, she certainly could have been. The projectile was a common AA battery, quite small, certainly, but heavy enough to have severely bruised or even blinded the infant (who was clad in nothing but a nappy) had the polt's aim not been so perfect.

But could Kirsty or Andrew, in the kitchen some metres behind Tony, have thrown the battery? It seemed that neither of them could have done so without risking being seen by the other, so if it *was* thrown then they had colluded in endangering the child. We found that impossible to believe.

At that point some sensible soul said it for all of us: "Ok – enough is enough – let's not provoke it anymore!"

"It *is* happening, isn't it?"

By this stage we'd seen almost enough to convince us that the polt was the real McCoy. We realise however, that some readers will be hesitant to accept that we – who have spent 35 years investigating such things as lake monsters, yetis, mystery big cats, UFOs and spook lights, and who, like agent Mulder, really *want* to believe – were capable of a truly objective investigation.

It is therefore worth repeating that all the investigators who visited the site before we did – three priests, three *Litchfield Times* reporters, the five-man "Today Tonight" crew, journalist Max Anderson, plus the freelance cameramen Brendan Gowdie, Danny Sim and Jarrod Suttee – had all been convinced the phenomenon was genuine. We later talked to two Darwin-based journalists who had also seen utterly mind-boggling events at the house.

During our five days at McMinns Drive only one journalist visited the house. He was a distinguished member of his profession: Walkley Award-winning Frank Robson, of the *Sydney Morning Herald*.

Very professional and thorough, Frank conducted several interviews – with Fr. Steven, Fr. Tom, the staff of the *Litchfield Times* and others. He rented a cabin behind the nearby Humpty Doo pub and spent two days and evenings at McMinns Drive.

Although he arrived at the house with a properly sceptical attitude, he was also determined to remain open minded – which was just as well, because he soon witnessed so many inexplicable events that he was forced to accept that something paranormal really was occurring.

With that realisation came another: as a worldly-wise journo he knew that any reporter who dared to state, in a major national newspaper, that he'd seen poltergeist activity risked being pilloried, not only by other writers and editors but also, quite possibly, by ABC Television's dreaded "Media Watch" program. ("Media Watch's" acerbic host, Richard Ackland, had already skewered Channel Seven for its coverage of the story – and taken an uninformed, gratuitous slap at the McMinns Drive residents for good measure).

On his first day at the house, after one of many weird incidents, Frank turned to us and said, "I just hope that when I write my article I have the guts to tell the truth about all this." Holding in his hand an object that had fallen, apparently from nowhere, a few minutes earlier, he spoke again: "It really *is* happening, isn't it?"

Frank Robson. (Healy/Cropper)

Fortunately for us, for the polt-plagued tenants, and for all the others who'd told the truth about their experiences, Frank is a man of integrity. In his article, which appeared in the *Sydney Morning Herald Good Weekend Magazine* on 13 June 1998, he made no bones about it: everything he'd seen at the house and everything he'd learned in interviews with multiple eyewitnesses indicated that the Humpty Doo poltergeist phenomenon was entirely genuine. The only joke in his article was a good one, and didn't reflect on the credibility of anyone concerned. As he was casting around for a catchy title for the piece an inspired colleague suggested this gem: "HUMPTY BOO!"

On his first evening at McMinns Drive Frank was drinking beer at the outdoor bar with Dave, Kirsty and Jill when, just before 10 pm, a shower of gravel fell from above their heads and rattled onto the bar. Frank noted that the sound, which he caught on his tape recorder, seemed to be "… much louder than the sound eight or 10 pebbles should make falling from that height" Just as weirdly, he had the distinct impression that although they had made an unnaturally loud noise on impact, the stones, some of which passed within a few inches of his face and onto his arms, had also fallen at an unnaturally slow speed.

When the phenomenon occurred, he'd been no more than a metre from the three housemates and was looking directly at them. None of them had moved. Furthermore, there was no sound of the pebbles striking the underside of the unlined tin roof about a metre above their heads – as they would have done if thrown upwards.

Later that night and on the following day Frank witnessed several other inexplicable falls, some of which, like the initial pebble shower, seemed to make an excessively loud noise. Once, when he and Paul were in the kitchen, a 20-cent coin struck the wall a few metres behind them with, as Frank put it, "amazing force". They watched it roll to a stop, "stunned that something this size could make so much noise."[25]

A mismatch between the size of thrown objects and the noise they make has been noted during many other polt episodes. We noticed it at Humpty Doo, as did many others, including Father Stephen. When Frank interviewed him, the priest pointed out that if a drinking glass is thrown against a wall it "… creates only a certain amount of noise" whereas a glass he saw flying into a wall at McMinns Drive "… sounded like 100 tumblers smashing … Wow, what a sound!"

We were at the house when Frank visited for a second time. As Kirsty's housemates were all at work, the three of us agreed that it was a good opportunity to spot anything in her behaviour that suggested hoaxing.

As things seemed a little quiet, Paul opened play by reading a few psalms in the "spooky" back room and in Jill and Dave's room.

The polt returned serve at 11.25 am when, from somewhere above Frank's head, it pitched a small battery onto the kitchen floor. A knife and a stone soon followed. Paul then checked Jill and Dave's room – and found gravel scattered across the bed. It hadn't been there when he'd read the psalms.

Shortly thereafter, as he entered the bathroom, a pair of scissors hit the floor behind him. Although Kirsty was within range, she was making a telephone call at the time – with the phone in one hand and a cigarette in the other.

The polt pranks continued for 40 minutes or so, culminating in an event that would have been, given the circumstances, very difficult if not nearly impossible to hoax.

---

25 Frank Robson, *Sydney Morning Herald*, 13 June 1998.

Show us your cross

When one of her chores required Kirsty to fetch something from the garage Frank accompanied her, partly to take a few pictures, but mainly to keep her under observation. As they neared the outbuilding, about 30 metres from the house, he asked her to pause for a photograph. Meanwhile Paul was in the process of walking towards them across the covered patio beside the house. Suddenly something hit the concrete just behind him. It was Father Tom's much-travelled, much-abused crucifix.

It would take a determined sceptic to believe that Kirsty had fitted the crucifix into some kind of catapult and triggered it remotely while being photographed by Frank 30 metres away. The device would then have had to retract undetectably into the bare ceiling of the breezeway.

An impudent imp

Shortly thereafter, seated in the kitchen during a lull in the action, Tony was reflecting on the tenants' belief that the polt eavesdropped on their conversations. Recalling a suggestion by British researcher Colin Wilson that polts may even be capable of picking up on peoples' thoughts[26], he impulsively attempted to project a suggestion along the lines of, "OK – let's see your next trick!"

Seconds later three Scrabble tiles bounced off the base of the kitchen wall. There was an "S", another "S" and an "A". If they were meant to form a word, the only one we could think of was – embarrassingly – "ASS". With the chuckles of Paul, Kirsty – and possibly the unseen imp – echoing in his ears, Tony left the room, unsure whether he should feel pleased that he (might have) communicated telepathically with a polt, or mortified at being insulted by a smart-arse from the Twilight Zone.

At this stage, although he believed the testimony of others, and although he had witnessed many flying objects shortly before impact or in the process of ricocheting off walls, Tony, unlike Paul, had yet to witness any single event that he felt couldn't possibly have been faked.

Out of thin air

He didn't have to wait much longer. That afternoon, as Kirsty sat at the kitchen table, he happened to ask her about a recent *Litchfield Times* article. In response, she picked up the paper and began to read aloud. Seconds later, Tony saw an object fall onto the small, bare table between them. He was facing directly towards the object and had the distinct

---

26 Colin Wilson, *Poltergeist!*, p. 162. Liz Fleming, focus of paranormal phenomena in the "Caressa" case (Chapter Four) also claimed that a polt could read her mind.

Kirsty at the table. (Healy/Cropper)

impression that it simply materialised in mid air, about a foot and a half (45 cm) above the table.

It proved to be a well-known "frequent flyer": a small brass plug, originally part of an air compressor that resided in the back of the garage.

While a skilled conjurer could probably accomplish such a trick, Tony thought it near-impossible that Kirsty could have flicked the plug into the air. She'd been holding the newspaper with both hands and reading aloud at the time, Tony had been looking straight at her, Frank was less than three metres away and Paul was also in the room. The object's behaviour on landing – a dead-fall with barely a bounce – also seemed to rule out anything other than a vertical trajectory. Such "deadfalls" have been observed many times during other poltergeist episodes.

Shell shock

While Frank Robson was the only journalist to visit the house while we were there, we met (in addition to the staff of the *Litchfield Times*) two other seasoned journalists who'd been there previously. Nikki Voss, Chief of Staff at the *Northern Territory News*, and ABC radio reporter Tracy Farrar were both convinced they'd observed genuinely paranormal phenomena – phenomena that was, in fact, considerably stranger than anything we'd seen.

Nikki told us that she and her photographer had their "extreme scepticism" jolted as soon as they arrived at the property. As they walked down the driveway and drew level with the side of the residence they'd been greeted by a beer mug that shot with great force and uncanny accuracy through a small pre-existing hole in the kitchen window and bounced off a fence to their left. Taking the object inside, they found it had passed through the hole with only millimetres of clearance.

Still doggedly sceptical, Nikki's veteran cameraman suggested that to foil hoaxers they stand with their backs to an internal wall. The polt, however, was way ahead of them: no sooner had they backed up against the wall than they were hit in the nape of their necks with a shower of gravel that came – impossibly – from behind them.

Because one of the tenants might conceivably have thrown it, Rachelle Barnett of the *Litchfield Times* managed to remain sceptical after witnessing Father Tom's crucifix fly across the living room. But she began to have second thoughts after looking into the bathroom, where she noticed several felt-tip pens from the child's colouring set. They'd been carefully arranged on the floor to spell out the letters "TRO".

"As we left the bathroom something landed with a bang on top of the [vanity] cabinet. It was the TV remote control from the lounge room, which seemed to have dropped through the roof or the wall. There was no way for someone to have thrown [it] because everyone had just left the bathroom.

"When we went back to the bathroom shortly afterwards, the rest of the word had been completed to form 'TROY'". The pens were still quivering[27].

Tracy Farrar experienced something even weirder. In her spare time, she makes jewellery from seashells and on the day before the Humpty Doo visit she'd spent hours collecting a particular type of small, brown shell at a Darwin beach. Next morning, while interviewing Kirsty (who she'd never met before), she watched in amazement as an identical shell sailed over her shoulder and landed on the table between them. Rachelle entered the room moments later to witness more shells falling, apparently from the ceiling.

Shocked: Tracy Farrar. (Healy/Cropper)

During her interview with Kirsty, Tracy received several electric shocks from her microphone – something that had never happened before – and also saw the much-travelled TV remote *lift off a table just a couple of feet to her right and fly up into the air.*

Before joining the ABC she'd been a science technician. Yet, as she told Frank Robson later, "I can't explain it in [scientific] or any other terms. But I know what I saw … and it wasn't a hoax." Although thrilled by the polt experience, she was, like Nikki Voss, plagued by bad dreams for several nights afterwards.

Like us, Nikki, Tracy and Rachelle couldn't see how all of the phenomena could have been faked or *why* anyone would do it. The money from Channel Seven (only $2000, or $400 each) was not significant, the tenants clearly didn't relish the public attention and they absolutely did not want to leave the house. A hoaxing individual

---

27   *Litchfield Times*, 9 April 1998.

or clique within the group would have risked "murder" by the others if discovered.

So, after spending the better part of five days and evenings at the site, we left the Northern Territory 99% sure that a poltergeist really was infesting that little blue house at Humpty Doo.

But, convincing as the positive testimony of so many independent witnesses was – not to mention the evidence of our own eyes – we couldn't make an honest assessment of the case without coming to terms with what Greg Quail insisted was Kirsty's "confession".

Lies and videotape

During our time at Humpty Doo and for a long time afterwards we didn't think much of the alleged confession. It seemed clear that, during the crucial midnight telephone call to Humpty Doo, Quail was under intense pressure to deliver the negative outcome his bosses demanded. Given the lateness of the hour and his stressed-out condition, we thought it likely he'd simply misinterpreted one of Kirsty's responses.

In 2011, when we finally interviewed him, it was evident that he still strongly believed she'd confessed. He was adamant she'd admitted she did it "because she [was] desperate to convince people the house [was] haunted by a poltergeist". She'd also, he said, promised to submit to a later interview in which she would explain her actions.

The irony was that although he believed she'd faked that particular incident, he was still convinced that most of the phenomena he and his crew experienced at Humpty Doo really did defy explanation. "Weird things were going on", he told us, "the place was insane … crazy shit happened … we had all that stuff … [but] that woman undid everything. We busted her on tape cheating"[28].

He'd previously told freelance journalist Max Anderson much the same thing: "*You know there's something [genuine] in there, I know there's something in there, but what can I do? With that one incident, she's blown the whole story.*"[29]

It seems that even though his crew had failed to obtain much film of objects in flight, Quail had hoped that the footage of his very thorough investigation would be enough to convince most viewers that the phenomenon was genuinely paranormal. But by faking the pot lid incident Kirsty had entirely destroyed the story's credibility. Even thirteen years later he appeared to be absolutely furious that she'd "messed up" his project, making him, for a while, the butt of some humour in television circles.

So, since Kirsty adamantly denies the alleged confession, the truth of the pot lid incident hinges entirely on a tiny fragment of film. The man who shot the footage, Jarrod Suttee, was presumably best placed to judge the truth of the matter. Interviewed by Frank Robson just days just after the event, he unreservedly backed Kirsty. The pot lid wasn't the only object to move that evening. Things, he said, "were flying everywhere",

---

28   Paul Cropper, interview with Greg Quail, 2 September 2011.
29   Max Anderson, *The Australian*, 9–10 May 1998.

many from impossible angles. After repeatedly viewing the film, he and his boss Danny Sim could see no evidence of her throwing the lid.

Kirsty had been behind him and to his right, ironing clothes. "From the angle she's supposed to have thrown the thing it would have had to change course by about 70 degrees – in mid-air – to strike where it ended up". He pointed out that the supposedly incriminating shot of Kirsty consisted of only two frames of film – which at normal speed would last just one twelfth of a second. The object was moving at "around a metre in one twenty-fifth of a second. How could [she] throw something faster than test bowler Glen McGrath can bowl?"

As mentioned previously, before we travelled to Humpty Doo in 1998 we'd videotaped the "Today Tonight" episode containing the supposedly incriminating footage and viewed it many times. The quality of our tape, however, was so poor that, although the pot lid was discernible towards the end of its flight, we couldn't make out its entire "flight path". And while Kirsty, to judge from her dim reflection, *might* have risen slightly just as the object flew, we could see no hand movement or other indication that she'd thrown it. Because of that, and because of our low opinion of Australian tabloid television, we'd been very much inclined to accept Kirsty's version of events.

Recently, however, when we obtained a much higher quality copy of the crucial footage and viewed it repeatedly on widescreen digital television, we somewhat modified our harsh judgment of the film – and of the "Today Tonight" editors and executives. It was now possible to discern the pot lid as it flew in an arc past the glass doors of the cabinet. And that "flight path", to be fair to sceptics, *does* seem to originate in the vicinity of Kirsty's reflection.

It is clear, also, that Kirsty appears to bob upwards – perhaps even *sharply* upwards – just as the object first comes into view. As mentioned earlier, she claimed that she was shaking out her baby's clothes and simply looked up as the object flew, and that may have been the case. Because of the extreme brevity of the incident, however, we simply can't make a definite "call", on the basis of the film alone, as to whether or not she threw the object. But we can understand why Greg Quail and the "Today Tonight" bosses might think she did.

Jarrod Suttee and Danny Sim both insisted that if Kirsty had thrown the object it would have had to turn sharply in mid-air to enter the corridor as it did. After repeated viewings of the film we can't make out any such deviation, but as Jarrod and Danny were right there on the spot, and as, having only her reflection to go by, we can't be sure of Kirsty's exact position, we must defer to their judgement.

There *are* a couple of things about the sequence, however, that may suggest a polt didn't hurl the lid.

The object flies in a distinct arc, and, to our eyes, doesn't seem to be travelling any faster than it would have if thrown by a mere mortal. And the sound it makes upon impact is pretty unremarkable – unlike the unnaturally-loud whacks noted at other times. Also, the lid bounces quite normally – there is no suggestion of the "dead fall" observed during some of the earlier incidents.

Like us, Frank Robson found it interesting that although he'd delivered the "hoax" conclusion desired by his bosses, Greg Quail still believed in the polt. "There's no way in the wide world," Quail told Robson only two days after the final program went to air, "that anyone could have [contrived] some of the things that happened before my eyes."

Robson also stressed this important point: we'll never know for sure what transpired during the contentious phone call because, "Curiously, given what was at stake, Quail did not record [the] supposed confession."

This might also be considered: given all the electronic gadgets that she knew he had at his disposal, Kirsty must have known there was a very good chance that Quail *had* taped the call. Yet she confidently refuted his version of their conversation.

Reasons to believe:

The Humpty Doo case displayed many of the hallmarks of a genuine polt outbreak: showers of stones both indoors and out, dangerous objects thrown with great force but without causing injury, objects falling unnaturally slowly yet producing unnaturally loud sounds on impact, objects observed levitating, objects observed materialising in mid-air, rappings, scratchings, violent reactions to prayers and religious paraphernalia, threatening messages and nasty mind games.

As pointed out previously, everyone we know of – priests, cameramen, soundmen, radio, television and print journalists – who actually visited the house to investigate the phenomenon, became convinced it was genuine.

When Andrew told us about it, we'd never heard of anything like the frequently-disappearing bottle opener that always returned brightly polished – but we have since learned that that same very odd and unexpected detail occurred in the United States in the 1850s. During a long drawn-out and very interesting polt episode recorded by J. Frank Dobie in *Tales of Old-Time Texas*, many objects vanished or were moved around in locked and guarded buildings in a region known as The Navidad. On one occasion a saw and a 12 foot long, 30 pound log chain disappeared from under the noses of guard dogs, and then reappeared just as mysteriously, "scoured and polished as bright as a looking glass ... no one knew before that this familiar metal was susceptible of such a gloss". We consider it extremely unlikely that Andrew could have stumbled across that very obscure American story.

We have also discovered a nineteenth-century case wherein bullets disappeared and reappeared in a similar way to the .44 magnum cartridges at Humpty Doo.

That well-documented episode occurred in 1829–30 at John McDonald's homestead near Wallaceburg, Ontario, beside a branch of the St. Clair River. It featured levitation of furniture, materialisation of objects, scores of inexplicable little fires and, as a grand finale, the total immolation of the homestead.

There were dozens of eyewitnesses. As at Humpty Doo, many bullets – in this case musket balls – landed inside the homestead. Members of the family, their neighbours and other visitors, marked the soft leaden balls and threw them in the river – only to see them promptly reappear inside the house[30].

In none of our interaction with them at McMinns Drive, in none of our phone conversations before and since, and in none of the interviews they gave to print, radio and television journalists, did we detect anything in the residents' statements or demeanour that even faintly suggested they weren't truthful.

As Kirsty spent much more time around the house than any of the others, most investigators – including ourselves – decided that if any individual was hoaxing, it virtually had to be her. But none of her housemates doubted her for a moment. Another consideration is that Andrew and Kirsty had been together for several years. If she was a conjurer of stage magician standard she'd managed to keep that talent to herself throughout their entire relationship.

Furthermore – as her housemates and the Channel Seven team pointed out – polt phenomena also occurred when Kirsty was away from home. When the pistol bullet was filmed falling, for instance, neither she nor any of the other tenants was indoors.

We think it impossible that all of the strange phenomena could have been produced by simple sleight of hand or other trickery. Several events, like the vertical shower of pebbles that hit Paul, the fall of the bullet onto his knee, the fall of the crucifix behind him on the patio and the apparent materialisation of the brass plug in front of Tony's eyes – seemed almost unfakeable. Consider, too, the stones that pelted Nikki Voss and her photographer in the nape of their necks as they stood with their backs against a wall, the levitating TV remote that Tracy Farrar witnessed, plus the small brown shell – identical to the ones she'd been collecting the previous day – that fell onto the table in front of her.

Wise words

Something we unintentionally tape-recorded during our time at the house also inclines us to believe the phenomenon was genuine. At one stage, after trying to record the sound of objects bouncing off walls and floors, Paul inadvertently left his machine running in the family room while he stepped outside. During his absence it picked up a telephone conversation between Andrew and his father.

During the cheerful and unaffected long-distance chat his dad apparently asked about the poltergeist. "Yeah – it's still going on", said Andrew. His dad then apparently commiserated with him about the final "Today Tonight" program, whereupon Andrew said "they hounded her [Kirsty] for hours in the middle of the night demanding that she confess to throwing the plastic lid …" As he hangs up he says to someone nearby, "[Dad] says we should never have let them [the 'Today Tonight' crew] in". Wise words.

---

30 McDonald, Neil T., *The Belledoon Mysteries, An O'er True Story*, Wallaceburg News Book and Job Print, Ontario, 1905. (Princeton University copy, digitised by Google).

What triggered the Humpty Doo episode?

The outbreak of weirdness may not have had just a single cause; it seems likely, in fact, that it was triggered by a combination of factors.

Trouy's death?

Trouy and his mate died when their vehicle, loaded with paint thinner, crashed and exploded in a ball of flame. The timing of his death – in January, shortly before the first stone falls – cannot be ignored.

Many times throughout the centuries it has been suggested that polt phenomena is caused by restless spirits of the recently deceased. The following chapters contain a few other Australian cases in which similar strange events occurred shortly after someone's violent, gruesome, premature or unexpected death. Trouy's death was certainly premature – he was, as they say, "too young to die" – as well as unexpected and extremely gruesome.

As mentioned earlier, however, despite all the references to his death – "FIRE", "CAR" etc. – that were scrawled on their walls and floors, Trouy's friends strongly rejected the notion that it was he who was haunting them. They could think of no reason why he, a good friend to all, should give them trouble. They concluded instead that the scrawled messages, in which his name was misspelled, were just one of the polt's nasty mind games. After they loudly challenged it on the matter all references to Trouy, cars and fires ceased.

Murph?

Murph had been one of Trouy's best mates, and it was he who seemed most affected by his tragic death, who found the polt activity most annoying and who most resented the media attention.

He was sensitive to ridicule and had a very volatile personality: his muscular arms, in a way, told the story: they were (and given the manner of Trouy's death this seemed weirdly appropriate) covered with tattoos of *flames*. While most of the words and phrases spelt out on the walls and floors seemed to refer to Trouy's death or to the Channel Seven TV crew, one cryptic message, which consisted of only two letters – "MF" – puzzled the housemates. The only theory they could come up with was that it might have been a reference to Murph.

We had rarely met anyone who appeared to be nursing as much bottled-up rage as Murph. Given that many researchers have suggested polts somehow gain strength from psychic energy given off by people going through emotional turmoil, it seems reasonable to suspect that Murph's grief, anger and frustration contributed to the intensity of the Humpty Doo episode.

Kirsty a medium?

Father Stephen's "take" on the situation was that a restless spirit may have been drawn to the house, possibly because one of the occupants was, without being aware of it, a natural medium.

As we have seen, Andrew was fairly sure the phenomenon was focused on Kirsty. He pointed out that they'd experienced strange incidents at previous residences and suggested that the polt, in a weaker form, may have followed them from Batchelor to the NSW central coast and back again. When they reached Humpty Doo it decided, for some reason, to go ballistic.

On the other hand, when Andrew and Kirsty finally left the McMinns Drive property, they experienced, as far as we know, no further strange phenomena. (As of 2010, when we last checked with them, Jill and Dave, living happily in the Territory, were also polt-free).

An Aboriginal curse?

The surreptitious visit by the two unknown Aborigines, during which they began to dig a hole right next to the house, certainly suggests that they were trying to influence the polt activity.

If one accepts that curses cast by Aboriginal shamans – "clever men" – really can cause supernatural mischief, it is possible to imagine that the Humpty Doo phenomenon was the result of a curse put on Andrew a couple of years earlier, at Batchelor. Perhaps the "bush Aborigines" visited McMinns Road to lift the curse – or perhaps they came to renew or intensify it.

Many, if not most, Aborigines believe that shamans are capable of remarkable feats such as psychic healing, remote viewing, teleportation and levitation, and many knowledgeable non-Aborigines, including the great anthropologist A.P. Elkin, have become convinced that such "men of high degree" possess, at the least, strong telepathic and clairvoyant ability[31].

While we know of no Australian case, other than Humpty Doo, where it has been suggested shamans are capable of inducing stone falls, there *has* been such a case in South Africa.

Don't knock the Doc

In early July 1980 two 17-year-old tennis players, Okkie Kellerman and Andre Wulfse, were on their way to Maritzburg for a major tournament. When their train pulled into a siding near the city they made the mistake of mocking an oddly-dressed man who described himself as a "witch doctor". As he gestured angrily, they went away laughing – but soon regretted their rudeness.

---

31   James Cowan, *Aborigine Dreaming*, pp. 86–101.

After a practice session the next day, Okkie found himself being pelted with stones that seemed to come from nowhere. For several days thereafter, whenever he and Andre ventured out of their lodgings, "suddenly the stones would be all around us". Matters came to a head on the night of 11 July when stones rained down for three hours inside the boys' bedroom. When interviewed by the South African *Sunday Times*, their landlord, Peter Dove, confirmed the story. "The rocks", he said, "started flying virtually from the time Okkie and Andre arrived at the house and stopped only when they left."[32]

A Greek curse?

Journalist Ross Irby, of *The Northern Territory News*, uncovered another very interesting possibility. He interviewed Stavros Kanaris, who built the McMinns Drive house and lived there happily for 20 years before being forced to leave. Mr. Kanaris believed the polt activity was the result of his family's anger at being evicted after his building business failed in 1993. The words he chose were loaded with emotion, his bitterness palpable: "The bank took my blood – 30 years of hard work." Now reduced to renting in Darwin, the family yearned to return to the property: "My spirit every night is there. Every night I'm there in my dreams. My wife is always there too. It was our life."

As she was forced out the door on the final day, Maria Kanaris didn't curse her beloved house. She did, however, put a heartfelt curse on the bank[33].

The Kanaris's seething, unappeased anger and constant yearning for their lost dream home could very well have contributed to the psychic stew that spawned the Humpty Doo polt. The fact that Maria Kanaris quite literally "put a curse on the bank" also has to be taken into account. (Mind you, if a poltergeist was generated every time someone cursed a bank every home would have one!)

A history of weirdness?

Irene Winters, who cleaned the residence some weeks before the group moved in, recalled that "there was this horrible feeling in the whole house"; it was unnaturally cold, and doors seemed to open and close of their own volition. She said that a tradesman who was working there at the time became spooked and left without even beginning the work he was contracted to do. "He just said, 'I'm out of here!' It was really freaky."

It would be natural for sceptics to assume that Ms. Winters' recollections were coloured by newspaper articles she read later. But she wasn't the only person to suggest there was something weird about the place prior to January 1998.

---

32 *Sunday Times* (South Africa), 20 July 1980, quoted in *Fortean Times* no. 35, pp. 42–43.
33 *Northern Territory News*, 6 April 1998.

One of Father Tom English's parishioners claimed that she, too, had been puzzled by self-closing doors and other odd things when she played on the property as a child.[34]

Annette Taylor, the schoolteacher who was struck by the levitating vice-grips while visiting the property in March 1998, had lived there during part of 1997. She told Frank Robson that although no actual poltergeist phenomena occurred during her occupancy, she "… knew that there was something there. I used to say so to people, and they looked at me as though I was weird."[35]

Dave Clark suspected that Kosta and Angela Boubaris, the people who bought the house when the original owners were forced to sell, had also experienced frightening phenomena on the property. As he pointed out later, it seemed very strange that while they were renting-out the comfortable, spacious house to Dave and his friends, they themselves, along with their five children, were cooped up just down the road in a stiflingly hot tin shed. Had they been too frightened to stay in the larger residence?

A steamy, stormy spook?

The Humpty Doo episode began during "The Wet" – the stormy monsoon season, and when he arrived at the property the psychic ghost-buster, Stephen Bishop, mentioned his belief that "storms unsettle polts"[36] That suggestion didn't surprise Dave Clark, who'd noticed the connection some weeks earlier: "when thunderstorms and lightening were around 'it' appeared to use this energy to do what it wanted"[37].

Stormy weather has been mentioned during other Australian poltergeist episodes, notably the ones that occurred in 1935 at Cannibal Creek, at Mayanup in the 1950s and in the brothels of Canberra in 1994–96 (see Chapters Two, Four and Five). In this context, it is worth mentioning that in a great many cases, both in Australia and overseas, polts have apparently manipulated a wide range of electrical appliances.

Very appropriate!

While he was writing his article for the *Sydney Morning Herald* Frank Robson thought to check the derivation of the name "Humpty Doo" and came up with an interesting result. According to the Place Names Committee of the Northern Territory, Humpty Doo is named after the cattle station "Umpity Doo", whose name derives from a colloquialism meaning "everything was going well" or the complete opposite: *"everything done wrong or upside down"*.

---

34   Ken Llewelyn, *Caressa*, p. 134.
35   Frank Robson, *Sydney Morning Herald*, 13 June 1998.
36   Max Anderson, *Australian*, 9–10 May 1998.
37   Ken Llewelyn, *Caressa*, p. 136.

Up, up and away

Perhaps the strangest of the Humpty Doo incidents occurred about half way through the four-month-long haunting. One morning after a particularly wild night of polt activity the tenants woke to find a thick covering of pebbles on their cars and the outdoor bar. They then noticed long, shallow troughs in the gravel driveway – as though the pebbles had been "vacuumed up" in their thousands. Shortly thereafter, one of Murph's mates, Brett Styles, glimpsed what might have been a polt in the process of "reloading". While seated in the covered barbeque area, he observed a strange object approaching from the direction of the driveway. It flew past him under the breezeway roof and away. It appeared to be spherical, jet-black and smaller than fist-size – and *it had a two-foot-long stream of gravel trailing behind it*. Freaky.

Frank Robson with Brett Styles. (Healy/Cropper)

Half a star is born

When we penned the first draft of this chapter in 2010 we confidently awarded the Humpty Doo case a five-star rating, but the possibility – some readers might think probability – that Kirsty gave in to a mad impulse and faked the pot lid incident, caused us to very reluctantly downgrade it by half a star.

That is not to say we doubt that a poltergeist really was infesting the little blue house on McMinns Road. The downgrade is simply an acknowledgement of the slight blot left on an otherwise flawless case by the alleged confession.

Another consideration was that, impressive though it certainly is, the Humpty Doo case is not the most remarkable in our Australian files. As we will show in the following chapter, when it comes to which Aussie polt deserves the coveted five-star rating, the Mayanup Poltergeist wins hands down.

Sources:

Litchfield Times, 2, 9, 16, 23 and 30 Apr 1998.

Northern Territory News, 3, 4, 6, 7, 16, 17, 20–23 and 25 Apr 1998.

Sunday Territorian, 3 May 1998.

Frank Robson, "Humpty Boo!" *Sydney Morning Herald Good Weekend Magazine*, 13 Jun 1998.

Max Anderson, "Ghost Writer", *The Australian Magazine*, 9–10 May 1998.

Tony Healy and Paul Cropper, "Stone Me!", *Fortean Times* No. 116, Nov 1998.

Ken Llewelyn, *Caressa, From Call Girl to God's Child*, Sandstone Publishing, Leichhardt NSW, 2002.

"Today Tonight", Channel Seven, Sydney, videotapes, Apr 1998.

Paul Cropper, interviews with Greg Quail, Brendan Gowdie and Jimmy Hamilton, Sept 2011.

CHAPTER TWO

A serial pest: The Mayanup Poltergeist

MAYANUP, PUMPHREY AND BOYUP BROOK,
WA, 1955–1957. RATING: ★★★★★

This remarkable episode – a series of very strange events that began on a large property near Mayanup and spread to three other farms in south-west Western Australia – is by far the most impressive in our files.

The weird activity continued for an unusually long time: it was very intense from 1955 to 1957, recurred sporadically throughout the 1960s and persists, in a less dramatic form to this day. Over the years the phenomena was witnessed by hundreds of people. A particularly interesting aspect of the case is that the polt's attention was focused initially on a couple of indigenous families and that Aboriginal shamans attempted to corral the spook using traditional magic.

Very few poltergeist events anywhere in the world are better documented. Bill and Ethel Hack, who owned the property, "Keninup", where it all started, were interviewed many times during and after the episode, and Ethel kept a detailed record of events as they happened. Her journal formed the basis of *The Mystery of the Mayanup Poltergeist*, written by her daughter-in-law Helen Hack. That excellent book is the definitive account of the episode and every polt researcher should have a copy.

While researching the episode, Helen recorded the testimony of dozens of eyewitnesses and folklorist John Meredith conducted interviews with the Hacks on behalf of the National Library of Australia. We, too, have interviewed key figures in the saga, and visited two of the affected properties. Veteran journalist, author and ghost buster Keith Smith drew on Ethel's journal to write a good summary of the events in his 1993 book, *Supernatural 2*, and in July 2009 ABC Television screened a documentary, "Spirit Stones", about the case.

Because many of the journalists who visited the polt-plagued properties actually witnessed stone falls and other weird phenomena, contemporary press coverage was unusually detailed and refreshingly well balanced. There was little of the jokey scepticism that has marred the coverage of some other Australian cases.

Seriously spooked

As far as Bill and Ethel Hack were concerned the story began at about 10 pm on 17 May 1955, when Gilbert Smith, an Aboriginal employee, came to their door to plead for help. Like many large landowners, the Hacks employed several farm hands, some of whom lived on site. The cottage that Mr. Smith, his wife Jean and five of their children occupied was situated on a hilltop 500 metres from the main homestead.

The Smith residence. (*Weekend Mail*, Perth, 18 June 1955)

Although Gilbert Smith was a tall, powerfully-built, 36-year-old man, he was clearly quite frightened. He told the Hacks that some lunatic was throwing stones and other objects onto, and into, his house. The episode had begun at dusk, when his big "kangaroo dogs" suddenly went berserk, yelping and howling as if they were being savagely attacked. When Jean ventured outside to investigate, she heard a very long, low, eerie whistle. At that, the terrified dogs broke their chains and fled. As the family sat down to dinner, stones and an old iron ring clattered against the galvanised iron walls and roof. Mr. Smith went outside and circled the house but could see nothing. Shortly thereafter, when a golf ball flew though an open door and bounced around the living room, he decided enough was enough, and went for help.

Because he was their most competent and reliable employee – he'd been with them for ten years – and was so seriously upset, the Hacks agreed to help guard Mr. Smith's house for a couple of nights, even though they assumed the stone throwing was nothing more than a prank or the result of some petty grudge. It wasn't long, however, before they saw why the Smiths were so freaked out: the next evening Bill and his brother Ron saw stones apparently materialising in the air above the cottage before falling at unnaturally slow speeds and odd trajectories. Indoors they watched, gob-smacked, as a stone flew towards them from within the fireplace and a piece of charcoal fell from near the ceiling.[38]

From then on the weirdness intensified, continuing on an almost nightly basis for four months until 20 September, after which it decreased and almost stopped entirely. About six months later, however, it resumed and continued until 26 May1957.

Gilbert Smith. (*Australasian Post*, 1 March 1956)

During that time the Hack family and a great many other people observed hundreds of stones and other objects including tins, potatoes and bits of iron falling apparently out of nowhere.

As at Humpty Doo and many other polt sites, many of the objects didn't fall normally: some "floated" gently to the ground; others changed direction, hovered, levitated, materialised out of thin air and otherwise mocked the laws of physics. Many witnesses noted that the stones, even those that had been flying very fast, landed with a soft thud – a "plop". As Bill's brother Doug put it, it was "as if they were made of cork". And they never rolled when they hit the ground: they simply stopped dead, "as if they had no momentum at all."[39]

Many stones and other objects also landed *inside* the Smiths' cottage. There was, in some places, a three-inch (7.5 cm) ventilation gap between the roof and the walls, but as the objects falling indoors displayed the same disregard for the laws of physics as those outside – hovering, floating, etc. – none of the many eyewitnesses considered it possible they'd been thrown through that narrow gap.

---

38   Helen Hack, *The Mystery of the Mayanup Poltergeist*, pp. 7–8.
39   Helen Hack p. 8 and John Meredith (National Library of Australia) interviews with Doug and Ethel Hack, 9 September 1991.

Nearly all of the odd phenomena occurred from dusk to dawn, but as the site was only thinly-treed and often illuminated, sometimes on all sides, by headlights and spotlights, it was possible to observe the objects' weird trajectories and to see that they could not have been thrown by hoaxers. Sometimes so many stones fell at once that hoaxing was out of the question. As Bill and Ethel Hack were driving towards the Smith cottage one night they saw, illuminated by their headlights, "showers of stones falling like hail". Not infrequently, in fact, stones and other objects flew in broad daylight. Whenever that occurred the Smiths and Hacks knew that, come nightfall, they were in for unusually intense episodes of activity.

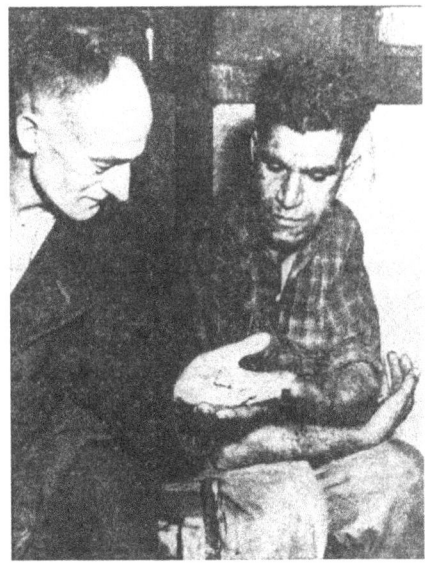

Bill Hack and Gilbert Smith. (*Weekend Mail*, 18 June 1955)

The "ghost break"

Because its hilltop position made it vulnerable to bushfires, Mr. Hack had for years maintained a wide, horseshoe-shaped firebreak around the Smiths' cottage. After the first week or so of stone falls, to make dead sure hoaxers couldn't approach the back and

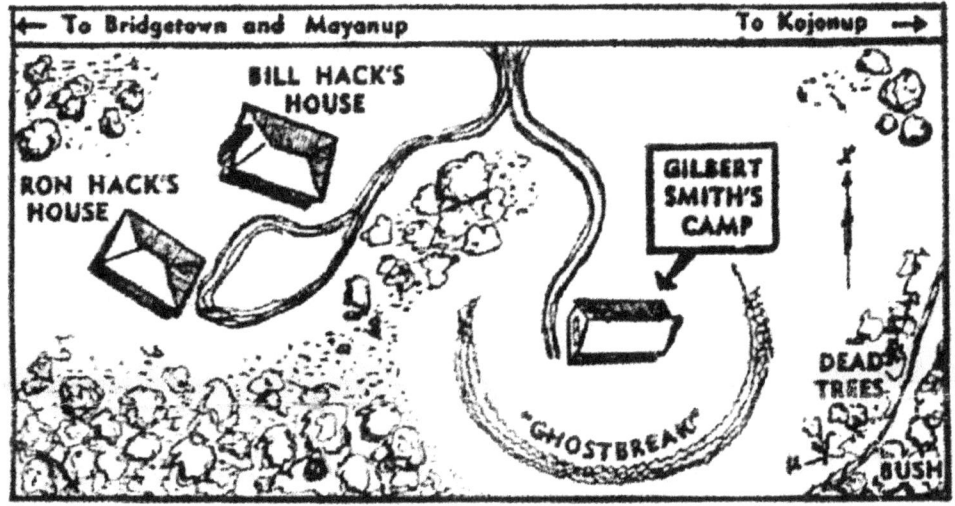

Map of the "ghost break". (*Weekend Mail*, Perth, 18 June 1955)

sides of the dwelling without leaving tracks, he ploughed the strip afresh. No suspicious tracks were ever found on the "ghost break".⁴⁰

The focus

Stressed and stormy: Jean Smith.
(*Weekend Mail*, Perth, 18 June 1955)

Ethel Hack noticed right from the start that the phenomena seemed to be focused primarily on Jean Smith. The stone falls occurred only when Jean, who seems to have had something of a volatile personality, was at home. They were particularly intense when she was angry with her husband and, as Ethel's daughter-in-law Helen put it, Jean and Gilbert were "known to have frequent and stormy arguments."⁴¹ It would have been surprising, in fact, if Jean Smith was not somewhat stressed in the period preceding the stone falls. Going through an apparently difficult stage in her relationship with Gilbert, worried about her terminally-ill father and pregnant with her seventh child, she nevertheless had to cook and care for her other children, plus a 15-year-old nephew, Aden Eades.

There isn't space here to list all of the remarkable events that were observed at "Keninup" during those three wild and weird months, but the following synopsis will give some idea of the "high strangeness" that was the order of the day.

Too big to throw

While most of the stones that fell ranged from pea-size to fist-size, some were far too large to have been thrown or catapulted by hoaxers. One evening while standing outside the Smiths' cottage, 18-year-old Julie Hack glanced up to see a pumpkin-sized rock descending slowly through the air, "as if it was being lowered", before settling very gently on top of a 1000-gallon galvanised iron water tank. In the morning, when Bill Hack put it on his scales, he found it weighed 35 pounds (15.9 kg).⁴²

---

40   *Weekend Mail*, 18 June 1955 and Paul Cropper interview with Ethel Hack, 30 April 2000.
41   Helen Hack, p. 74.
42   John Meredith interviews.

Hot stuff

As mentioned in the preceding chapter, many of the objects that fell at Humpty Doo in 1998 were found to be quite warm to the touch. Given the Territory's tropical climate that may not seem particularly odd, but when the same phenomenon was noticed at "Keninup" during the cold, wet, West Australian winter it was considered quite remarkable. None of the stones that fell at "Keninup" were cold. As Doug Hack put it, most were "about blood heat"[43].

Bill Hack with the largest rock. (*Perth Daily News*, 21 March 1957)

Many witnesses noticed the anomaly. On one cold, rainy night, seated inside the Smith cottage with a journalist and a couple of policemen, David Millington saw several golf-ball-sized stones appear from nowhere and "float" down to the floor. Every one he picked up was distinctly warm and dry despite the wet, wintery weather.

As time went by some of the stones were found to be not just warm, but very hot. Doug Hack noticed that it was the somewhat larger stones, those "about the size of your fist" that were the hottest. Some were too hot to handle. This phenomenon was noted in Ethel's journal and confirmed by several independent witnesses, including *Weekend Mail* reporter Hugh Schmitt. One young couple, who were visiting "Keninup" when hot stones fell, put some of them in an empty kerosene tin and drove to their home in Mayanup. After the one-hour drive, the stones had lost very little heat. On another occasion it was noticed that some fallen stones remained warm an hour after landing on the cold ground.[44]

Doug Hack with other objects that fell. (*Perth Daily News*, 22 March 1957)

Gravity defied

On one occasion young Alex Hack saw a slowly-gliding stone execute a neat ninety-degree turn in mid air. His aunt Ethel watched as another sailed towards her on a

---

43 John Meredith interviews.
44 Helen Hack, pp. 22–23 and John Meredith interviews.

perfectly horizontal trajectory just a few inches above the ground before lightly striking her ankle.[45]

One bright, sunny afternoon, Bill and Ethel watched as a bottle floated through the air towards the Smiths' house, turning over and over as it flew. When it descended onto the sloping iron roof, it defied gravity once again by simply staying where it landed without rolling off. On another occasion young Kim Hack was actually standing on the roof, with an uninterrupted view all around, when two more bottles came cart-wheeling through the air. They, too, simply landed on the roof without breaking or rolling off.[46]

Stones thrown by the polt also clung to the roof in some inexplicable way. When the Hacks, the Smiths and others experimented by throwing stones onto the roof they always bounced or rolled off. When they lobbed bottles up there they invariably broke or rolled off.

Levitation

As at Humpty Doo, household objects were prone to lifting up and flying though the Smiths' cottage. One night as Doug Hack looked on, "Jean Smith was brushing her daughter's hair ... she put the brush down and it just took off and flew across the room."[47]

Apports

One rainy night fifty people including some journalists were at "Keninup" when stones fell constantly inside and outside the Smiths' house. In the living room, Rona Nicholson watched as stones simply appeared in mid-air, floated down and *passed through* a table to land on the floor below.[48]

Many household objects disappeared from their places within the cottage. "I think you'd call it dematerialisation", said Doug Hack, who was present when a teapot suddenly vanished, "they'd be gone for about an hour and then they'd be back ...".[49] Psychical researchers refer to objects that disappear and reappear in that manner as "apports".

Several stones even found their way inside the Smiths' hurricane lanterns. This happened both indoors and out. A tinkling would be heard and then a stone would be seen coming to rest inside the glass.[50]

---

45 Helen Hack, p. 12.
46 John Meredith interviews.
47 John Meredith interviews.
48 Helen Hack, pp. 22–23.
49 John Meredith interviews.
50 Helen Hack, p. 13.

Scary but harmless

As Helen Hack and others have observed, many of the stones were large enough and were travelling fast enough to have killed a person. But people who *were* hit said the impact was remarkably gentle. No one was even slightly injured.

The polt, in fact, seemed intent on teasing, rather than hurting, people. When Ethel Hack was hit in the small of the back by a flight of three potatoes, she felt only a series of soft impacts as, one after the other, they struck her: "… the potatoes felt soft and when they landed they didn't roll." Another wayward vegetable, an onion, "made a line for a point just above my knee [struck lightly] and then dropped straight down to the ground and didn't roll. When I picked it up and dropped it, it *did* roll."[51]

No property damage

It is well worth noting that despite the hundreds of stones that rained on the Smith Cottage not a single window was broken. Nor did any of the objects that fell indoors cause the slightest damage. One incident in particular, witnessed by Colin Barron and documented by Helen Hack, shows how the polt apparently took pains to avoid causing serious damage. On that occasion "a stone the size of a cricket ball" fell with a bang onto the Smiths' kitchen table – landing on the only spot that was clear of crockery.[52]

There was only one exception to the spook's apparent "no damage" policy: as Ethel Hack recalled, it once "… caused an explosive bang which shook the Smiths' house and shattered a cup on a kitchen table".[53]

Murray Hack and Don Halligan stand guard. (*Weekend Mail*, Perth, 18 June 1955)

It stands to reason that if the hundreds of flying stones and other objects were simply thrown or catapulted by hoaxers lurking in the dark some distance away, at least some injury and considerable property damage would have been done.

---

51   John Meredith interviews.
52   Helen Hack, p. 18.
53   Smith, Keith, *Supernatural 2*, Pan Macmillan, Melbourne 1993, p. 119.

The dogs that didn't bark

It is also worth looking once again at the odd behaviour of the Smith's dogs. Normally, if strangers approached the cottage they reacted, as most farm dogs do, by simply barking. But immediately before the first wave of stone falls they went totally berserk, broke their chains and fled – a strange overreaction. Even more strangely, for the following two years, as noisy, weird events occurred all around them, *they never reacted at all*.[54]

The polt steps out

On 19 June, one month after it began its activities at "Keninup" the polt extended its activities across the Boyup Brook-Kojonup Road to another large property, "Lynford Hill", owned by Bill Hack's brother Doug. There, it began pestering another Aboriginal family – a family that bore a name destined to become famous in the annals of Australian Rules football.

Alf and Molly Krakouer had worked at "Lynford Hill" for some years. The shack in which they and their seven children lived was only about 600 metres from the Smiths'. As well as living in such close proximity, the families were blood relations – Molly was Jean Smith's niece – so the Krakouers became involved in the mysterious events right from the beginning: frequently visiting the polt-plagued dwelling and even staying overnight to provide comfort and support. Their acts of kindness, however, landed them in a weird world of trouble: the polt evidently took a shine to them, and followed them home.

A reporter from the local *Blackwood Times*, who was just across the road when it began on the evening of 19 June, became one of the first witnesses to the "Lynford Hill" polt outbreak. Between 8.30 and 9.30 that night he witnessed nine stones falling onto the Krakouers' roof. While he noted that their house, unlike the Smiths', was surrounded by trees and scrub, he saw nothing, including the demeanour of the family, to suggest hoaxing.[55]

Over the course of the next week, according to Doug Hack, stones too numerous to count – hundreds of them – fell at the Krakouer house. It is important to note that the polt didn't cease its activities at "Keninup" during that time: *stones fell simultaneously on both properties.*[56]

---

54 Helen Hack, p. 33.
55 *Blackwood Times*, 24 June, 1955.
56 *Blackwood Times*, 1 July 1955.

An eye for the ladies

Whereas the phenomena at "Keninup" seemed to be focused on Jean Smith, it soon became clear that the entity troubling the Krakouer residence was interested mainly in Alf and Molly's 14-year-old daughter Audrey. In later years her cousin Aden Eades recalled, in an interview with Ken Hayward, that when Audrey walked around the property "the stones would follow her everywhere ... they were falling around her ... she thought it was quite funny".

One of the Hack girls was also named Audrey. One evening, while visiting the Krakouer family, she witnessed a particularly remarkable event: a large stone suddenly materialising at knee-height and soaring very slowly upwards before settling on the roof.

On another night Gordon Barron, his two sons and several others observed something similar to – but one degree stranger than – the pebble showers we saw at Humpty Doo: while indoors at the Krakouer residence, they looked up to see "a handful of small stones about half the size of peas" *hovering* above them. After about five seconds they dropped to the floor.

Like the objects that seemed to cling to the Smith's roof, those that struck the Krakouers' dwelling also acted very oddly. Gillian Peebles, a gifted artist who later illustrated Helen Hack's book, saw a stone hit the building's corrugated iron wall, cling to it for a moment, and then slide "gently down the wall following the contours of the corrugations as if held to the iron by a magnet". When she tried to pick it up it proved too hot to handle.

Another witness, a Mrs. Richardson from Kulikup, watched, amazed, as a large stone rose from the ground two or three metres in front of her, flew up and hit her gently on the shoulder.[57]

Ethel Hack had the unique experience of seeing a stone materialise high above the Krakouer house in broad daylight: "I was looking up into a clear, grey sky when a tiny [object] took shape ... [the materialisation process] was a bit like a kaleidoscope: a few jerks this way and that and it was there". The stone fell onto the roof and, when retrieved, proved to be quite warm. [58]

Marbar vs. Jannick

Very soon after the first stones fell at "Keninup", Gilbert Smith suggested that the strange goings-on were the work of an evil spirit – a type of entity that his people, the Nyungar, referred to as a *Jannick*. Although the Hacks initially scoffed at the idea, it wasn't long before they came around to, as Ethel Hack put it, "the reluctant conclusion that no human agency could be responsible".[59]

---

57 Helen Hack, pp. 17, 19, 28, 37 and 54.
58 John Meredith interviews.
59 Ethel Hack quoted in Smith, p. 114.

Although a few odd things happened elsewhere – like a work party being pelted with sticks and stones in a paddock on "Lynford Hill" and a brass tap suddenly materialising and dropping onto a table in the "Keninup" homestead – it was also clear that the Jannick was focused almost entirely on the two Aboriginal families.

So, when Gilbert Smith, having put up with frights, disturbed sleep and crowds of visitors for a couple of weeks, suggested that he seek out an Aboriginal shaman or *marbar* to exorcise the spook, Bill Hack told him to go ahead.

The best-known marbar in the district was old Sammy Miller, who was famous locally for having found a lost child, apparently by clairvoyance, near Mt Barker. Readily agreeing to help, he soon arrived at "Keninup" to assess the situation.

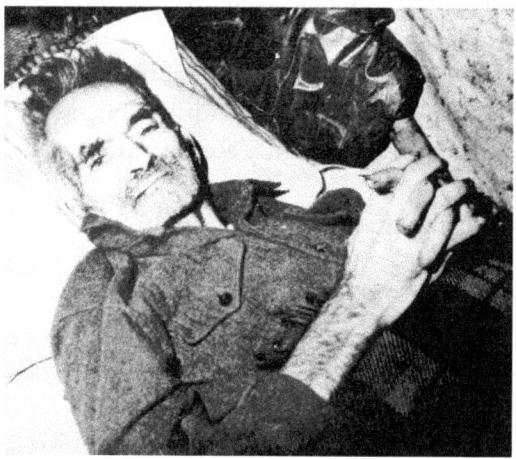

Alf Eades on his deathbed. (*Australasian Post*, 1 March 1956)

He got off to a promising start: as soon as he set foot on the property the paranormal activity stopped. It didn't resume until he left. Later, after conferring with other "clever men", he told the Smiths that the trouble was probably being caused by the spirit of Jean's father, Alf Eades, who'd suffered a severe stroke at "Keninup" shortly before the haunting began. Even though Mr. Eades was still alive, being nursed by relatives in Kojonup, the marbar said that because he was so gravely ill his spirit was capable of leaving his body.

He thought it likely that, as Jean had always been his favourite child, Mr. Eades' spirit had been drawn to her at "Keninup". The spirit, he told her, was not to be feared: it was friendly and wouldn't hurt anyone. He believed that with the help of another marbar, Freddie Winmar, he could "catch" the spirit and return it to her father's body.

Jean Smith, however, was far from convinced that her father's spirit had anything to do with the stone falls. She had two good reasons for scepticism. Firstly, her father, when well enough to speak, indignantly denied that his spirit was doing anything untoward. Secondly, at least one, albeit very minor, instance of polt activity had occurred four years *before* her father became ill. In about 1951, as Gilbert was reading beside the fire, a handful of pebbles fell, apparently from nowhere, onto his newspaper. As nothing further happened at the time, he and Jean put the incident out of their minds.[60]

On the other hand, Jean admitted to being very impressed when the old shaman unhesitatingly identified the exact spot on the "Keninup" fence line where her father had collapsed. So she and Gilbert agreed the ceremony was worth a try.

---

60   *Blackwood Times*, 17 June 1955.

The wizards of Oz

On 5 July, at an Aboriginal camp near Kojonup, in the presence of many indigenous and some non-indigenous people, including Bill and Doug Hack, the marbars attempted to corral the wayward wraith.

There was very little ritual involved. "No", Sammy Miller told a *Blackwood Times* reporter, "we just catch it and put it back in the body." When asked what form the spirit took, he replied that to him it was a definite form but "to you white fellas it only looks like a puff of smoke."[61]

At dusk Mr. Miller stood silently outside the cottage in which Mr. Eades lay, and stared in the direction of Mayanup. Freddie Winmar, meanwhile, descended into a nearby gully, closely watched by the still sceptical Jean Smith. There she saw him chase, and throw a blanket over, something small and white. As he returned to the cottage, witnesses had

Sammy Miller and Freddie Winmar. (*Australasian Post*, 1 March 1956)

the impression that whatever was inside the blanket – animal or spook – seemed to be struggling to get out. As the *Blackwood Times* reporter watched, the marbars then opened the blanket above Mr. Eades' prostrate body, ostensibly returning the slippery spirit to its proper location.

It is interesting that Mr. Eades, who had previously, when lucid, been scathingly sceptical of the marbars, said later that as the blanket was opened, "It felt just like a big gust of wind hitting me in the chest".[62]

So, having accomplished their bit of ghost busting, did the shamans claim that henceforth all would be well at Mayanup? Well ... not quite. Sceptics might chortle at this: the marbars left themselves with an "out". Mr. Winmar told the *Blackwood Times* reporter that while in the gully he'd seen not only Mr. Eades' spirit but also another that he didn't recognise. So, while he hoped the stone throwing would cease, the unidentified spirit might have other ideas.[63]

Be that as it may, the "ghost catching" exercise did absolutely nothing to lessen the activity at "Keninup" and "Lynford Hill". The intensity of the polt pranks, in fact, increased. As the *Blackwood Times* reported on 22 July, "… stones at Mayanup are

---

61 *Blackwood Times*, 8 July 1955.
62 Helen Hack, p. 42.
63 *Blackwood Times*, 8 July 1955.

falling faster and more furious than ever ... now activity has been great during daylight hours ..."

It is worth considering, however, that the intensification of activity, while proving the "ghost catching" failed, might also indicate that the marbars' ceremony had, at least, some effect on the poltergeist, albeit negative. We make this suggestion because similar intensifications of activity have occurred after attempted exorcisms at several other poltergeist sites, including, as mentioned in the previous chapter, Humpty Doo.

Another thing that makes us reluctant to dismiss the shamans as complete charlatans is that, as we will see, another marbar later succeeded (apparently) in stopping a polt episode in a different part of the state. A final, minor consideration is that a prediction made by the marbars at the Kojonup ceremony proved to be very accurate: they told Mr. Eades' wife that he would die in six weeks time – and he did indeed die on about 18 August. Although his death, like the "ghost catching" ceremony that preceded it, didn't bring the weird events at Mayanup to an immediate end, the stone falls gradually decreased from then on, and after another month ceased completely.

The polt takes a holiday

For almost seven months after 20 September 1955 peace reigned at "Keninup" and "Lynford Hill". But in April 1956, just as the Hacks and their employees were beginning to hope it had gone forever, the Jannick returned from its holiday, refreshed and full of mischief.

Things get creepier

Stones fell as before, and other objects flew, but this time around, the tricks seemed to have a nasty edge not previously evident.

One night, just outside the Krakouers' house, something took hold of a little boy and began to drag him slowly out of the tent in which he and his older brother were sleeping. Fortunately, when the older boy grabbed the child, the spook let go.[64]

A couple of things particularly upset the Krakouer girls: the Jannick took to scattering dirt and gravel in their beds and tugging at their hair both day and night. Gilbert and Jean Smith, who'd become quite blasé about simple stone falls, became increasingly nervous when floor boards began creaking in their kitchen during the night and when something shiny and white suddenly fell onto their bed. Creepiest of all was the sound of heavy breathing and whispering that Gilbert heard one night, followed by the discovery,

---

64   John Meredith interviews.

on the bedroom floor, of a half a cupful of sticky, odourless fluid.[65]

By the end of 1956, the Krakouers had had enough. They packed up and left "Lynford Hill", never to return.

When the Smiths followed suit on 26 May 1957 peace finally descended on "Keninup". Not a single pebble fell except on two occasions when the Smiths dropped by to visit their old employers. On both occasions, as the Hacks greeted them, so too did the Jannick: with showers of sticks, stones and bottles.

Apart from targeting them during those brief visits, the Jannick left the Smiths alone for the next few months as they moved from job to job around the state's south-west. On 26 June 1958, however, while they were camped at the Mayanup Race Course, the stone/bottle/stick falls began again. From then on, wherever they went, they experienced, intermittently, the same sort of thing. It continued, in fact, right into the next decade. When Bill Hack visited them at their house in Boyup Brook in the 1960s he again witnessed a stone fall. "It happens all the time", said Jean Smith resignedly, "I just don't tell anyone anymore."

The Pumphrey Poltergeist

Whether it had to clone itself, bifurcate, or enlist a franchisee from the spirit world to accomplish what it did is anybody's guess, but on 15 March 1957, not content with harassing the residents of "Keninup" and "Lynford Hill", the Jannick extended its creepy reach 150 kilometres north to a farm near Pumphreys Bridge. On that 2500-acre property, "Carabin", owned by 64-year-old Alan Donaldson, it once again focused on two Aboriginal families.

Twenty-two-year-old Cyril Penny and his young wife Lorna had a two-year-old baby; Kevin and Alma Ugle also had a young family. They were itinerant workers so, unlike the Smiths and Krakouers, they had no permanent quarters. When at "Carabin" they lived in tents, although Mr. Penny and his wife sometimes used a galvanised iron and canvas shack. At the time of the first

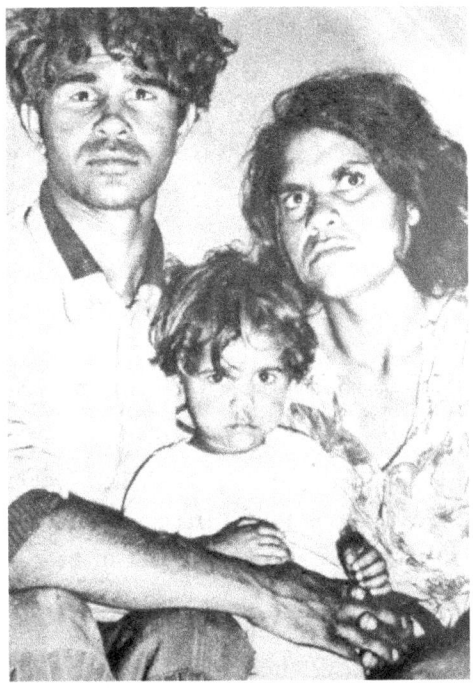

Terrified: Cyril Penny and family. (*People Magazine*, 17 September 1958)

---

65   Helen Hack, pp. 55 and 59.

stone falls their camp was situated in an open area backed by a sparsely timbered hill. As there seemed to be nowhere for hoaxers to hide, they became quite frightened.

Although the Pumphrey "rain of terror" was brief (it lasted only seven days) and consisted only of stone falls it was every bit as remarkable as the Mayanup episode.

Alan Donaldson and his sons Brian and Ian, who quickly responded to their workers' pleas for assistance, often saw stones raining down, apparently out of thin air, onto about an acre of ground around the Aborigines' camp. At first it was only pea-sized pebbles, but as time went by larger and larger stones fell. Although they were never discerned high in the air, they were easy enough to focus on as they passed through the trees. As at Mayanup, some slowly "floated" down, landing with an unnatural, dull thump – a "dead fall", as Brian Donaldson put it – and most did not roll on landing. On the rare occasions people were struck, the impact was too soft to cause even the slightest injury.

Alan Donaldson and sons at the site. (*West Australian*, 20 March 1957)

Although most of the stones fell at dusk or later, the terrain was so lacking in cover that the Donaldsons, like their employees, considered hoaxing virtually out of the question. Some stones, in any case, fell in broad daylight, and thorough searches revealed no suspicious tracks.[66]

A careful experiment dispelled any lingering doubts. Twenty-year-old Ian, his brother Brian, 26, a neighbour and a couple of the Aborigines entered one of the tents, lashed the entrance shut and covered the floor with clean chaff bags. There they watched, fascinated, as a succession of stones passed straight through the canvas roof without damaging it in

---

66   *Weekend Mail*, 23 March 1957 and Paul Cropper interview with Brian Donaldson, 29 January 1988.

Witnessing the impossible: Donaldsons and Ugles inside the tent. (*Perth Daily News*, 20 March 1957)

any way. Eventually, the entire floor was covered with them. The Aborigines had, in fact, mentioned previous stone falls inside the tents, but until they experienced the phenomenon themselves the Donaldsons couldn't credit the story.[67]

They ran but couldn't hide

After three nights of terror, the Aborigines decided they'd had enough, so on the night of 18 March, they moved camp to a creek 16 kilometres away. Their effort was rewarded by a few hours' peace, but by the early hours of the 19th the polt had zeroed-in on them again. When Ian Donaldson visited the new camp just after dawn, they were again being showered with stones. Resignedly, they packed up once again and moved back to "Carabin" – where they were duly greeted by a pebbly barrage.[68]

Before long there was another instance of stones falling inside a tent. As Brian Donaldson watched incredulously, the stones thudded gently onto a rug on which two Aboriginal toddlers lay sleeping.[69]

Journalists and sightseers

Word of the new poltergeist event spread very quickly and within a couple of days scores of sightseers descended on "Carabin". One evening, Brian Donaldson recalled, 60 or 70 people congregated at the Aboriginal camp to watch the show. Several reporters, some of whom had already covered the Mayanup events, also arrived and seemed inclined to believe the phenomenon was genuinely supernatural.

A *West Australian* journalist observed that the topography and vegetation around the camp would have made it very difficult for hoaxers to conceal themselves, and Tony Taylor of the *Sunday Telegraph*, who stayed for four days, witnessed several uncanny events. "I was slightly frightened and very perplexed", he wrote, "when eight stones dropped with soft thumps near me". Another missed his photographer's head by a fraction of an inch. "There is no possibility", Taylor insisted, "that this freak affair is a hoax."[70]

---

67   *West Australian*, 20 March 1957.
68   *West Australian*, 20 March 1957.
69   *Weekend Mail*, 23 March 1957.
70   *Sunday Telegraph*, 19 March 1957, the *West Australian*, 20 March 1957 and *Two Worlds* magazine, 11 May 1957.

Sightseers. (*Weekend Mail*, 23 March 1957)

Rob Lenton of the *Weekend Mail* also saw stones falling and observed that, given the lack of cover and the lay of the land, any "crackpot prankster" would have to possess "the superhuman ability to throw stones ... up to 100 yards with uncanny accuracy at a target he can't see."[71]

The Southern Districts officer of the Natives Affairs Branch, Mr. C.R. Webster, who had heard of similar happenings while in India, also visited "Carabin". After witnessing a couple of stone falls he was convinced they were truly supernatural.

A dubious story

Although the journalists saw no evidence of hoaxing, Athol Douglas, who'd been sent to the site by the Western Australian Museum, was loudly sceptical.

While it is unclear whether Mr. Douglas, an entomologist, actually witnessed any stone falls, he lost no time in branding as liars not only the Donaldsons, their employees and neighbours, but also the journalists who'd reported seeing paranormal phenomena. He went on to claim that, after using a compass to establish the direction from which the stones had come, he'd discovered a footprint and then extracted a confession of hoaxing from an unnamed "friend of Cyril Penny".[72]

Apart from the blanket accusation of lying, he offered no explanation for the slow descent of many stones or for the stone falls that occurred inside the tents and his discovery of a solitary footprint in an area where plenty of people had been wandering around seems entirely unremarkable.

Call us hardened old sceptics if you will, but we, like Helen Hack, the Pennys, the

---

71 *Weekend Mail*, 23 March 1957.
72 Helen Hack, p. 64.

Ugles, the Donaldsons and just about everyone else, find Mr. Douglas's story pretty lame. We think he was simply determined, in defiance of all the evidence, to "explain away" a problem that offended his scientific sensibilities.

A better story

To us, the conclusions of Jack Coulter, a Perth-based crime reporter, seem a lot more reasonable. Mr. Coulter, who spent three days in the area, was initially very sceptical. "The general theory", he said, "was that these stones were … being flicked or thrown by [the] Aborigines … but that was pretty quickly dispelled … because [they] were obviously in considerable fear". Coulter was also very impressed by Alan Donaldson, "a very practical man … a successful farmer … an infantry officer in World War One … he wasn't the sort of chap to be fooled by anything."

Any remaining doubts vanished as Coulter watched his cameraman, Max Holtern, gather all of the Aboriginal people together for a group shot. He and Holtern were the only outsiders on the property at the time, yet, as Coulter stood there, "with an unobstructed view of about half a mile" and with all the indigenous people lined up in front of him, "… four stones actually fell around us."

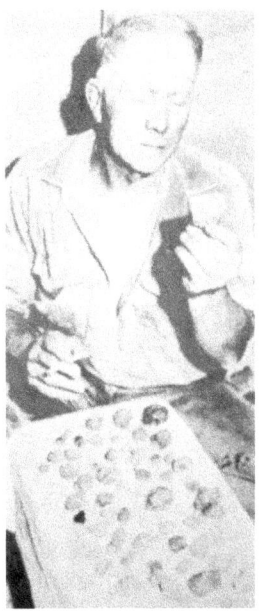

Alan Donaldson. (*People Magazine*, 17 September 1958)

Jack Coulter. (Access Press, Northbridge, WA)

Coulter noted that when those stones and others struck the ground it was with an unnaturally soft "plop". Any that landed on a tin roof did so "with just a dull thud". Having served for four years as an artillery officer during World War Two, he "… was well versed in the science of ballistics and the trajectory of projectiles, but the way these stones were, for want of a better word, appearing, entirely confounded all those … ideas. They [seemed] to be dropping vertically, they were not dropping heavily … I was quite convinced they were, in some peculiar way, dropping out of the sky."[73]

---

73 Transcript of interview with Jack Coulter by the producers of the "Spirit Stones" documentary.

Inspector Sunter investigates

While Coulter was still at the property a senior policeman arrived to investigate. Inspector Slom Sunter was a very experienced officer "who knew the bush, knew the Aborigines and was a straight down the middle, hard-nosed cop". Although he didn't see any stone falls himself, he became firmly convinced they did occur.

According to a report he sent to the Acting Commissioner of Police on 19 March, Sunter, like Coulter, had been very favourably impressed not only by Alan Donaldson, "a well respected citizen, a Justice of the Peace, and a man of some substance" but also by "all the other persons … people of intelligence … who have witnessed these happenings …"

As well as quizzing the Donaldsons and their employees, Sunter interviewed several neighbours who'd been struck by falling stones. A Mrs. Garrigal, who was hit on the chest, told him that the impact was very gentle: it was as if she'd been struck by a cork. Mr. Quartermaine, a farmer, received a similar, oddly gentle impact to his neck. Their testimony was particularly interesting because when they (and two companions) were at the camp being showered with stones, the Donaldsons were attending a sale in town and all the Aborigines were working on a fence line two miles away.

Apparently because of that incident, Inspector Sunter began to favour the theory that the stone falls were not linked to any particular person or persons, but were "apparently due to some geological disturbance … this could have been occurring for some time past and has only just been discovered owing to the natives having camped in the immediate vicinity. The number of small stones in the area … would give one the impression that this is so." As good a theory as any, perhaps, given what Sunter had learned at "Carabin" – but one that would have been revealed as inadequate had he extended his investigation to include the two Mayanup properties.

In conclusion, Inspector Sunter endorsed the accuracy of Jack Coulter's version of the events.

Mr. Jinx

At Pumphrey, as at Mayanup, it seemed obvious the polt was concerned almost entirely with the Aboriginal people. Whereas hundreds of stones fell around and inside their camp, only a few fell on the nearby Donaldson residence. Significantly, all of those fell at about 9.30 pm on 18 March – when Lorna Penny and Alma Ugle were visiting the homestead.

Because he was related to the Smiths (he was Jean's nephew) and because he'd visited Mayanup during the polt activity, Cyril Penny concluded that the Jannick had latched onto him there and hitched a ride back to Pumphrey. As we will see, there is every reason to believe he was right. In any case, because most of the phenomena at "Carabin" seemed to be focused on his family, Cyril became convinced that he was jinxed. So he and Lorna packed up once again, and on March 20th Alan Donaldson trucked them to a new camp at Williams, 40 kilometres to the south.

The stones, however, continued to fall at "Carabin" and Kevin Ugle, now convinced it was *he* who was jinxed, drove down to Narrogin to plead for help from an Aboriginal *marbar*.

A successful exorcism?

Whereas the Catholic priests at Humpty Doo and the marbars at Mayanup had managed only to irritate the spooks, the Narrogin "clever man" seems to have succeeded in exorcising the Pumphrey poltergeist: after he visited "Carabin" and performed rituals designed to "catch the spirit" the stone falls ceased, never to recur.

The final insult

While things may have gone back to normal at Donaldson's farm, the Jannick, it seems, wasn't quite finished with Cyril Penny. In later years Aden Eades – who, interestingly, was related to both the Pennys *and* the Smiths – told Helen Hack that, after the Pumphrey episode, he and his Uncle Cyril experienced a brief polt event near Borden, 200 kilometres to the south-east.

One rainy night, while sheltering under a tarp, they'd been pelted with sandalwood nuts which were, they noted, bone-dry. When they threw a handful out into the darkness with the challenge, "Here – have another go", a "shovel full" was hurled back at them.[74]

We don't know exactly when this odd incident occurred – it could have been any time after 21 March 1957, when the Pennys were known to be en route to Borden.[75]

The polt goes west

During the period of intense activity at "Keninup" and "Lynford Hill", George Dickson of "Eastington", near Boyup Brook, was a frequent, fascinated, visitor. Sometimes he brought his 11-year-old son Harvey with him, and sometimes they took home a few "Jannick stones" as souvenirs.

Ethel Hack noted that George and Harvey visited the Smith cottage on the evening of 25 May 1957 – the night before the Smiths left "Keninup" for good. They stayed until 2 am, witnessing "showers of gravel" and other phenomena – the last of the polt activity at the property.

As all strange phenomena ceased at "Keninup" that night, but resumed later on the

---

74 Helen Hack, p. 65.
75 *West Australian*, 22 March 1957.

Dicksons' own farm, 20 kilometres to the north-west, it seems reasonable to suggest the polt had taken a shine to young Harvey, as it had previously to Cyril Penny, and hitched a ride back to "Eastington".

For some reason, however, the weird phenomena didn't begin immediately at "Eastington". As at Mayanup between September 1955 and April 1956, the polt apparently decided to award itself a well-earned break: nothing in the way of paranormal activity occurred for four whole months at the Dickson property or anywhere else.

Apports

The first round of weirdness – a series of "apports" – began at the Dickson farm on 27 September 1957. On that afternoon, and for a couple of days thereafter, various objects, mainly pencils and sets of pencils, repeatedly disappeared and reappeared. After they noticed what was happening, the Dicksons assembled all the pencils on the kitchen table – yet they continued to vanish and reappear right in front of their eyes.

On the following day stone falls occurred from morning till night, following Mr. Dickson, his married daughter Leila and young Harvey about the farm. Remarkably, the stones followed Leila and Harvey even as they drove into Boyup Brook that afternoon – falling not only on the roof and bonnet but also *inside* the car as it moved along. Stones continued to fall about them as they did their shopping.

It seems the spook was out to impress, because the phenomena that occurred at "Eastington" between 27 September and 16 October, when it almost entirely ceased, was arguably a degree or two weirder than what had preceded it at Mayanup and Pumphrey. Many witnesses other than the Dicksons saw stones, potatoes, tin cans, and many other objects falling, appearing and disappearing both indoors and out. Some, like Bill and Ethel Hack, who came over from "Keninup", and Keith and Mildred Smith, witnessed scenes reminiscent of Disney's "The Sorcerer's Apprentice", when shovels and a three-

George and Harvey Dickson. (*Sydney Truth*, 6 October 1957)

legged stool jumped around inside the milking shed. On different occasions, two journalists, Ritchie Hand, of the *Sunday Times* and Andrew Wauchope of the *Blackwood Times*, saw stones passing right through galvanised iron roofs. Mr. Wauchope later watched, gob-smacked, as other objects appeared and disappeared in front of his eyes.[76]

Like polts at many other locations, including Humpty Doo, the Boyup Brook spook seemed to delight in pulling the covers off neatly-made beds and, as in the Krakouer house, stones frequently appeared under bedclothes. One visitor, Sylvia Yates, told Helen Hack how she once watched, terrified, as a growing bulge of what later proved to be stones made a quilt move as if alive.[77]

"Uncle Bobby"

When the weirdness began at "Eastington", the Dicksons suggested, half-jokingly, that an eccentric, deceased relation might be responsible. The man in question was George Dickson's late brother Robert, who'd been considered rather "odd", particularly in his later years, when he sometimes spoke of seeing ghosts and strange lights on the property. "Uncle Bob was a gentle, kind, old man", Leila recalls. "He lived in a world of his own and never left the farm. He was a diabetic and quite deaf, so he couldn't speak very well – particularly towards the end, but he absolutely loved the little kids: he made toys for all of them."

So, because the stone falls, levitations and apports commenced ten years to the day after his death, and because the "Eastington" polt appeared to be harmless (and at times downright benign) the Dicksons always referred to it as "Uncle Bobby".[78]

"Sometimes we'd ask 'Uncle Bob' to throw something and, sure enough, he would do it", Leila recalls, "and once, when he made the baby's dummy disappear, I said 'Oh, that is disgusting – to take a baby's dummy!' And it came back instantly."

Another of "Uncle Bobby's" tricks would make him popular with anybody: once, when Leila and Harvey returned from a shopping trip, the exact sum of money they'd just spent in the Boyup Brook bakery dropped, out of nowhere, onto the kitchen table. On that occasion pebbles had again dropped inside the car as they drove along, but Leila noticed that the only ones that fell on her baby were "little tiny ones – nothing that could hurt her."

On several occasions "Uncle Bob" performed a party trick more-or-less on demand. Before the family sat down for dinner Mr. Dickson would mark several coins and put them aside, then ask everyone to look under their plate to make sure there was nothing there. At the conclusion of the meal a marked coin, usually a florin, would be found under every plate.[79]

---

76 *Sunday Times*, 6 October 1957, *Blackwood Times*, date uncertain, probably 8 October 1957 and Tony Healy interview with Leila McCreery, January 2011.
77 Helen Hack, pp. 69–70.
78 Tony Healy, interview with Leila McCreery, January 2011.
79 Tony Healy, interview with Leila McCreery, January 2011.

"I couldn't care less"

Although it played quite a few tricks when he was absent from the farm, it soon became clear that the polt was focused mainly on young Harvey. Although none of them were particularly outspoken, some people who had either not been to the farm at all or who had observed only simple, outdoor stone falls, suggested that the 11-year-old was cleverly hoaxing the whole thing.

On more than one occasion, fed up with the accusations, George Dickson, in the presence of several observers, placed various marked objects in his son's pockets, bound his arms to his sides and covered him with a securely-buttoned coat. Though the tightly-trussed lad was under constant surveillance, the objects still managed to leave his pockets and appear in various parts of the house.[80]

Coolheaded: young Harvey. (*Sydney Truth*, 6 October 1957)

Because the uncanny events occurred not only at night but also in the full light of day, it seems well-nigh impossible they could have been faked. One broad-daylight incident that particularly impressed Leila involved "a good-sized rock, about six by six inches" that flew along slowly, about three feet above the ground, as she and several companions watched closely.[81]

While some people singled out for special attention by polts have been scared witless by the experience, Young Harvey remained remarkably cool within the maelstrom of weirdness. "I couldn't care less", he told a journalist, "I don't mind when it finishes. I don't worry."[82]

After occurring continually for 19 days, the phenomena ceased entirely on October 16. Or perhaps we should say that it ceased almost entirely – because decidedly odd things *still* occasionally happen at "Eastington".

Although objects still move around or, more commonly, disappear from their usual place and reappear later, the phenomena, in recent years, has consisted mostly of (very) strange noises and ghostly apparitions.

As mentioned in the introduction, Colin Wilson and some other psychical researchers have pointed out that there is often a very fine line between poltergeist episodes and "ordinary" ghostly hauntings. There have been many instances, throughout the centuries, of events involving the usual range of polt phenomena – indoor/outdoor stone falls,

---

80   Helen Hack, pp. 69–70.
81   Tony Healy, interview with Leila McCreery, January 2011.
82   Sydney *Truth*, 6 October 1957.

levitation/disappearance/reappearance of objects, etc. – gradually morphing into hauntings involving inexplicable footsteps and apparitions of wraithlike or more solid-looking people, etc.

While this may well have been what happened at "Eastington", it is important to mention that there was a long interval between the end of the classic polt activity of 1957 and the commencement of the ghostly phenomena that has occurred in more recent years. The period of normality, in fact, lasted until about 1970.

Phantom cars

Perhaps the most interesting of the more recent phenomena occurred several times throughout the 1970s, '80s and '90s but hasn't persisted into the present century. It was an auditory phenomenon that corresponded exactly to the sound of a car approaching the homestead. The vehicle would be clearly heard coming down the long, gravel driveway and stopping near the front porch. This was followed by the sound of car doors opening and closing. Harvey's dogs would rush out barking, followed by Harvey, his wife Rose or their daughter, who would find … nothing: no visitor, no car, no dust – nothing.

One day a friend of Harvey's was actually standing out front as a phantom car approached. He kept his nerve as the sound of the engine and the crunching of gravel came to a halt right in front of him, but lost it when he heard the "car door" open. Harvey, who was home at the time, recalls with a laugh that his mate didn't just retreat into the house – he ran right through it into the back yard!

The ghost who walks

The activity most favoured by the spook is simply walking, with distinctly audible steps, throughout the house. It often walks downstairs and proceeds across the living room, leaving Harvey and Rose with the powerful impression that a person with some weight and substance – but completely invisible – has passed right in front of them. And it seems the resident phantom doesn't particularly like change. In early 2011, when furniture was moved aside and new carpet laid in the living room, the footsteps became distinctly heavier, as if someone was stomping around rather indignantly. When the familiar furniture was reintroduced, however, the spook settled down.

Harvey and Rose Dickson. (Healy/Cropper)

Sometimes the homestead's kitchen door, after being securely closed, is found to be wide open. As the door is old and very prone to jamming, it seems the intangible interloper has strength enough to give it a determined shove.

A good attitude

As an 11-year-old, during the wild, weird days of September/October 1957, Harvey remained remarkably composed and, as the years have gone by, his laid-back attitude doesn't seem to have changed. When we first contacted him in 1995 and met him in person in 2002 we found him to be extremely affable, hospitable and still completely unfazed by the continuing activities of the spook – be it "Uncle Bobby" or something else. As "Eastington" has been in his family since 1882, he has never contemplated leaving the property, so under the circumstances his good humoured, down-to-earth, accepting attitude seems exactly suited to the situation.

Only one incident tested Harvey's nerve a little. One night he heard the phantom footsteps walk right into his bedroom. Then someone or some*thing* – a quite heavy, invisible something – sat down on the side of his bed.

Another incident, perhaps a shade less scary, involved a woman in what looked like 1940s-era clothing who materialised at the foot of the bed.

Rose, like her husband, is remarkably relaxed about their mysterious housemate. When she hears the phantom footsteps or when, as has happened a few times, the spook helpfully lights fires in the fireplaces, her attitude is that, as it hasn't hurt anyone over the past fifty years or so, it is unlikely to do so now.

The only time she and Harvey became concerned was when their daughter experienced a couple of unnerving episodes of sleep paralysis, where something seemed to be preventing her from getting out of bed. After she moved to a different bedroom, however, the experience was never repeated.

Like the Hacks and the Donaldsons, the Dickson family has never attempted to profit from the poltergeist episode. Although Harvey now hosts country music festivals on "Eastington", he doesn't refer to the 1957 polt episode or to the more recent ghostly incidents when publicising the events. But if anyone contacts him to enquire about the three weeks of weirdness in 1957 or about "Uncle Bobby's" more recent tricks, he is always willing to share his recollections. Indeed, on several occasions over the years, he has allowed researchers such as ourselves to visit "Eastington" and look around.

Fright lights

Most of the phenomena observed during the West Australian poltergeist wave of 1955–57, though unusually intense and extremely weird, were nevertheless far from unique. Indoor/outdoor stone falls, levitation, hair-pulling, apports, dragging of people from their beds, etc., have all been reported many times throughout the centuries in other countries. But interestingly – and perhaps quite significantly – the West Australian episode involved something else: something very Australian.

One of the country's greatest mysteries is that of the so-called Min Min Lights. These "spook lights", usually estimated to be between tennis ball and basket ball size, have baffled thousands of people –Aborigines, drovers, farmers and tourists – in many corners of the country since time immemorial. Some witnesses say Min Mins seem to be aware they are being observed; others say they engage in playful and tricky behaviour. On several occasions, right from the beginning of the Mayanup episode, such lights were seen on and around the Hack property, often acting in concert with the stone falls.

Ethel Hack wrote that "we began to see lights … some about sixty metres away and others much further afield … like dull torch lights going on and off". Some were "quite bright, yet none seemed to actually throw a beam." Some were plain white but others were blue, orange or yellow.[83] To Doug Hack they seemed to be about nine inches [23 cm] in diameter and to "float about twenty feet [6 metres] above the ground." It was soon noticed that immediately after the lights disappeared stones would fall in or around the Smiths' house. At those times a low whistle was often heard.[84]

Being intimately familiar with the terrain, the Hacks were certain the lights were not carried by hoaxers, but one evening, in an attempt to rule out that possibility, Ethel stationed herself near a fence about 200 metres from the Smiths' cottage to listen for twanging of wire that might reveal an intruder. There, in the twilight, she saw a glowing object suspended about five feet [1.5m] from the ground, "sort of like a bicycle light but … it didn't cast light on anything [it was] a dull yellow [and] seemed to follow the line of a brook that ran through the property … it was a smooth movement and very fast." There was no road or track in the vicinity. Almost simultaneously, three stones landed on the roof, and one inside, the Smiths' dwelling. Bill Hack, who was there at the time, jumped into his truck and drove completely around the hilltop site without seeing a soul.[85]

As time went by some of the Mayanup lights grew in size. On June 10th Ethel's sister-in-law, Marjory Hack, told a journalist that at six o'clock that evening she'd seen a "powerful light travelling fairly fast about two feet above [the same] brook. It, too, moved "very smoothly [with] no variation in height" and could not, she was certain, have been any conventional light. Seconds after the sighting, a pebble dropped lightly onto her car's roof and several others fell inside the house.

One night, to his great alarm, young Aden Eades was stalked by a Min Min. As he was walking back to the Smiths' house from "Lynford Hill", the blue light blocked his way, then followed him as he made a wide detour, jumped a fence and ran for his life.[86]

Apparently the link between Min Mins and polt activity was well known to Aboriginal

---

83 *Blackwood Times*, 17 June 1955 and Ethel Hack, quoted in Smith, p. 116.
84 John Meredith interviews.
85 *Weekend Mail*, 18 June 1955 and Paul Cropper interview with Ethel Hack, 30 April 2000.
86 Helen Hack, p. 50.

shamans. When interviewed by the *Blackwood Times* prior to the "ghost catching" episode, Fred Winmar said that while they were always mischievous, he had never known a Jannick to harm anyone. He added that the tricky spirits were often accompanied by lights.[87]

UFOs?

As time went by, Ethel noted, "the lights got bigger and brighter – as big as a car headlight", and some of the larger lights behaved in a manner that is highly reminiscent of (sceptics, sharpen your pencils) UFO activity. One night on Whistler Road, which forms the western boundary of "Lynford Hill", Doug Hack's sons, Rod and Kim, were illuminated, dazzled, and then chased by a full-moon-sized disc of light. The "moon disc" appeared at least three more times, chasing or pacing cars on the same stretch of road. In 1967 Chris and Neil Sambell were chased by a similar light on Kojonup Road, which runs east-west between the two Hack properties.[88]

When we met her and her husband Tom at "Keninup" in 2002, Helen Hack told us that sightings of, and encounters with, large flying lights continued to occur on theirs and neighbouring properties well after the stone falls ceased in 1957. Such incidents occurred, in fact, right up to 1996, and many of the lights displayed behaviour – rotating, projecting blindingly-bright beams, hovering, zooming up and away at great speed – that is often associated with UFOs. One event in particular, which involved a car being pulled to a stop by a hovering oval object, and the driver illuminated for some time by a beam of light, could certainly be classified as a Close Encounter of the Third Kind. That occurred about two kilometres east of "Keninup" on the Kojonup Road.

Earth-ripping

Whatever the Min Mins and "UFOs" were, they weren't entirely insubstantial: they seem to have left physical traces in one of Bill and Ethel's paddocks, where a patch of ground was torn up in an inexplicable way. It was a corner of the property where several lights had been seen, and it seemed, said Ethel, "as if a strong force had swept over" the 10 by 20 metre area, up-ending many large clods of earth and turf. Curiously, while the paddock was otherwise saturated by overnight rain, the underside of the clods and the holes from which they came were quite dry.[89]

---

87   *Blackwood Times*, 8 July 1955.
88   John Meredith interviews.
89   John Meredith interviews.

Glowing hands

Perhaps the strangest of all the strange things seen during the West Australian episode(s) were luminous, disembodied hands. The first such sighting was by young Tom Hack, who saw a luminous green hand under the floorboards of the Smiths' Cottage. Alf Krakouer at "Lynford Hill" and Harvey Dickson at "Eastington" also saw luminous hands – but in their case the spectral hands were blue.[90]

While phantom hands have been reported in a couple of foreign cases, the only other such reports in our Australian files occurred during the extremely creepy "Coalbaggie Bogey" case of 1891–94 (see Chapter Eleven) and during an episode at Adelong in 1891 (Case 12, Chapter Twelve).

Marks of the geist

Readers will make up their own minds about the Mayanup – Pumphrey – Boyup Brook case, but we have no doubt that it was a genuinely paranormal episode, every bit as strange as anything that has been recorded elsewhere in the world throughout the centuries.

Most of the phenomena observed at the three locations – scratching noises, stone falls, levitation and materialisation of objects, even hair-pulling and the creation of a pool of anomalous fluid – have been reported at many other apparently polt-haunted locations around the world and could be considered veritable hallmarks of genuine poltergeist activity.

Strange lights, too, have been mentioned in a small number of other cases, although we know of none that have featured as many "spook lights" and large ufo-like flying lights as this West Australian case.

One thing that makes the case uniquely interesting is the way the polt didn't simply focus on one particular family or residence, as is usually the case. At one stage it was pestering, *simultaneously*, the Smiths at "Keninup", the Krakouers at "Lynford Hill" and the Pennys 150 kilometres away at "Carabin". Later, when Cyril Penny was again targeted at Borden, the Jannick was still operating at Mayanup, 160 km to the west. Later, as we have seen, it took a shine to young Harvey Dickson and moved to Boyup Brook.

It's unlikely we'll ever find out how the Jannick managed to torment so many different people, in so many locations, simultaneously, but the fact that nearly all its targets were Aboriginal, and that most of them were related must, one assumes, have had a lot to do with the intensity and spread of the phenomenon. This suggests the possibility that (as was suggested at Humpty Doo) the long series of weird events was started by some kind of Aboriginal curse.

During several other Australian outbreaks, including, as we have seen, the Humpty

---

90   Helen Hack, p. 44.

Doo episode, sceptics have loudly proclaimed – often from a safe distance – that the events in question were the work of human tricksters. Few such suggestions were made during the West Australian wave of weirdness. This was largely because the Hacks, Donaldsons and Dicksons were such long-established, wealthy and well-respected families.

As an *Australasian Post* journalist observed, both Alan Donaldson and Bill Hack "are serious about the [poltergeist] matter… Both could have cashed in on the phenomena by charging admission to the farm or selling the stones, but they are above that. They genuinely want to find a solution to the mystery."[91] The same goes for George Dickson and family.

Although, in the mid-1950s, many Aboriginal people still suffered considerable racial and class prejudice, it is clear that their white bosses and neighbours thought very highly of both the Smiths and Krakouers. There is no suggestion that either family tried to profit in any way from the Jannick events.

Idiots

Some amateurish, spontaneous hoaxing did occur at Mayanup. On Sunday 27 June, a *Blackwood Times* reporter, who had previously observed several genuinely strange stone falls at both "Keninup" and "Lynford Hill", witnessed some stone throwing by thrill-seeking meatheads. "Later [that] evening", he wrote, "about 100 people arrived [at the Krakouers' house] and I thought it rather unfortunate that a number of them had come determined to hear stones on the house – even if they had to throw them themselves.

"Many people who arrived did just this, which, of course, made it impossible for anybody interested to record authentic supernatural stone falling. I cannot understand why responsible persons should travel many miles to witness phenomena and then … immediately decide to become themselves amateur 'poltergeists'."[92]

Occasional pranks of that nature didn't concern Bill and Ethel Hack, who made a special point of mentioning that they, the Smiths and Krakouers, could easily distinguish the impact of genuine Jannick-thrown stones and those thrown playfully by humans. The sounds made by stones propelled or dropped by the polt were quite distinctive, and couldn't be replicated.

In any case, the odd stone thrown by idiots cannot account for the many objects that were seen to levitate and fall *inside* the Smith and Krakouer houses – not to mention those that materialised within the "Keninup", "Carabin" and "Eastington" homesteads.

None of the many journalists who visited the affected properties – neither those who observed objects defying the laws of physics nor those who didn't – mentioned any cause for scepticism. And none of the several police who visited the Mayanup and Pumphrey

---

91   *Australasian Post*, 11 April 1957.
92   *Blackwood Times*, 1 July 1955.

sites found any evidence of hoaxing. The only outspoken sceptic was Athol Douglas who, to maintain his negative position, was reduced to branding everyone else at "Carabin" – the Donaldsons, the Pennys, the Ugles, their neighbours and several journalists – as liars.

Camera-shy spooks

The Mayanup – Boyup Brook – Pumphrey episode was the earliest Australian case for which we have a good photographic record. That being the case, sceptics might well ask, why do none of the pictures show stones or other objects in flight? Surely some of the objects, particularly those that supposedly floated so slowly past the eyes of witnesses, should have been caught on film. Good question – and one that has frustrated polt researchers since the invention of portable cameras. In the previous chapter we described how the Humpty Doo polt managed to frustrate every attempt to film objects in flight. It seems the WA polt was just as camera shy.

Although television broadcasting didn't commence in WA until two years later, TV coverage of the 1955–57 poltergeist episode was attempted on at least two occasions, presumably by freelancers or by crews from the eastern states. Leila McCreery recalls that one camera team made Boyup Brook their base for a couple of days, but "Whenever they came to the property the poltergeist wouldn't perform. But then, a couple of times, after they'd packed up and were starting to drive away, it would start up again!"

According to the *Sunday Times* (our copy is almost illegible) there was also an attempt to film the stone falls at Pumphrey in March 1957. It seems that although the cameramen saw stones falling they couldn't catch them on film.

Hoaxing very unlikely

It is reasonable, when researching some supposed polt episodes, to suspect – or at least to leave open the possibility – that the strange phenomena were hoaxed. In most of the questionable cases the person on whom the activity appears to be focused is usually "in the frame" as the possible hoaxer. Sometimes brothers or sisters of that person, or neighbourhood larrikins are reasonably suspected to have assisted the ring leader. In the case of the extended Mayanup – Pumphrey – Borden – Boyup Brook episode, however, such suspicions are hard to maintain. Quite apart from the sheer number of solid eyewitnesses, there is the consideration that the episode didn't involve one particular unwilling "medium". Instead, the polt (or polts) latched onto several different people, most of whom were extremely unhappy to have been chosen.

It is difficult to believe all of those people would have taken it into their heads to perpetrate hoaxes, throwing all those stones, indoors and out, for days, weeks and months on end without being detected, and, in the case of the Aboriginal people, maintained a very convincing pretence of being scared half to death by their own hoaxes.

One thing that strongly suggests hoaxing was not involved in the West Australian episode(s) is that the hundreds of stones that flew around never hurt anybody; neither did they break windows or lamps or crockery. It stands to reason that if hundreds of stones – some quite heavy – were thrown or catapulted at night, at long range, by hoaxers, injury or property damage would have been inevitable. As at many other polt locations, however, it was noted that the flying objects displayed "amazing accuracy" and, one might say, restraint: always managing to either just miss people and their more fragile possessions or to hit them at such an unnaturally slow speed that no injury resulted.

One experiment conducted at "Keninup" strongly suggests the property was infested by a genuine polt: the Hacks selected exactly 100 stones, coated them with silver paint and scattered them widely over the general area. After just a few days they had all been pitched back into the Smiths' camp. It seems downright impossible that a hoaxer or hoaxers, sneaking around in the dark, could have located every single one of those painted stones.

During other polt episodes both here and overseas, people have reported being dragged or tipped out of bed by invisible forces. The incident of the sleeping boy being dragged from his tent at the Krakouers' camp therefore conforms to known polt behaviour. And as Helen Hack points out, the child's brother, who reported the incident, "had never been to school so it was impossible for him to have read about [such polt behaviour] elsewhere".

Possible causes of the episode

When interviewed in 1991 Doug Hack was still baffled by the events of 1955–57. "If this poltergeist was trying to tell you something", he said, "you couldn't work it out – there was no sense to it." Ethel agreed: "One suspected there was a pattern to it but what that pattern was we never found out."[93]

Pregnancies?

Ethel, however, did wonder whether it was merely coincidental that Jean Smith had been pregnant when the phenomena began at "Keninup" and that Molly Krakouer became aware that she, too, was pregnant just before the first stone falls at "Lynford Park."

---

93   Ethel Hack, quoted in Smith, p. 119.

Stormy weather?

She commented, also, on the unusually wet, stormy weather that prevailed before and during the Mayanup events. As we have seen, the Humpty Doo episode also began during wild, stormy weather. So, too, did the 1935 Cannibal Creek incident (see Chapter Five) and a couple of others.

Land clearing?

Aborigines involved in the making of the "Spirit Stones" documentary suggested that the Jannick may have been stirred into action by the large amount of land-clearing that took place around Mayanup in the mid-1950s.

Alf Eades' spirit?

As we will show in the following chapters, the Mayanup episode is not the only one in which a comatose, seriously ill or dying person was either on the premises or associated somehow with the strange phenomena. But while the phenomena *did* taper off shortly after Mr. Eades' death and cease a month later, it resumed in earnest after a seven-month break.

Wilton Hack?

When the stone falls began at "Keninup", Bill Hack wondered for a while if the strange goings-on could have had anything to do with his late father Wilton, who, *very* unusually for the era, had converted to Buddhism in the early 1900s. When he died, Wilton was, as per his instructions – and to the consternation of many in the district – cremated on a funeral pyre. When the stones began to fall in 1955 Bill and Ethel couldn't help but remember that he'd occasionally suggested he might "come back" one day.[94]

Uncle Bobby?

When the strange events began at the Dickson farm it didn't seem entirely unreasonable, given how benign it seemed to be, to suggest that the polt was dear old Uncle Bob, who'd died exactly ten years earlier.

---

94   Helen Hack, p. 24.

No room for doubt

While we harbour varying degrees of scepticism about some of the other cases in our files, we have no doubt that what transpired at Mayanup, Pumphrey and Boyup Brook was genuinely paranormal. We're confident that any open-minded reader will have come to same conclusion.

We encourage anyone who still harbours doubts to obtain a copy of Helen Hack's excellent, in-depth account of the episode. If that doesn't dispel any lingering scepticism, we don't know what in heaven, or elsewhere, will.

Sources:

Helen Hack, *The Mystery of the Mayanup Poltergeist*, Hesperian Press, Carlisle, Western Australia, 2000.

Ethel Hack, Journal 1955–57, quoted in Keith Smith, *Supernatural 2*, Pan Macmillan, Melbourne, 1993, pp. 113–121.

Blackwood Times, 17 and 24 Jun, 1, 8 and 22 Jul 1955.

Weekend Mail, 18 Jun 1955, 23 Mar 1957.

West Australian, 19–22 Mar 1957.

Sunday Times (Perth), 6 Oct 1957.

Truth (Sydney), 6 Oct 1957.

Two Worlds, 11 May 1957.

Psychic News, 20 Aug 1955 and 23 Nov 1957.

Paul Cropper, interview with Brian Donaldson, 29 Jan 1988.

John Meredith, audio taped interviews with Ethel and Douglas Hack, 9 Sept 1991 (National Library of Australia Bibliographical ID no's. 491839 and 2014397).

Frank Cusack, *Australian Ghost Stories*, Pan Macmillan, Melbourne, 1993, pp. 135–139.

Tony Healy, interviews with Harvey and Rose Dickson, 1995–2011.

Paul Cropper, interview with Ethel Hack, 30 Apr 2000.

Tony Healy, interview with Helen and Tom Hack, Jul 2002.

"Spirit Stones", ABC television documentary, Jag Films, 2009.

Transcript of interview with Jack Coulter, made by the producers of "Spirit Stones", 2009.

Tony Healy, interviews with Leila McCreery, 2011 and 2012.

CHAPTER THREE

A Ghost in the Machine

1949. Tarcutta, NSW. Rating: ★★★★

During this remarkable episode a milking machine belonging to dairy farmer Laurence Wilkinson malfunctioned in a weird and dramatic way: its metal pulsator plates repeatedly, inexplicably vanishing and landing up to 250 yards from the shed.

Other objects were seen to levitate. The phenomenon, which persisted for eleven months, was observed and documented by Alexander Portors, an engineer of 30 years experience, who was very familiar with the machine in question.

The story broke on 19 January 1949, when the *Wagga Wagga Advertiser* learned that Mr. Portors had asked the newly-established Commonwealth Scientific and Industrial Research Organisation (CSIRO) for assistance.

When interviewed by the *Advertiser*, Mr. Portors said the phenomenon began on 10 January and had occurred almost every day thereafter. It involved a common five-stand milking machine that had operated normally for several years until, inexplicably, its pulsator plates started to vanish. It always happened so fast that none of the witnesses, not even those who were looking directly at the plates at the critical moment, actually saw them disappear from the machine or exit the shed: one moment they were there, the next they were gone. As most of them were later found on a stony ridge to the north, it was assumed that some mysterious force had caused them to fly out of the shed at phenomenal speed.

The disc-shaped, brass-and-Bakelite plates weighed 13 ounces (368 grams), were about one and a half inches thick and three inches long (3.5 x 7 cm). To exit the shed they would have had to dip downwards to clear the sloping edge of the roof. Then, to reach the area where they commonly landed, they would have had to swoop upwards to clear a stockyard fence. On landing, they either buried themselves in the ground or tore two-foot-long, one-inch-deep (60 x 2.5 cm) scars in the earth.

"Flung to glory": the flight of the discs. (*Sunday Herald*, 4 December 1949)

The milking shed and surrounds, 2010. (Healy/Cropper)

Another strange aspect was that the phenomenon happened regardless of how fast or how slowly the machine was operating, and occurred even when the power was off and it was being turned by hand. Equally strangely, the "flight" of the plates was absolutely noiseless.

Because they couldn't normally be removed unless the machine was stationary, and then only by manipulating them in a certain way, the plates' behaviour seemed to defy explanation.

Mr. Portors claimed that he "could get signatures from 20 adults, sensible men who have seen the phenomenon to swear to it", and several of them did indeed step forward.

Roy Donahue, who owned a similar milking machine, said "It is impossible, but I saw it happen". Another, Clem Gorman, said "I saw it, but I wish to God I had not seen it. It is frightening. There's no reason … why this should happen, and I'm a mechanical man … it disturbs me greatly."

Mr. Wilkinson's 15-year-old son, Robin, was on the property throughout most of the episode. On one occasion three Tarcutta residents watched him touch one of the plates with a short iron rod. The plate suddenly flew from the machine, and at the same time the rod was wrenched from his hand and embedded in the concrete floor. The plate was found about 200 yards away, embedded in a mud heap and emitting an odour "like that of a burning arc lamp, but [it] was cold when we picked it up." A slight blue haze hung about the spot.

Laurence Wilkinson.

On January 18th a technician from the company that sold the machine arrived to examine it, and found it worked perfectly. The plates behaved themselves for a few days after that, but if Mr. Wilkinson thought his troubles were over he was badly mistaken: on the night of Saturday 22nd they again flew off "with terrific force".

In desperation, the flummoxed farmer bolted down the steel bar that kept the plates in position – but they still flew off. He also experimented by cutting the fibre faces off the brass plates and substituting leather, but they were then thrown further than ever. After ten days of weirdness he decided the machine was simply too dangerous to use and abandoned it. Despite being handicapped by, as the *Advertiser* put it, "a maimed hand", he resorted to milking his 100 cows manually.

In spite of the technician's report and without bothering to visit Tarcutta to see for himself, L.C. Thurston, the President of the Dairymens Association, suggested the plates might have been flung away because the pump was blowing instead of sucking. That idea was quickly scotched by an indignant Mr. Portors, who pointed out that if such was the case the phenomenon would hardly be noiseless. "I have been in engineering since 1917 and I know that the milking plant is without any fault. The machine is perfect."

A boffin's brush-off

The CSIRO's response to Mr. Portors' appeal was also rather disappointing. Without deigning to leave his office in Canberra, one of the organisation's officers, D.T. Dickson, suggested that the machine be inspected by a dairy expert (which had, of course, already been done) and by an electrical engineer, who should then send their reports to CSIRO headquarters in Melbourne. Mr. Dickson also told journalists that a 60,000-volt power line that passed close to the property could have something to do with the phenomenon: "High tension wires sometimes become awry and remarkable things occur."

Mr. Portors was furious. The line in question, he pointed out, carried only 33,000 volts and was located 11 miles away. "These people in the cities", he seethed, "are apt to think everyone in the country is a nitwit". He insisted that a force strong enough to hurl metal plates long distances faster than the eye could see obviously warranted official investigation. At no time did he suggest poltergeist activity; he believed, rather, that the plates were hurled by power that was built up by the machine in some way. If scientists could detect the source of the unknown power, he said, the discovery could be of great value to the country. "There's a build-up of power there … [it] is only exerted for a fraction of a second, but the plate picks up tremendous speed, and the momentum carries it on … it is noiseless, too. I've watched for a plate leaving the machine, but could not sight it. It's just so fast you can't see it. Dairy farmers from all around [have come to see] and it has just flung the plates to glory. They've all been … amazed."

The CSIRO's suggestions were, he said, "just side-stepping … what we need here is a scientist … but if the experts do not hurry up there will be little or nothing to see. My reaction to the [CSIRO] attitude is one of complete disgust … as luck would have it, the discs so far have not struck anyone. If they did it would mean serious bodily harm, perhaps death."

Ben Chifley lends a hand … but not for long

Ben Chifley.

After the inaction of the CSIRO and the Dairymen's Association chief, Mr. Portors must have been heartened (albeit briefly) by the response of the Federal Member for Hume, Mr. Fuller, who, on about 28 January, personally requested the Prime Minister, Ben Chifley, to intercede.

We'd love to report that the PM, a former engine driver, donned his overalls and sped down to the farm to sort things out, but in fact he didn't budge from his desk in Canberra. He did, however, communicate with the town clerk of Tarcutta to "gain the closest impression of the reason why" the plates were flying, and then contacted "high scientists" at CSIRO headquarters in Melbourne. Predictably, however, the "high scientists" ducked the issue again. The matter, they said, was not one for scientists, but for the manufacturers of the milking machine.

As the boffins knew very well that the manufacturers had already found the machine to be faultless, Mr. Portors and Mr. Wilkinson found this second round of butt-covering particularly galling. The president of Kyeamba Shire, Councillor A. O'Brian, shared their frustration: "It seems … they won't send a scientist down here until someone is killed or seriously injured", he said.

So the exhausted Mr. Wilkinson was left to cope with the weirdness and run his farm as best he could.

Mr. Dowsett "solves" the mystery

What would a good polt event be without a confirmed sceptic making a flying visit to the site and attempting to debunk it?

On 29 January a Chartered Engineer, J.H. Dowsett, wrote to the *Wagga Wagga Advertiser* to say that local residents "may now sleep soundly … for the mystery has been solved". He and one or two companions had visited the Wilkinson property on the previous Tuesday and satisfied themselves that young Robin Wilkinson was hoaxing the whole thing. But how they came to that conclusion is far from adequately explained.

They arrived some time before the evening milking, examined the machine, which appeared to be working properly and, using a compass and other devices, found nothing unusual about the magnetic

Robin Wilkinson. (*Sunday Herald*, 4 December 1949)

deviation and the pull of gravity. The brass pulsator plates were, unsurprisingly, found to be non-magnetic. They were told that during the morning the master plate had flown off and dived into a six-foot-tall water tank. Dowsett found that implausible. "Remarkable", he commented sarcastically but not unreasonably, "how someone knew to look into this tank to find the plate, as they cannot be observed when in actual flight."

He saw that Mr. Wilkinson had taken the precaution of covering most of the machinery with wire netting and checked that everything was properly grounded. During all this, he noted, there were two children present, "a boy and a girl, both between about … nine to twelve years." The boy, in fact, was 15-year-old Robin, who proceeded to round up the cows and help his father attach them to the machine, which began to work perfectly.

But Dowsett was keeping a sharp eye on the lad who "… was quite a power in his actions about the dairy, and his eagerness to assist with milking was outstanding; his movements were keenly observed."

The engineer then states, rather oddly, that "We were all rather puzzled, but had by this time formed our opinions, so we packed up … and started on our journey homewards."

They'd driven only 400 yards when someone (with, apparently, a particularly loud voice) called them back. On their return they were told a pulsator plate had attempted to fly but had been immediately replaced so that milking could continue. The machine had resumed working normally. Dowsett didn't say where the plate was found, but implies that it was inside the wire netting. He thought that very suspicious. If the mysterious force was really strong enough to hurl objects 200 yards, he suggested, and then surely it could "drive a plate through wire netting." That doesn't sound entirely unreasonable, until we remember that Dowsett knew full well that Wilkinson had not claimed every object was thrown a great distance. Several – including the one that landed in the water tank that same morning – had been found quite close to the machine.

But Dowsett had made up his mind. Plates found some distance from the dairy, he told the *Advertiser*, "have been thrown or placed in position … the whole situation is fantastic and utter rot." In conclusion he pointed the finger of blame straight at young Robin: "I suggest that no further trouble will be experienced … after the termination of the present school holidays."

In that and in several other respects, Dowsett was wrong.

Mystery unsolved

Far from finishing when Robin returned to school at the end of January, the weird events continued for the next ten months. That included a period of three weeks when Robin was 140 kilometres away in Albury.

11 Months Of Strange Events In …
THE 'HAUNTED' FARM Scientists Puzzled As Tins Float In Air
FIRST-HAND STORY
Early this year weird, unaccountable happenings began to terrorise visitors to the lonely dairy farm of Mr. Lawrence A. Wilkinson, near Tarcutta.

By early October the phenomenon was affecting not only the milking machine, but also the diesel engine that drove it and an auxiliary engine. "All the moveable parts of both engines and milking machines, and also the separator", wrote W.A. Breaden, Secretary of the Tarcutta and district Progress Association, "have been flung away."

Mr. Wilkinson said that one part of the milking machine, weighing 2.5 pounds (1.13 kg) was found 250 yards from the shed. On one occasion a cast-iron axle weighing 65 pounds (29.48 kg) was lifted two feet (61 cm) off the ground with what he described as "a terrific bang."

A *Sydney Morning Herald* journalist who visited the farm in November wrote that "in an effort to stop the machine from flying to bits, Mr. Wilkinson had tied every moving part to the walls and rafters with bits of chain, wire and rope … yet parts of the machine, both moving and stationary, continue to fly about, twisting the heavy dog chains that secure them as if they were soft copper wire."

They saw nothing

Given what we know of the notoriously contrary nature of polts, we weren't surprised to learn that whenever Mr. Wilkinson and Mr. Portors managed to persuade experts to examine it, the machine worked flawlessly.

When dairy inspectors from the NSW Department of Agriculture inspected the machine, they, like the technician from the company who sold the machine, could find no fault with it. Public Works Department engineers also drew a blank.

In November, when the CSIRO finally bowed to pressure and sent out a couple of scientists, the polt again kept a low profile. In the presence of Roger Morse and Chester Gray, both Electrical and Mechanical engineers, the machine worked perfectly, and Morse, the senior of the two, duly reported that they "were satisfied the occurrences are not related to any new source of energy. It does not appear, therefore, that any scientific investigation, such as this organisation, with its present far from unlimited resources, could undertake, would be of any value in explaining the happenings."

Morse seems to have been intent on coming to a negative conclusion. He dismissed the testimony of the eyewitnesses with the odd remark that they could all have been fooled "by a simple form of conjuring … or by some form of hypnotism", and then took a couple of nasty, gratuitous swipes at the long-suffering Wilkinsons: "Although the boy has been a suspect … Wilkinson himself would have had the opportunity of interfering with the plant … it is quite possible that a psychiatrist might get to the bottom of the matter …".

Pretty damning stuff – until we consider this: Chester Gray revealed later that he had not been in full agreement with his colleague.

Unlike Morse, Gray was very favourably impressed by the eyewitnesses: "We had sworn declarations [from] four people … who made them at considerable hazard to their reputations …we cross-examined [them and other witnesses] … without in any way shaking them, or revealing noticeable flaws or inconsistencies … accordingly these statements constitute unusually powerful authentication of the phenomena reported.

"I was far less inclined to wipe the whole thing … In my opinion it would have taken a whole coterie of professional magicians … to have brought off the tricks".

They saw lots

When one reads their compelling testimony, it is easy to see why Mr. Gray found it hard to dismiss the eyewitnesses as hoaxers or dupes.

In November 1949 a *Sydney Morning Herald* journalist interviewed Alexander Portors, two other engineers who had visited the dairy repeatedly over the course of eleven months, and eight other eyewitnesses.

As well as witnessing many disappearances of pulsator plates, Mr. Portors had watched an empty grease tin lift from the top of the machine's vacuum pump and "rise slowly in the air … spinning as it rose. It cleared a 6 foot wooden partition with 18 inches [46 cm] to spare, then turned and fell with terrific force to the ground about 18 inches from where I stood. A peculiar thing about it was that it seemed much bigger than it really was – as big as a football. I suppose that was because it was spinning diagonally. We were so astonished we thought we'd see what happened to an empty 50-cigarette tin. We put it on … the vacuum pump. A minute or two later it also rose over the 6ft partition."

Interior of the shed in 2010. (Healy/Cropper)

Another mechanical engineer, R.V. Donahue, and his daughter Veronica witnessed those amazing events. Veronica told the journalist that she was standing beside her father and Mr. and Mrs. Portors "when I saw the grease tin rise in the air and crash at my feet with a loud bang. I got a terrible fright."

Mr. Donahue also witnessed the sudden disappearance of several pulsator plates: "One moment they were there, the next moment they were gone."

One day Edward Brown helped Mr. Portors examine the plates, and "… made sure they were fixed firmly on … then started up the engine. Suddenly the master pulsator flew off … we had a look at the other pulsators and found two of them were missing."

A radio and electrical engineer, Mr. R. Mumford, provided the journalist with some particularly interesting observations: "When I first heard about the strange events … I didn't believe them, but thought I'd go and see for myself." He visited the dairy about twenty times, sometimes spending entire weekends there.

"I was with the party who saw the grease tin and cigarette tin rise in the air, but there were many other remarkable experiences. I once kept the master pulsator block … under observation for four hours. Suddenly I became aware it had gone. We found it later 50 yards away in the paddock.

"One Sunday … I saw the lid of a cream can lift itself off the creamery shelf, rush through the air and strike the opposite wall. No one was present … but myself. *Mr. Wilkinson's boy was in the cottage 100 yards away* [our italics].

"It's impossible to explain these things by any known law. I've thought of magnetic deflection and electrical interference, and at one time I made a lot of … tests with instruments I brought to the farm for the purpose, but all … proved nothing. It's the biggest mystery I've ever experienced."

Magic moments

The *Herald* also reported the findings of someone who had interviewed young Robin Wilkinson. The man in question was a stage magician – a member of the Magic Circle of London. "When I went to [the] dairy", he stated, "I had two things to settle in my mind. Was the rampaging milking machine in a state of neglect and disrepair? And was there any loophole for trickery? The answer to the first question was patently 'No'".

Nor could he believe Mr. Wilkinson was a hoaxer: The farmer "is too stolid and hard-working … to want to play tricks on himself. The continued disintegration of his machine has imposed a tremendous physical strain upon him and reduced his nervous system to a wreck."

The man then focused his attention on young Robin, "a strong, healthy boy of 15, obviously interested in machinery, always doing odd jobs in the dairy". While the sceptical Mr. Dowsett had thought it suspicious that the boy was "the indefatigable retriever of missing engine parts", this investigator, noting that the lad was miles from the farm when some phenomena occurred, was "convinced Robin intentionally was not responsible for these strange goings-on."

"Yet", he continued, "it was the boy … who gave me a clue. He said, in answer to my question: 'Not much happens when I'm away.'

"Nearly all poltergeist phenomena occurs in the presence of a human agent, usually an adolescent boy or girl … I think it reasonable that the absurd happenings at Wilkinson's farm are of poltergeist origin and that the human agent … is Mr. Wilkinson's son."

Gone but not forgotten

As we can find no newspaper articles about the "haunted cow shed" dated later than January 1950, it seems likely the polt activity eased off as the new year began. One document in our file, however, hints that strange events occurred occasionally until at least 1956.

As mentioned above, one of the CSIRO scientists, Chester M. Gray, was never completely happy with the negative report lodged by his colleague Roger Morse after their visit to Tarcutta in November 1949. So it is very interesting that, when he retired in 1971 after a long and distinguished career, he "decided to follow-up the investigation, to the extent that this was possible after so long a time."

Consequently, between 1973 and 1975 he corresponded with senior officers at the

CSIRO, the National Library and the Australian Archives, seeking copies of all relevant documents, particularly statutory declarations of eyewitnesses, as well as copies of several photographs he'd taken on the farm.

In one letter he gives a brief account of his return visit to the site in January 1975: "I … found, against all expectations, that the principal dramatis personae were still going strong … with Mr. Breaden I … obtained from Mr. Wilkinson and his wife information about *what transpired, allegedly, in the seven years or so following my previous visit* [our italics]."

While Mr. Gray "was particularly impressed by the simple, unreserved words of Mrs. Wilkinson", he found her husband "very secretive about certain important aspects". Sceptics might find his reticence significant, but perhaps the farmer was just sick to death of scientists and media attention. Or perhaps, after belatedly accepting that something paranormal really *was* lurking about the farm, he was reluctant to talk for fear of stirring it up.

Despite Wilkinson's reticence, Mr. Gray did not "despair of obtaining further cooperation" and believed the strange phenomena to be genuinely paranormal. Declaring that "the main lines of the story are now fairly clear", he resolved to write a full account of his investigations for the London-based Society for Psychical Research (SPR).

It would have been very interesting to learn what he was referring to when he alluded to events that "transpired, allegedly, in the seven years after [1949]". Unfortunately, however, as the SPR has no record of receiving his report, it seems Mr. Gray, for some reason or other, never got around to sending it.

Robin's end

As we didn't become aware of the Tarcutta mystery until 2010, we have been able to locate only one member of the Wilkinson family. Although she was at the farm during parts of 1949, the lady, who requests anonymity, was then very young and has forgotten most of what transpired – it was "just a part of life".

She did, however, tell us that although she visited Robin Wilkinson regularly in later years, they never once talked about the strange events of '49. Robin, she said, was never chatty – he often "clammed up". He lived in Junee and died there in 2002.

To conclude:

A good feature of the Wilkinson case is that it involved plenty of eyewitnesses, but, because of its location, not *too* many. In some other cases excessive numbers of sightseers have made it difficult to decide whether or not hoaxing was involved.

After one brief visit to the property Mr. Dowsett asserted that the phenomena were being faked, but there is very little, if anything, to suggest he was right. He seemed to think that the mere fact that he was suspicious of young Robin was enough to prove that the entire series of events was "utter rot". Roger Morse of the CSIRO, after a similarly brief visit, also suggested hoaxing and implied Mr. Wilkinson was responsible. But three other professional engineers and many knowledgeable locals, who spent a great deal more time on the site than either Dowsett or Morse, and who'd actually witnessed the phenomena, stoutly defended the Wilkinsons.

One would expect that if hoaxing was involved a highly trained conjurer would be able to detect it. Yet the stage magician who visited in October 1949 concluded that no such hoaxing had occurred.

Because stormy weather has been associated with poltergeist activity during several other notable episodes it may be significant that the only time pulsator plates disappeared completely was during a severe storm on 25 January 1949. Three of them disappeared that night and the remaining two vanished three days later. Although the Wilkinsons searched "until they were footsore" they never found a trace of them.

It is interesting to note that although other people suggested something supernatural was going on at his farm, Laurence Wilkinson strongly resisted the notion. Like his stoutest supporter, Alexander Portors, he clung to the idea that the phenomena, though extremely weird, was the result of some undiscovered natural force.

As we know, Mr. Portors thought that the force – if only the government could harness it – would be a great boon for mankind. Given his engineering background and apparent unfamiliarity with poltergeist lore, his materialist "take" on the situation was not unreasonable. The episode had, after all, occurred just four years after the general public was made rudely aware of the awesome, almost incomprehensible power of the atom.

To us, however, it is pretty clear that for some reason or other a poltergeist really did decide to play merry hell in the Wilkinsons' cow shed.

Sources:

Wagga Wagga Advertiser, 19, 20, 21, 22, 29 Jan and 1 Feb 1949.

Canberra Times, 19, 20, 24, 25 and 29 Jan 1949.

Sydney Morning Herald, 20 and 21 Jan, 4 and 7 Dec 1949.

Adelaide Advertiser, 20 Jan 1949.

West Australian, 20 Jan 1949.

Mercury (Hobart), 29 Jan 1949.

Psychic News, 14 Jan and 25 Jun 1950.

Two Worlds, 3 Jun 1950.

National Archives of Australia file: "Dairy research, machinery and equipment, report on incidents at Tarcutta". Date range: 1949–1975. Series A 9778, Item D4/20/44E. (The file contains, among many other documents, Roger N. Morse's report, dated 8 Nov 1949, and correspondence from and to Chester Gray dating from 2 Feb 1973 to 28 Feb 1975).

Paul Cropper, interviews with Tarcutta residents Bill Belling and Ted Brown, Oct 2009.

Paul Cropper, interview with Wilkinson family member, 1 Sept 2010.

CHAPTER FOUR

"Caressa": Sex and the Supernatural

1992–1997. CANBERRA, ACT. RATING: ★★★★

In early 1999 we were contacted by the Director of Public Information for the RAAF, Reserve Wing Commander Ken Llewelyn. The call, however, had nothing to do with his "day job"; he wanted to compare notes about the Humpty Doo, Northern Territory, poltergeist episode.

Ken is an interesting guy. Born in Scotland in 1944, he worked as a journalist, served in both the RAF and RAAF and has, for many years, been actively involved in psychical research. In 1991 he wrote a fascinating book, *Flight into the Ages*, about the paranormal experiences of his fellow aviators.

Since late 1994, he told us, he'd been researching the strange case of a Canberra-based prostitute, Liz Fleming (working name: "Caressa"), who'd been at the epicentre of an amazing five-year-long series of poltergeist events. For a couple of years he'd been working on a manuscript that dealt not only with her paranormal experiences, but which also chronicled – sometimes in eye-popping detail – her very unusual professional life[95].

Ken Llewelyn. (Ken Llewelyn)

In late 1998, as his "Caressa" project progressed, it occurred to him that, for purposes

---

95 Many of the key witnesses were sex workers or their clients and therefore didn't want to be identified. So when Ken documented this remarkable case he changed the names of everyone involved – including that of the main protagonist, "Liz Fleming".

of comparison, it would be helpful to include details of at least one other strong Australian poltergeist case. Right on cue, our old friend the "Cosmic Prankster" helped him out: with an unexpected five-month posting to Darwin – just up the road from Humpty Doo. "It seemed", he joked, "… that some external agency was … guiding me on to my next case."

Although the Humpty Doo episode had finished a few months earlier, Ken put his time in the Territory to very good use, visiting the site and interviewing many of the people involved. As a result his book, *Caressa – From Call Girl to God's Child*, published in 2002, contains, in addition to Liz Fleming's own amazing story, an excellent 28-page chapter about the Humpty Doo case.

Caressa is well written, well illustrated, well documented and quite enthralling. It has also, we might add, the most eye-catching cover we've ever seen on a book about the paranormal. It stands alongside Helen Hack's *Mayanup Poltergeist* as one of the two best books about Australian poltergeists.

We don't want to steal Ken's "thunder" and it would, in any case, be impossible for us to adequately cover, in this short sub-chapter, all the strange phenomena he catalogued during his investigation. But we hope the following summary will give some idea of the high level of sustained weirdness that was involved in "Caressa's" strange saga.

Haunted brothels, haunted homes, haunted phones

Caressa. (Photo by Exclusive Photography, Canberra Pty Ltd.)

Although she'd previously had a few strange experiences, such as brief episodes of "astral projection", the poltergeist(s) didn't latch onto former public servant Liz until she started work at one of Canberra's legal brothels in 1992. Interestingly, occasional instances of apparently paranormal activity had been occurring there for some time prior to her arrival.

One woman, for instance, told of seeing a make-up bag thrown across a room by an unseen force. Several years earlier, before prostitution became legal, a man who died in the brothel, apparently while "on the job", had been carried out to his car and driven a couple of blocks down the road. It seemed reasonable to wonder if his disgruntled spirit was responsible for the phenomena.

In any case, as soon as Liz arrived, the brothel's weirdness rating shot right through the roof, and it soon became clear to her employers and workmates that the polt(s) found her presence very stimulating.

Although all the windows and doors were locked, as is the usual practice in a brothel, many small objects such as pencils, cutlery, shoes and candlesticks fell at her feet or were thrown around "with great force" but (as in so many other polt episodes) without injuring anyone. Although some of her workmates were terrified, most of them – and Liz in particular – found the phenomenon very entertaining.

As time went by she came to believe that several disembodied spirits were involved, and, being an adventurous, inquisitive person, began to speak to them, encouraging them to ramp-up their activities. She claimed that (like amiable "Uncle Bobby" in Western Australia) they often obliged, conjuring up and throwing various objects as requested. Even more strangely, she asserted that her requests didn't necessarily have to be verbal, as the "spirits" were capable of reading her mind.

When she moved to another brothel called The Golden Apple, the spirits – like the "hitch-hiking" West Australian spooks – went along for the ride. Soon, because of the tricks she encouraged the polts to play, her workmates began to refer to her as "the ghost lady". While most of them were fascinated by the phenomena, some were too frightened to work with her, and before long the manager asked her to leave.

Because she was so popular with the clients she was soon reinstated and, as time went by, the weird activity intensified. Among many other strange events, a two-metre-tall potted palm was hurled down a corridor and objects such as baseball bats levitated.

At about that time, Liz began making serious efforts to understand what was going on. After trying in vain to persuade an Australian National University academic – a member of Canberra Skeptics – to investigate her case, she contacted a local clairvoyant, Monica Hamers, who used hypnosis to try to work out whoever – or whatever – was behind the phenomenon.

Because Liz saw an image of a shepherd while under hypnosis, Ms. Hamers suggested that she leave a lipstick in front of her mirror at the brothel and ask the "shepherd" to communicate. Sure enough, a message – "I love you, Liz", complete with a heart pierced by an arrow, soon appeared. Others followed, including one in which a friendly entity named "Matt" claimed to be an associate of the "shepherd". Two other spirits, identifying themselves as "Roscoe" and "Marty", made contact later.

Despite the friendly messages, the poltergeists' behaviour became, at times, quite violent: loud rapping shook the walls; a large mattress hit Liz in the face, knocking her to the floor; vases full of flowers were thrown around, narrowly missing people, and a male prostitute was pummelled and thrown against a wall by an invisible assailant.

Liz eventually chose to work alone, apart from a receptionist, at her suburban home. Many of her regular clients followed her there – and so did her devoted "spirits", who carried on their shenanigans as before. At the suburban location, however, it seemed the spooks particularly enjoyed throwing certain types of objects around. The "frequent flyers" included potatoes and gold-painted stones.

The weirdness continued unabated through 1994, and in October of that year Ms. Hamers put Liz in contact with Ken Llewelyn.

"Exciting and scary"

Ken found her to be a very engaging, intelligent character, but when she poured out her amazing story in an excited, non-stop monologue, he thought she was "way over the top … I thought she was on drugs". It wasn't until he'd gathered corroborating testimony from nine other eyewitnesses and seen several inexplicable events himself that he could accept she was telling the truth as she perceived it.

Peta, who'd worked with Liz at The Golden Apple, confirmed her account of messages appearing on the mirror in the empty room. She also saw many objects appear, apparently out of thin air, saw doors open and shut of their own accord and testified to the fact that the phenomena often occurred immediately after Liz asked the spirits to perform. Inexplicable anomalies affected the telephone and answering machine on several occasions when, out of boredom, Liz asked the spirits to make a call.

Peta's reaction to all this weirdness was highly reminiscent of the mixture of fear and excitement that we felt, and observed in others, at Humpty Doo in 1998: "I was scared – it was like you were on the Big Dipper and screaming to get off, yet when you were on the ground you couldn't wait to go for another ride. It was both exciting and scary."

Another friend, Tereza, disapproved of Liz's spirits and the feeling, apparently, was mutual: her car was afflicted by strange electrical malfunctions while parked at Liz's house and, back at her own house, while she was on the phone to Liz, a vase smashed to pieces and electrical equipment malfunctioned.

Early one evening, just after arriving at Liz's house, 55-year-old Ray, one of her regular clients, realised he'd locked his keys in his truck. No worries: Liz simply asked "Matt" to retrieve them – and they dropped, apparently out of nowhere, onto the bedroom floor. Ken Llewelyn interviewed Ray just five minutes after the event, while he was still struggling to accept what his eyes had seen. "There was no way", the man insisted, "that those keys could have got inside the house." Liz's receptionist corroborated the story.

The teleported keys. (Ken Llewelyn)

People other than prostitutes and their clients witnessed the polts' pranks. Thirty-six-year-old David, who visited Liz a number of times in his capacity as a social worker, had always been sceptical of things supernatural. But he changed his mind when he witnessed objects, including a pot plant, move of their own accord. As three potatoes appeared, one after the other, and flew across a room, he kept a close eye on Liz and a friend – the only other people in the house. "It wasn't the two girls", he concluded, "… I can't explain what happened."

Hair raising

Nichole, the owner of Liz's favourite hairdressing salon, saw many inexplicable events, such as brushes teleporting from one spot to another, or the radio turning itself on or off, when the haunted hooker was on the premises (and even, interestingly, *just before* she phoned to make appointments).

But the weirdest episode occurred one day in September 1994, when Liz and three other clients were being attended to. It began with a child's pram, untouched by anyone in the salon, repeatedly tipping over; then two potatoes rolled though the open door from the deserted street, followed by a gold-painted rock that "for a few seconds jumped around the floor with an energy of its own". Then many pieces of rolled-up bark fell "through" the ceiling and a coin and a key appeared out of nowhere. The whole episode "… took about 25 minutes", said Nichole. "My staff were confused and frightened … I have no idea how these objects appeared, but I know they did. We all observed the event and I'm convinced that Liz was the catalyst."

Things that go bonk in the night

Ken saw no reason to doubt the veracity of his informants because, during the time he spent with Liz, he witnessed many similar events himself.

He saw several objects, including the ubiquitous potatoes and gold-painted stones – appear seemingly out of nowhere. Interestingly, one stone, like those at so many other polt locations, was distinctly warm to the touch. The appearance of one object – a tiny "party popper" firework – was

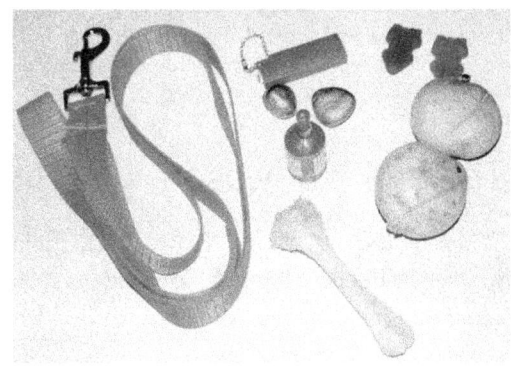

Some of the polt's playthings. (Ken Llewelyn)

preceded by a massive noise, like that of a large-calibre rifle shot, which caused the girls to scream. As the shock subsided, Ken noticed a potato rolling along the floor, and picked it up. Interestingly, it was distinctly warm to the touch.

Impulsively, in an attempt to replicate the "rifle shot" noise, Ken then threw the potato against the wall, but the spud produced only an ordinary sound and, on rebounding, rolled under Liz's bed.

That led to another remarkable event. As he tried to retrieve the potato Ken asked Liz for a torch. Just as she was replying that she didn't have one, "… a small red object, which at first appeared to be a cigarette lighter, fell on the floor beside us … it proved to be an Eveready torch – a small pocket torch. It looked brand new and worked perfectly."

He also heard loud thumping on the walls but, like the baffled victims of the "Guyra

Ghost" (Chapter Ten) he couldn't trace the source of the noises – or even determine whether they came from indoors or out.

The most remarkable thing Ken witnessed was "a cigarette lighter flying gently through the air and [lighting itself] in mid-air". After travelling a couple of metres the object seemed to lose power, and descended to the bedroom floor. As it had last been seen on the kitchen table, it must have passed through a wall and a closed door to get to the bedroom. When it first caught his eye it was about 1.5 metres above the floor. "The extraordinary thing ... was that it remained vertical, as though carried very slowly by an invisible hand ... not only was [it] vertical, so was the flame, which moved as though 'protected' by an air pocket." He found it impossible to carry the lighter on a similar trajectory without the flame flickering.

Gutsy and determined, Ken persisted with his investigation even after the polts turned their attention on him. Once, in the street outside, he was hit by a flying stone and on another occasion found that two gold-painted pebbles had been placed on his motor bike: one in the exact middle of the petrol cap, the other in the exact middle of the seat. Both mirrors had been pulled inwards at precisely the same angle: 45 degrees and, most unsettlingly, the carburettor idling screw had been manipulated so that the engine revved uncontrollably.

After an investigation lasting, on and off, for two and a half years, he spoke to Liz for the last time in May 1997, shortly before leaving for an eight-month stint in the UK.

The end – or was it?

When he learned, on his return to Australia, that "Caressa" had taken her own life he was very saddened, but not surprised, as she'd often said she would do so when the time came that men were no longer captivated by her. At the time of her death, in July 1997, she was just 42 years of age.

No worries, though: Ken and his clairvoyant friend, Monica Hamers, both suspected that "if anyone were to try to 'talk' with us from the 'other side' it would be the very determined and single-minded Liz". Sure enough, in April 1998, while Monica was in a deep trance, she came through loud and clear. As in life, she was very animated and talkative, telling Monica (among many other things) that she was happy – in a beautiful place, with "Marty" and all her other spirit friends. Not a bad end, you might say, to an often troubled, naughty – but never dull – life.

The "Caressa" episode had a great many interesting aspects – including several messages left on audio tape by, apparently, "Matt" and the other spirits – that we don't have space to deal with in this brief chapter. We strongly encourage anyone who wants to know the whole story to buy a copy of Ken Llewelyn's amazing book.

A very strong case

This unusually long-running episode, involving multiple eye-witnesses and a lengthy on-the-spot investigation by a competent, courageous and knowledgeable person, constitutes one of the strongest cases in our Australian files.

Readers will have noticed that most of the tricks attributed to "Caressa's" poltergeists – the wall-thumping, the many objects that flew without hitting people, the objects that apparently passed through walls and ceilings, the eavesdropping and mind-reading, even the "hitch-hiking" of the spooks from place to place – conform very well to phenomena observed at Humpty Doo and Mayanup.

Throughout the two and a half years that he knew her, Ken saw nothing to indicate hoaxing by Liz or anyone else. None of the other eyewitnesses found any reason to suspect trickery.

We found one small detail of the "Caressa" case particularly interesting: Ken mentioned that Liz's poltergeists "seemed to draw strength from stormy, humid conditions". During his subsequent investigation of the Humpty Doo episode he noted, as we did, that it, too, produced its most dramatic phenomena during the stormy northern monsoon season. As we have seen, the Mayanup poltergeist episode also occurred during an unusually stormy period.

Sources:

Ken Llewelyn, *Caressa – From Call girl to God's Child*, Sandstone Publishing, Leichhardt NSW, 2002.

Tony Healy, interviews with Ken Llewelyn, 1999 and 2014.

CHAPTER FIVE

The Vengeful Spook of Cannibal Creek

MARCH 1935. PALMER RIVER GOLDFIELDS, 100 KM SOUTHWEST OF COOKTOWN, QLD. RATING: ★★★½

This weird episode is of particular interest not only because it involved a malicious, invisible firebug but also because it occurred in such a colourful location – the notorious Palmer River goldfields.

For a few hectic years after the discovery of gold there in 1872 the region was the scene of much greed-stoked mayhem. Gun-toting prospectors battled with courageous but poorly-armed Aboriginal warriors, and violence flared between European and Chinese gold-seekers. Robberies, murders and apparent instances of cannibalism (by Aborigines driven to desperation by the destruction of their hunting grounds) did nothing to lighten the atmosphere.

While some good times were had on the Palmer in the '70s, life there, by and large, can't have been a barrel of laughs. Historians have estimated that during that rush and the one that followed, on the nearby Hodgkinson River, scores of gold-seekers were speared to death and hundreds of Aborigines were shot or starved to death. Many Aborigines, Europeans and Chinese also died of disease.

It seems therefore, rather appropriate that the polt which sprang from that bloody ground was one of the most violent and malevolent in our Australian files.

Slim pickings on the Cannibal

After most of the gold was played out a few diehards stayed on at the Palmer, and for several decades prospected for tin along the river and its tributaries. It was during the depths of the Great Depression, in early 1935, as Joe Jones and his mate Dick Clarke were eking out a living on Cannibal Creek, that the poltergeist began its rampage.

Joe's account of those terrifying events, written in 1938, was published by the Cairns Historical Society in October 1971 and formed the basis of a booklet, *The Palmer Poltergeist*, published by local historian Lennie Wallace, in 2004.

A "loathsome disease"

On Granite Creek, four miles north of Joe and Dick's camp, lived Jimmy Ah Quay, who'd been brought to the 1870s gold rush by his father at the age of twelve. He lived alone, grew a few vegetables and recovered sufficient tin from the creek bed to pay for incidentals.

Ah Quay's only neighbour was another old Chinese man who, as Joe put it, was "suffering from some loathsome disease", possibly leprosy. At some risk to his own health, Quay cooked for the man and generally looked out for him.

In January, when the poor man eventually died, Quay buried him, then burnt his camp and everything in it.

A month later, Joe and Dick visited Quay and showed him how he might retrieve more tin from his claim by using explosives. Enthused, the old man took his pack horses 70 miles to Laura and returned with gelignite and provisions for six months. He brought with him a young Australian-born Chinese, Willie Hip Wah, who was expected to help extract the tin.

After showing Quay how to drill holes and fire them, Joe and Dick returned to Cannibal Creek. Just a few days later, however, they were surprised to see the old man and his off-sider approaching through the heavy monsoon rain, "carrying their swags on bamboos".

Trouble in the camp

"My place haunted," Quay told his incredulous friends, "we can't live there; ghost come; he break up everything."

Joe was then in his mid-sixties and Dick, a veteran of the Great War, was in his forties. "Neither of us", Joe insisted in his well-written memoir, "believed in ghosts or spiritualism". So when Ah Quay asked them to help muster his horses and retrieve his other possessions the men readily agreed, saying "we will catch the ghost for you as well … [you won't] have to shift your place …"

"No matter", replied Quay, "you see." And next morning, when the party arrived back at Quay's camp, Joe and Dick *did* see …

No sooner had Joe unsaddled his horses than they "took fright, broke down a panel of [the] horse yard and galloped away, swimming over Granite Creek, which was in flood, with the hobbles on."

Still unfazed, and suspecting that young Willie, who probably wanted to get back to civilisation, was hoaxing the old man, Joe asked Quay not to start packing until he "could investigate matters and catch his ghost". No sooner had he spoken when "I noticed some coils of fuse were jumping onto the floor. There were six coils hung on a peg … They jumped down one at a time … I put it back [and] it all jumped back [down] a few minutes afterwards."

And so it began: all afternoon plates lifted off the table and hit the roof; cups and billy cans jumped about, bouncing off the walls and hitting old Quay, who was frantically packing.

By nightfall "… it was just a tornado; bottles, dishes, and cooking utensils were thrown about, striking the iron roof and walls and making a terrible din". Interestingly, Joe observed that when objects levitated at night "… you could see a faint light moving in and out through the room".

Joe was now in no doubt the phenomenon was truly paranormal, but he was managing to keep his nerve. At 9 pm he suggested they all go outside to see if the activity was confined to the building. That seemed like a reasonable idea, but the polt didn't seem to like it at all; as they stepped out, poor old Quay was blitzed "with broken plates, bottles and other missiles" and something smashed the lantern Joe was carrying. He fetched another but managed to take it only 40 yards from the hut before it too was smashed. A rain of sticks, stones and old tins pelted them for the next half hour.

Returning indoors, they were greeted by a hail of dishes, kerosene tins and scrap iron that made "an awful din". We find Joe's recollection of an exchange between him and his mate very reminiscent of remarks made by ourselves and Frank Robson at Humpty Doo sixty three years later: "Are those things happening, or have I gone suddenly mad?" he asked. To which Dick replied, "Too right they're happening". The war veteran added that "a hop [battle] over in France was a picnic compared to this." Had it not been so dark and rainy, he said, he'd have "gone bush".

The uncanny events had progressed from being merely fascinating, in the bright light of day, to exasperating and then to quite frightening. As the night wore on, things started to become downright sinister. About five minutes after young Willie retired to bed the men heard a frantic call: "Joe, Dick. Come quick; he smother me." Rushing to his assistance, they "found a rug completely wrapped around his head" and had some difficulty in unwinding it – by which time the boy was unconscious. They took him outside and laid him on the verandah, where they kept him under constant observation. He remained completely unconscious until daybreak.

At intervals throughout the night the men heard tapping, apparently on cases outside the hut, but whenever Joe approached them the noise moved elsewhere. They also heard groaning, "like someone in pain". It was not coming from young Willie: as they watched his face by torchlight, the eerie sound continued. At that point Quay made a confident prediction: "Cock crow he stop", and sure enough, as soon as the rooster crowed all was quiet … until about 7 am, when all hell broke loose.

With the four of them outside, rapping and other noises came from inside the hut and objects, including a heavy cradle box, began to fly out the door. Quay's suitcase hit the ground and sprang open, scattering his best clothing. Shortly thereafter, several fires started inside the hut. Joe carried some of the burning objects outside, but it was no use: "I went back into the humpy and found fires starting in different places on the floor. I tried to smother them with a sack but blazes would start up where there was nothing to burn."

As the humpy went up in flames Joe noted, in addition to the inexplicable way it started, another odd thing about the fire: Only four feet (1.3 metres) from the blazing hut there stood a thatched-roofed fowl house, with green tomato plants growing along its wall, yet although "the tomato plants were turned to cinders … the fowl house did not catch fire" even though debris from the burning hut fell against it.

The phantom hitchhikes

With the remains of the hut still smouldering, the party packed the last of Quay's goods and rode back to Cannibal Creek, but if Joe and his party thought they were shot of the pesky polt they were wrong: it came along for the ride.

Joe and Dick's nearest neighbour on the Cannibal was an old Italian who, on listening incredulously to their breathless stories, made fun of them and their "ghost". That night however, Joe and his party visited the sceptic's camp and "no sooner had we sat down than the business started … tins and bottles jumping around, hitting walls … The old Italian nearly had a fit. He could not hunt the chinamen away quick enough."

The polt then followed Joe's party back to his camp. There, as Joe watched over him throughout the night, "everything in the place" – including a hurricane lamp – "started to jump down and hit Willie". That went on for an hour, and then Quay and Joe were pelted with old tins until dawn when, mercifully, the pest seems to have decided it had made its point, and left them alone at last.

Ah Quay never returned to his camp; he obtained work elsewhere and in 1947 sailed for his old home, China. Willie Hip Wah took up baking and went on to become a prosperous and popular citizen of Cooktown.

Our comments:

This remarkable episode deserves a high rating for several reasons. Unusually in our Australian files, it involved a fire-starting polt. The fire had some very strange characteristics: the "blazes would start up … in different places on the floor … *where there was nothing to burn.*" The thatch-roofed fowl house right next to the blazing hut was strangely immune to the fire. Blazes that defy the laws of thermodynamics in similar ways have been documented in many foreign cases. (See Appendix A).

This polt also seemed bent on physically harming, perhaps even killing, one of its victims – behaviour that is extremely rare in Australia, but which has been reported occasionally in foreign cases.

Joe said the spook followed them from Granite Creek to Cannibal Creek – a distance of four miles. That detail corresponds with the reported "hitch-hiking "of poltergeists in many other well-attested cases.

The "faint light" that passed through the room when objects were thrown about at night is also of some interest. As we have seen, floating lights were reported frequently during the "Mayanup Poltergeist" episode of 1955–57.

The only weakness of the case is that everything we know about it stems from just one source: Joe Jones. His first-hand account is, however, very detailed, well-written and, to our minds, very credible. Mareeba-based historian Mrs. Lennie Wallace says that although it wasn't published until 1971, Joe wrote it in 1938, only three years after the incidents occurred. She first heard the story in the early 1950s from Sam Elliot, a contemporary of Joe's.

Joe mentioned that as his hut went up in flames Ah Quay remarked "No matter; I burn him, he burn me" – which clearly suggests he thought the spirit of his dead neighbour was persecuting him. But if he knew of any reason why the late lamented leper should torment him – apparently the only person who'd helped the man during his dying days – Quay kept it to himself.

The moaning sound "like someone in pain" might also indicate that the deceased neighbour was responsible. Others might favour the theory that young Willie, unhappy at having been dragged away from the comforts of town, had unwittingly triggered the events through spontaneous psychokinesis. Or perhaps the polt needed to "feed off" Willie's adolescent angst in order to operate. The weirdness, after all, didn't commence until he arrived on the scene, and ceased when he left. And although many of the objects targeted Ah Quay, the greatest violence appeared to be directed at Willie himself.

Sources:

Joe Jones, "The Granite Creek Ghost" MS, 1938, reprinted in Historical Society, Cairns, North Queensland, Bulletin 145, October 1971.

Lennie Wallace, *The Palmer Poltergeist*, Robyn's Nest Productions, 2004.

CHAPTER SIX

The San Remo Polt

1986. CENTRAL COAST, NSW. RATING: ★★★½

One evening in August 1986 George and Susan Sykes, then of Kalaroo Street, San Remo, received an excited phone call from Margaret and Ron Berrell, who lived in nearby Barkley Avenue. Something very strange and frightening was happening there.

At about 8.30 pm, soon after arriving at their friends' house, Sue and George experienced the phenomenon for themselves: someone – or some *thing* was pounding on the building's external walls. The walls, George told us later, were quite flimsy: fibro on the outside, and Masonite on the inside. But the noise, he insisted, "was coming from *within* the walls … inside the cavities … it wasn't someone banging on the outside of the house … and it was BANG! BANG! BANG! *Very* loud; very sharp and loud. I said [to Ron] 'You go out the front door and I'll go out the back, and there's no way [hoaxers] can escape', which we did – and there was nothing there – not a thing."

On other occasions George stationed himself on the roof, but still saw nothing to indicate hoaxing. The banging was clearly audible from outdoors, and to those outside it always seemed to be coming from inside.

"The banging would last for about thirty seconds to a minute", Sue recalls. "It would keep going if you ignored it, but would stop as

The Barkley Avenue house. (Healy/Cropper)

soon as you got up to look where it was coming from." Initially the thumping began "only when we turned out the lights", but later occurred in well-lit conditions and in broad daylight.

After the phenomenon had been going on for a few days the two couples noticed that although the noise sometimes emanated from other parts of the house, it usually came from a particular location on the wall – and that realisation led them to a rather unsettling conclusion.

"The old bloke"

The Berrell family hadn't been living in the house for very long. Until 18 months earlier it had been occupied by an old man, and the Berrells had been renting the place next door. As "the old bloke" was very frail, Ron often dropped in to check on him and to help with his chores. Throughout the same period, however, Ron also spent nearly every weekend in Sydney, taking care of his elderly, sight-impaired mother.

During one of his unavoidable absences tragedy struck: the old man collapsed and lay helpless on the floor for three days. By the time Ron found him he had developed pneumonia and was beyond saving. When the ambulance officers arrived, the dying man told them he'd been *knocking on the wall* for the entire three days, vainly trying to attract the Berrells' attention. Then, grabbing his neighbour by the wrist, he added rather enigmatically, "I will look after you, Ron."

Several months later, George recalls, "the old man's family said to Ron and Margaret, 'Well, there's nobody in the house, so you can rent it until you build your own place'. So it was after they'd moved into that house [in August 1986] that all the banging started – and I think it was the old bloke who may have been pissed off with Ron for not having been there to help him … I dunno." The section of wall where most of the mysterious banging came from was very close to where the old fellow collapsed.

While this suggestion – that the man's spirit was terrorising the neighbour who'd done so much for him – seems rather illogical, not to mention unfair, this isn't the only time a spirit is said to have harassed a Good Samaritan. As we have seen, the spirit of the old Chinese leper apparently tormented his benefactor, Ah Quay, in much the same way at Granite Creek in 1935.

In any case, the wall-banging and other strange phenomena began just after the Berrells moved into the "old bloke's" house. On 21 October Margaret told *Daily Mirror* journalist John Choueifate exactly how it all started. At 11.30 one Friday night they'd been woken by a banging noise in their son's bedroom. "At first we didn't pay much attention to it and thought it was possums in the ceiling. But the noise then moved across to my daughter's room. There was a large picture on the wall which started to move from side to side for no reason. All the time the noise was getting louder … we were all terrified." The thumping continued until 3.30 am and recurred each night.

"Sue and George … said we were imagining things [at first, but] they soon changed their minds."

A "usual suspect"

It will come as no surprise to many readers that one of the Berrells' two children was an adolescent who was "a little strange".

Nineteen-year-old Julie-Ann was, George Sykes told us, perfectly normal but Craig, who was about thirteen, "was definitely a little bit on the weird side ... a little bit slow ... definitely deep inside himself. He wouldn't talk to you, but he'd be down there [in his room or on the porch]

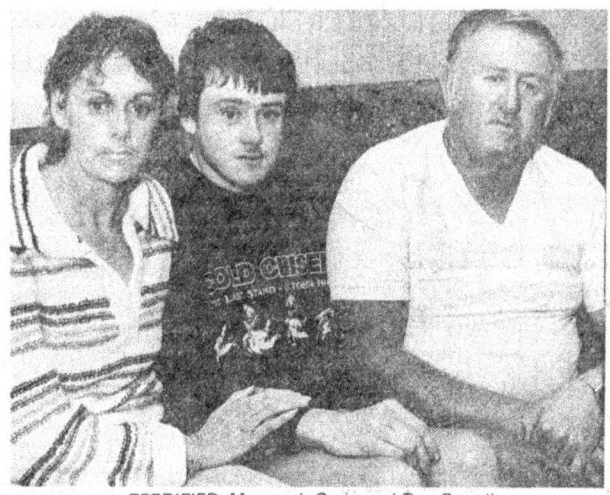

TERRIFIED: Margaret, Craig and Ron Berrell

(*Daily Mirror*, 21 October 1986)

talking to something or somebody ... you'd see his mouth moving, like he had a conversation going on."

As both of them were often in sight during the wall-banging, George and Sue were adamant that neither of the children could have hoaxed it. Nevertheless, George was convinced the phenomenon was linked in some way to young Craig: "I'm sure it was coming through him [but] I'm not saying he was faking it". Sue, who'd read accounts of other poltergeist episodes centred on troubled adolescents, agreed.

Although the Berrells, particularly Margaret, were very frightened at first, as time went by "they got sort of used to it". But then things changed drastically: on 4 September 1986, in another twist reminiscent of the Granite Creek case, the house was almost entirely destroyed by fire.

Sceptics may seize upon this: the blaze, Susan recalls, "... started in the room Craig was occupying". On the other hand, no one accused the boy of having started it, and there may have been something odd about the way it began; "The Fire Brigade said it came from the light globe but the insurance investigators said it came from the bottom – so I can't explain that. Margaret was in the house at the time. The wooden floor broke away ... all the damage was down low ... the bed was burnt."

Unhappy campers

After the fire George and Susan insisted the Berrells stay with them until they built a new house. With the children sleeping inside and Ron and Margaret living in a caravan outside, there was adequate space, and all was well until Sunday 19 October – when trouble came a'knockin' once again.

Ron told journalist John Choueifate that the second episode began with a strange tapping on the roof of the caravan at about 6 am: "At first it was like a tap leak but it began to grow and grow in intensity until it reached a violent bashing sound. The caravan started shaking and we thought it was going to tip over.

"Objects were being tossed about the place and smashed into the walls. Even the birdcage rose and travelled through the air. It was very scary and bewildering".

The racket was loud enough to wake George Sykes, sleeping inside the house: "It was a constant bashing. I raced down to see what was happening". But as he headed for the caravan he was "showered with pebbles … I was walking down the side of the house … and the pebbles just came up – I saw them actually come off the ground and hit me – they hit hard enough to hurt! Nobody could have done it …" (It is important to note that this occurred on the NSW Central Coast at 6 am in late October; that is, in broad daylight).

Another particularly freaky episode happened inside the caravan while Susan was present: "Marg and Ron were sitting on the lounge and Craig was there too. Then all the cupboards opened and all the plates shuffled out like cards – the plates flew out of every cupboard and then cushions started to fly around the room, like in a circular motion. It was very scary. Some plates fell on the lounge but a lot of others were smashed."

Who's in the loo?

Shortly thereafter, Susan "was getting the same thumping sounds in the ensuite off my laundry – exactly the same sound – like in the wall cavity." This happened day and night: "It didn't need the lights to be off. Then one evening the light was on in the laundry and I walked in to use the ensuite toilet and … the light bulb and the shade just smashed everywhere!"

That same night she woke at 2 am to hear water running in the back yard: "I went out … and [the hose] was gushing flat out. It was off when we went to bed and there is no way my Boxer and German shepherd would allow anyone into the yard". But that night her dogs, like those that were cowed by the Mayanup poltergeist, "were cringing and whining down the back."

On another evening, "when I was preparing tea and everybody was out of the house – Marg and Ron were in their caravan, Craig was up the back talking to himself and I don't know where Julie-Ann was – and the next minute … I had an [open doorway] through to the dining room with wooden beads hanging in the doorway … and then *thud!* I looked, and the beads were moving – and there on the [tiled] kitchen floor was a cushion from the lounge!" As with many of the objects that flew around the Humpty Doo house, the noise made by this cushion seemed unnaturally loud: "If someone throws a cushion it doesn't make a real thud like this did when it lands. And I got angry then, and *threw* it back into the lounge room and said, 'You're not going to scare me!'"

Other witnesses

The Sykes' two teenage children apparently witnessed some of the polt's shenanigans but we've been unable to interview them. At least one of the children's friends may also have observed some of the action.

The first print journalist to report the story, Paul Callaghan of the *Central Coast Express*, wrote that he and photographer Bill Rosier "heard the loud, unexplained banging noises" at the Sykes residence. "There was no plausible explanation."

It happened at about midday as the duo was talking to concerned neighbours outside. "At first no one noticed the front window shaking but then it became louder and almost instantaneously afterwards there was a loud, insistent banging noise from the rear bathroom. At the time the Berrells were being interviewed inside the house by a Mike Willesee television journalist."

Although the television journalist told Mr. Callaghan she'd heard the sounds, Susan Sykes says the team's sound man didn't manage to record any of it.

Still somewhat sceptical, Mr. Callaghan asked Margaret Berrell if her son had been on his own when the sounds occurred. "But she said he had only just left the room … and couldn't possibly have made the noise at the rear of the house. The sounds came from both extremities of the house." She insisted, also, that the banging had "… happened many times before when my husband and I and Craig have been sitting with friends."

Ron and Margaret impressed Mr. Callaghan as being "a genuine, though distraught, couple", who had "almost reached the end of their emotional resources."

Ghost busters

After their story was discussed on Radio 2GO the Berrells were disconcerted by the "flood of paranormal experts, religious fanatics … various ghost busters and nuts" who contacted the station. They decided, nevertheless, that they really did need expert help so, on 19 October, they contacted the Mizpah Clinic of Mind Dynamics, at nearby Wyong.

The clinic's staff seemed well qualified to deal with a polt infestation. One of the two principals, Marilyn Campling, was a clinical hypnotherapist and clairvoyant, and the other, registered psychologist Russell Kennard, had done courses in psychic healing and mediumship. Both had many years of experience as psychic investigators. A couple of other counsellors and a masseuse rounded out the team.

Marilyn Campling. (*Central Coast Express*, 31 October 1986)

Ms. Campling said that by the time the Berrells approached her for help, they were at their wit's end: "devastated". So between 21 and 24 October she, Mr. Kennard, and the crew suspended all other activity and concentrated exclusively on the case, spending long hours at the Sykes residence and counselling young Craig at the clinic.

She was convinced the events were paranormal. On one occasion, as she was making breakfast for the Berrells, "… the banging started. The intensity was amazing, tea cups were rising a foot above the coffee table and the banging was on the table itself … it was a strange, blunt knock that we couldn't emulate. It seemed to come from the table's centre."

The weirdness peaked, she said, on Wednesday 22 October, when the team "brought three ladies in who I believe have psychic knowledge … we found out a lot that day. On the Thursday we used hypnosis and really found out who the spirit was … [it] needed certain specific requirements met and we finally communicated with it and met those needs … and [at about 4 am on Friday] persuaded it to leave. I was physically and mentally exhausted."

Uh, oh – not so strange?

Everything we heard from the George and Sue Sykes, and every quote attributed to the Berrells and to Marilyn Campling seems to indicate that the San Remo episode was truly paranormal, but in the opinion of one very well-qualified witness, that was not necessarily so.

When we interviewed Ms. Campling's business partner, Russell Kennard, in October 2010, we found that his assessment of the case was quite different to hers. He thought, in fact, that young Craig could have faked the whole thing.

During many other apparent poltergeist episodes, both here and overseas, individuals have stepped forward to suggest that the activity was faked. Russell is different from nearly all of those sceptics in that he is not only a believer in paranormal activity but has actually experienced it on several occasions. He conducted his first investigation of strange phenomena at the tender age of seven and, particularly during his time with the Mizpah Clinic (1986–87), was involved in a lot of what he believes were genuinely paranormal cases.

Like Ms. Campling, he recalls that their investigation of the Berrell case was quite exhaustive – and exhausting: "[in all] we spent weeks with the family … we went to the burnt-out house to cleanse it … we'd go out [to the Sykes residence] and we had the son in the clinic doing counselling, because the issues seemed to be around him. But although I'm a believer in spiritual events, because I've experienced them, in this case I wasn't 100% convinced.

"There may have been something [paranormal] there but … because of my training as a psychologist … there was something around the boy that said to me that it could have been all [down to] him: him being mischievous. He had a lot of time to sneak around and organize things: nobody was watching him all the time … it [would have been] easy to arrange.

"He was a strange-appearing sort of character, but he didn't appear to be gifted with any psychic powers … didn't have any clairvoyance that was demonstrated … didn't seem to affect anything physically when people were with him."

Although he agrees that Ron and Margaret Berrell were genuinely "terrorised", Russell points out that "the relationship dynamics within the family were very stressed; I'd say that would have been the case without a poltergeist … I was open-minded to the possibility of a poltergeist but also to the possibility of the little boy … [the strange events] gave him a lot of attention … enormous power in the family."

Craig – just a clever prankster? (*Central Coast Express*, 22 October 1986)

Interestingly, whereas Marilyn Campling said at the time that "Russell and I both heard the knocking sounds", he can't recall hearing anything out of the ordinary: "The main memory I have is being at the house at one or two in the morning, trying to disperse any spirit presence and I remember no verification of a spirit. It was just quiet."

How could his recollection of events be so different from what Ms. Campling was quoted as saying at the time?

"Marilyn", he told us by way of explanation, "was a gifted person: definitely psychic. She started as a Tarot reader … she was also clairvoyant; she could sense things that might happen or were happening". But her experience "had been entirely in psychic phenomena – she had no training in psychology or science". So whereas she would get excited at anything that suggested the paranormal, Russell "… was the one who'd put the brakes on. [She] was a fairly emotive person."

"Enough's enough!"

The Berrells stayed with the Sykes for nearly three months, but eventually George and Sue felt they simply *had* to ask them to leave. In addition to the constant banging from the ensuite, the air in George and Sue's bedroom would often become icy cold. That seemed not only inexplicable (given San Remo's very mild climate) but distinctly sinister. Then one night Susan woke to find herself temporarily paralysed. "I didn't mind so much", said George, "when all this was only happening in the van, but when it came inside the house I said, 'Well – enough's enough.'"

It seems the Berrell's departure from the Sykes' house coincided, more or less, with the conclusion of the Mizpah team's polt-busting exercise. And at about the same time the strange phenomenon seems to have petered out. Whether it wound down because of the efforts of Ms. Campling and the three psychic ladies, or because the hoaxer (or the polt) tired of the game, is anybody's guess.

Even though the weird phenomena ceased, Russell Kennard doesn't think that the episode "… ended smoothly – everybody living happily ever after." That's putting it mildly. After the Berrells moved away and built a house of their own, George and Sue Sykes chose not to socialise with them anymore. That was because while George "was ok with Marg, Ron and Julie-Ann", he simply couldn't abide being anywhere near young Craig.

The Berrells hadn't been in their new house for very long before tragedy struck again. While on the expressway, driving back from his invalid mother's home in Sydney, Ron had a fatal heart attack: "He pulled over to the side of the road", said George, "and that's where they found him."

Our comments:

Russell Kennard genuinely believes Marilyn Campling got rather carried away – and saw what she wanted to see during her work with the Berrells. But whereas her statements were recorded by journalists immediately after the episode, we interviewed Mr. Kennard 24 years later. Could his recollection have been faulty? That seemed unlikely: the episode had consumed a lot of his time and was, we imagine, a very memorable case. The closest Russell came, during our interview, to conceding that the exorcism might really have driven the polt away was to say, "… that may have been the case, but not necessarily."

He mentioned that he'd had a falling out with Ms. Campling before they parted in 1987. Is it possible the tiff coloured his recollection of the case? Again, we don't think so: he impressed us as being too intelligent and good-natured to let an ancient dispute affect his judgment.

So – where does that leave us? On the one hand an eminently well-qualified person, who was involved in the final week or two of the episode and who probed the psyche of young Craig, suspected hoaxing.

On the other hand, leaving aside Ms. Campling's statements, we have the testimony of George and Sue Sykes, and Ron and Margaret Berrell, who lived though the episode from the very start. They testified to repeatedly experiencing, often in broad daylight, events that conform exactly to classic poltergeist activity.

Sceptics would probably seize on one remark Sue Sykes made during our 2010 interview: she said that even before the episode began, she and Margaret Berrell were "into all that" – i.e. they both had more than a casual interest in ghostly phenomena. But it's difficult to believe that a prior interest in the supernatural could have warped their judgement so badly that they became incapable of detecting a childish hoax.

Unlike his wife, George Sykes had never believed in the paranormal, but after being pelted by the levitating pebbles and experiencing the inexplicable knocking and pockets of frigid air he had no doubt the phenomenon was genuinely supernatural. The episode, in fact, upset him so badly that, even after the Berrells departed, he found he could no longer bear to live in his own house: "We sold up and got out of there. I'd had enough of it."

While Russell Kennard believes that young Craig "had a lot of time to sneak around and organise things: nobody was watching him all the time … it [would have been] easy to arrange", we find it extremely difficult to imagine how he could have arranged for all the cupboards in the caravan to fly open, for all the plates to "shuffle out like cards" and for other objects to fly in circles around his parents and Mrs. Sykes, as he sat beside them on the lounge. Or, for that matter, how he could have caused multiple pebbles to rise up from the ground, in broad daylight, in front of George Sykes' eyes.

Craig and his sister, according to their parents and the Sykes, were often in plain sight during the wall-banging and levitation of objects, and throughout the lengthy episode, at two different houses plus the caravan, neither of the children – or anyone else – was ever caught faking anything.

Most of the strange phenomena reported at San Remo – the shower of pebbles, the levitating objects, the unnaturally loud sound of the falling cushion, the banging that came from inside the wall, the reaction of the dogs, the sudden chilling of the air – conform very well to phenomena reported during many other well-attested poltergeist episodes. Exploding light bulbs, "sleep paralysis", fires – and even the apparently vengeful spirits of recently deceased people – while less common, have also featured in other episodes.

If we'd never interviewed Russell Kennard we would've had very few doubts that the episode was genuinely paranormal. But while his well-informed, reasonably-expressed opinion carries a lot of weight, does it outweigh the testimony of Ron and Margaret Berrell and George and Sue Sykes, all of whom spent a lot more time in the midst of the apparent polt episode, and who described phenomena that would have been difficult – to say the least – to fake?

Because everything reported there conformed so well with phenomena observed during other very well-attested cases, we think the San Remo episode probably did involve a poltergeist. But genuine or fake, the case contains so much of interest – to sceptics as well as to "true believers" – that we considered it good enough to be included here, as one of our best cases.

Sources:

The statements attributed to Ron and Margaret Berrell and to Marilyn Campling were taken from *The Central Coast Express*, 22 and 31 Oct 1986, and from *The Daily Mirror*, 21 Oct 1986 and 3 Nov 1986.

Paul Cropper, interview with Susan and George Sykes, 9 May 2010.

Paul Cropper, interview with Russell Kennard, 3 Oct 2010.

CHAPTER SEVEN

"Ghostly Missiles": The Cooyal Case

FEBRUARY–MARCH 1887, COOYAL, 20 KM NORTH-WEST OF MUDGEE, NSW. RATING: ★★★★

From the *Bathurst Free Press and Mining Journal*, 15 Feb 1887 (reprinted from The *Mudgee Independent*):

GHOSTLY MISSILES

… we glean [the following details] from Mr. J. Parker and several other reliable gentlemen who have been eyewitnesses ….

Some days ago, a farmer named Large … reported to the police that for several nights himself and his family had been almost terrified out of their wits in consequence of stones, some weighing one and a half pounds [680g] continually dropping inside the house, apparently coming through the roof. Strange to say these extraordinary occurrences are never apparent unless the man's wife is in the room … all who have visited the place, seeing for themselves, the police included, persist in applying the evidently appropriate term "ghostly missiles" to the huge "gibbers" that have dropped in the house when doors and windows have been secured.

The effect on the poor woman, who feels that she is the victim of an awful vengeance, is most alarming. At times whilst the stones are falling deathly chills affect her whole system, and almost prostrate her. One evening fearing to remain indoors, [she] sought quietude outside the house, but, strange to say, several large stones dropped close to her, whilst one, although falling upon some part of her body, left no mark – in fact, was hardly felt. A cold, deathly chill then crept over her and she had to be taken to the fire, but without restoring warmth.

It is an easy matter to convince superstitious people of these facts, but when sceptics go and see … and have stones dropping round about them, they are very glad to be rid of such *unpleasant associations. This was the case when Mr. Parker and others went out ...*

A large stone, which fell in the ordinary way, struck a little child on the side of the face, and strange to say left no mark, nor did the child appear to take any notice of the blow. At the time Mr. Parker was sitting in the house [with Mr. and Mrs. Large], *a number of friends ... were stationed outside to see that no person was on the roof. The house is without ceiling, so that no person could be secreted inside. We understand that Large has determined to remove his family from the place.*

A first-hand report by one of its own journalists appeared in the *Free Press* on 1 March 1887:

After a rough and not uneventful journey, we arrived ... and were greeted by Mrs. Large ... she was surrounded by a pack of "little Larges", the bantlings of a family of 15 ... We found her agreeable and communicative, fully competent to describe all the wonderful, yet to her startling incidents ...

She said it was not stone throwing, but "stones falling" ... coming so it seemed, through the roof, at times appearing to "float in on the air, and while floating looked white ... When [a] *stone fell on the floor, it fell with a dull thud, and looked black ...* [Her children were sometimes struck by stones] *but never hurt. The children described it "as though a small bag of feathers struck them".*

Mary Large in later years.

Mr. and Mrs. Large. (Courtesy Trevor Maranda)

On the first evening ... Mr. Large was returning home with a bag of flour on a pack horse [when] *the animal stood still, apparently afraid to move towards the dwelling ... with difficulty he was unpacked, and ... bolted as though maddened ... in every direction except near the house ... Just then, for the first time, the stones commenced dropping near the house.*

Mrs. Large at once concluded some of the young people were having a lark with her in revenge for her refusal to permit a dance being held there that night.

During that evening, and every succeeding evening from 5 o'clock until 9 or 10, the stones fell. On several occasions stones or mud would float in the room, sometimes diagonally, at other times horizontally. One evening ... a flat stone ... about three inches in diameter, nearly circular ... "floated in" at the door, struck against a kerosene lamp ... then knocked against a half dozen plates, causing them to roll to the floor, but, strange to say, none were broken.

None of the missiles fell whilst we were there, nor had any fallen for four or five days. Mrs. Large [said] that in the latter part of the manifestations, during last week, she felt as if all her strength was failing her.

The poor lady's respite from pebbly persecution was very brief: on Sunday 27 February an additional twenty-four stones fell inside the house. On hearing of the renewed activity, a Mr. Gettetlay decided to visit to the site. His report appeared in the *Mudgee Star Advertiser* on 5 March (and was reprinted in the *Broughton Creek Register* of 3 April):

I ... travelled 24 miles over a portion of the worst roads in the colony ... got bogged twice and with much difficulty succeeded in extricating myself and my wife, horse and buggy ... I had to leave the buggy and horse at the foot of a very steep range, up which there is no road or bridle track; the only mode of ascent is up the worn watercourse for about a mile ... at the top ... I could see that the Larges were located ... in a glen-like locality ... surrounded by very romantic-looking hills, all sandstone piled one on the other for hundreds of feet ...

On arriving ... Mrs. Large did not seem in any way disconcerted, but commenced ... to give a full description of the manifestations from beginning to end. She said the stones ceased falling for the last five days. She is the mother of 15 children ... is rather under middle size ... has a beautiful formed head, classical in shape, and a well-shaped body; her intellect to all appearances is clear, her descriptive powers were very good and quite natural. She is totally without education – so is her husband. In my opinion these people live very close to nature.

She said the stones seemed to float sometimes obliquely, sometimes horizontally, and when they fell vertically they fell with a thud as if some soft thing, such as wet clay would do. All who saw the stones floating verified her statement that the stones looked white, but when they fell on the floor they turned black. On examination the stones presented the usual appearance of those in the gully.

She also said that one evening she was under the impression that the house was about to be crushed in from some ponderous weight that was resting on the roof. The walls swayed from side to side, there was a rumbling noise overhead, and she saw some black object come through one angle of the house and go right through the opposite angle. This was verified by the young lady [Miss Blackman], *who accompanied us.*

A neighbouring farmer ... told me he went to the house [with the children – when the mother was two miles away] *and found that the floor was literally covered with stones, and they were then falling through the* [bark] *roof and a temporary ceiling of boards laid on the rafters.*

There must be mediumship among the children as well as the mother.

As the regional newspapers seem to have ceased writing about the episode by about the middle of March, the weird phenomena may have petered out shortly before that. All we have in the way of follow-up is an article from the Sydney *Sun* of 14 April 1921, prompted by the "Guyra Ghost" episode of that year, which mentions that the Cooyal episode, after lasting for several weeks, "ceased when the family left the house."

Sources:

Bathurst Free Press and Mining Journal, 15 Feb and 1 Mar 1887.

Broughton Creek Register, 5 Mar and 3 Apr 1887.

Kiama Independent & Shoalhaven Advertiser, 11 Mar 1887.

The Sun, 14 Apr 1921.

Our comments:

The Cooyal case displayed several hallmarks of a genuine poltergeist episode: stones falling or "floating" horizontally, indoors and out, apparently passing right through the roof, striking people without causing injury, and landing with a soft thud. As is often the case, the polt's attention seemed to be focused primarily on a particular individual.

The incident involving the flat stone that "floated in" through the door, struck a kerosene lamp and knocked half dozen plates to the floor – without breaking anything – is strikingly similar to incidents that occurred repeatedly at Mayanup in 1956–-57 and during other well-documented poltergeist episodes.

The behaviour of the pack horse is also worth noting. Horses have reacted in a similar way during other well-attested episodes.

The "cold, deathly chills" that affected Mrs. Large so badly are reminiscent of the pockets of frigid air reported in a few other Australian cases. But this case is slightly different in that only she, apparently, could feel the cold.

The case also contains some unique features: the white stones that turned black on landing, the "rumbling sound" and the reported swaying of the walls, as if the house was about to be "crushed in by some ponderous weight". Those things were witnessed not only by Mrs. Large but also by Miss Blackman.

The detail that interests us most is the "black object" that the two women saw "come through one angle of the house and go right through the opposite angle". That object is, as readers may have noticed, reminiscent of the black sphere that Brett Styles saw flying through the barbeque area at Humpty Doo in 1998.

Sceptics might suggest, quite rightly, that with fifteen children milling around it may have been difficult to spot a cunning juvenile hoaxer. But it is difficult to imagine a child, or clique of children, being so callous as to cause their own mother to become "almost prostrate" with "deathly chills" and to leave her with the feeling "that she is the victim of an awful vengeance". In any case, kids, no matter how naughty and resourceful, would have been incapable of making the whole house sway as if it was about to implode, or to cause stones to "float" horizontally through its rooms.

Some researchers, in fact, might consider that the presence of a seething mass of kids *increases* the likelihood of a genuine polt episode. The odds are that some of the kids were pimply, anguished adolescents – the very demographic that sometimes attracts (or triggers) polt activity. Certainly, Mr. Gettetlay seemed to think one or more of the kids were contributing to the psychic storm: "… there must be mediumship amongst the children …"

This is a strong case, well documented by *Mudgee Independent, Mudgee Star Advertiser* and *Bathurst Free Press* journalists and by Mr. Gettetlay – a seemingly very competent man. Although Gettetlay didn't actually see any strange phenomena several, if not many, people other than the Large family did. Those specifically mentioned were Mr. J. Parker "and several other reliable gentlemen", Mr. and Miss Blackman, some (admittedly unnamed) police officers, and the "neighbouring farmer".

We have recently made contact with one of Mrs. Large's many descendants, Trevor Maranda, who told us that the strange story of what happened to his great-grandmother and her brood was a valued piece of family lore.

He was also kind enough to supply us with a fine portrait of the lady herself, who looks, in our opinion, the very model of a tough, intelligent, good-natured pioneer.

CHAPTER EIGHT

The Gordon Street Polt

1977. NEWCASTLE, NSW. RATING: ★★★

Strange noises began to occur as soon as George and Jan Brown moved into a rented house at 18 Gordon Street, Mayfield. At first, Jan told us, it was "scratching noises in the walls; quite loud and constant of an evening, but not in the day". Next came loud thumping on (or in) the solid brick walls. "Then there was a sound like an egg-beater in the ceiling – that occurred very often, even sometimes first thing in the morning."

Interestingly, George and Jan, then in their early thirties, weren't particularly frightened. Even when they heard heavy footsteps tramping though the house, "we were just interested".

18 Gordon Street. (Healy/Cropper)

Although they came from various parts of the house, the sounds seemed to emanate most often from the walls and ceiling of the living room – which was "ice cold", summer and winter.

Theirs was a "blended family": George had two children from a previous marriage, Jan also had two, and they had a three-year-old between them. "It was very crowded", Jan recalls, "only a three-bedroom house, but we were all happy there apart from the eldest child, Michelle, who at that time seemed to think of me as 'the wicked stepmother'. She thought her dad shouldn't have left her mother to marry me."

But Jan and George thought it impossible that Michelle – only six years old – or the younger kids could have faked the strange noises. The footsteps, for one thing, were "too heavy for kids. They went down the corridor. We'd get up and find all the kids sound asleep."

After a while the polt came up with a new trick. Night after night paintings and ornaments were taken down and left leaning, very neatly, against the bottom of the walls. Jan points out that had they simply come loose and fallen down, they would have hit the skirting board and tipped over, face-down on the floor.

George wired all the objects very securely to their hooks but that made no difference apart from, perhaps, irritating the midnight rambler. The paintings and a decorative plaque continued to be taken down as before, but a replica antique pistol was torn from its wooden backing and broken in two.

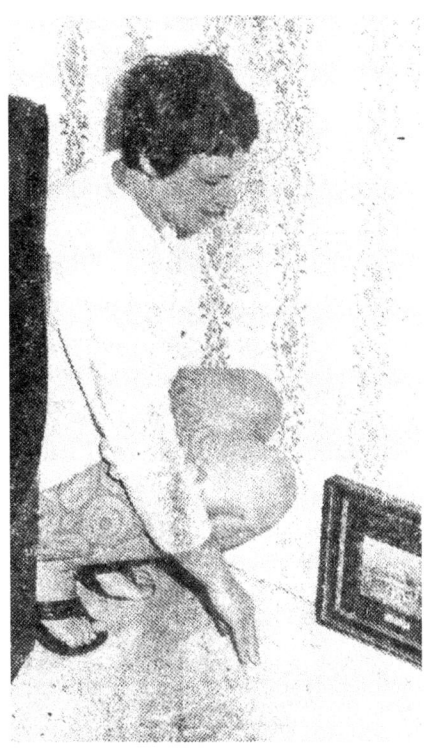

Floored: Jan with a fallen painting. (*Psychic Australian*, December 1977)

The episode attracted a small amount of media attention. One journalistic team arrived with infrared camera equipment, but on that occasion the phantom house guest, media-shy like so many other polts, kept a low profile.

Although it was pretty persistent, the Gordon Street spook wasn't malicious or (apart from destroying the replica pistol) destructive, and the Browns managed to put up with its strange little pranks for nearly a year. In fact, Jan insists, had the house been more spacious she would have been happy to stay there indefinitely.

In late 1977 however, she and George, having located a more roomy residence, moved out. The strange phenomena didn't follow them.

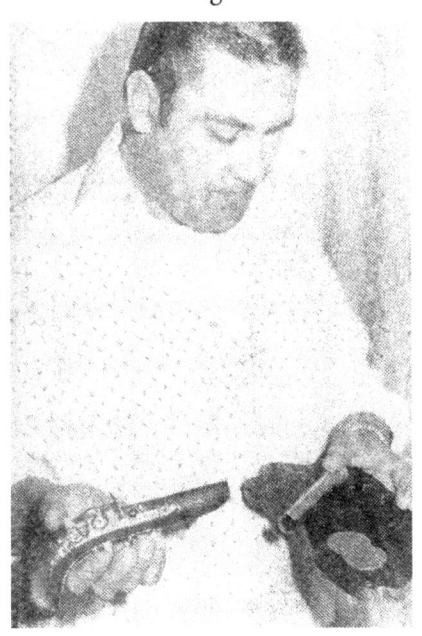

George examines the replica pistol. (*Psychic Australian*, December 1977)

Our comments:

The sequence of events at Gordon Street, beginning with scratching sounds, escalating to wall-thumping and to the moving of firmly secured objects, conforms very well to patterns of activity noted during many other well-attested polt cases.

There was no suggestion of hoaxing. The children – even the unhappy eldest – were much too young to have successfully faked the phenomena even for a short period, let alone for nearly twelve months. Contemporary journalists saw no reason to doubt Gordon's word, and we found Jan to be open, honest, and entirely credible.

Given that young six-year-old Michelle was so unhappy, it is tempting to assume that she triggered the phenomena through psychokinesis or because she was the unwitting "agent" needed by the polt. But the strange phenomena didn't follow the family after they left the house – as might have been expected if the child was the sole cause of the disturbances.

Was there something else helping to stir things up at 18 Gordon Street? Well, maybe: shortly after she and her family moved out of the house, Jan was told that a couple of gay men had lived there previously and that one of them had supposedly died, possibly murdered, *in the living room*.

Jan Brown in 2010. (Healy/Cropper)

There is a third possibility: that Jan, unknown even to herself at the time, possessed some psychic ability that facilitated the phenomena. She told us that some time after the Gordon Street episode she began to feel a bit "sensitive" to spiritual phenomena. In the mid-1980s, when she and George owned a pottery business in an old cottage at Morpeth, they had another brush with the "other side". Frequently, at dusk, just as they were shutting-up shop, they would see the shadowy figure of a woman walking past the front windows. Jan could never make out the face, but she saw enough of the clothes and hair to convince her it was the ghost of Eliza Cantwell, who had built the cottage a hundred years earlier.

Since moving to an old stationmaster's house at Kurri in 2000 she has often sensed the not-unfriendly presence of another female spirit – possibly the stationmaster's daughter, Miss Muriel English. And now that George has passed away – he died in 2009 – she sometimes senses his friendly presence as well.

Regardless of whether it was the result of psychokinesis produced by the sulky six-year-old, was orchestrated by the spirit of the murdered man, was connected in some way to Jan's apparent mild psychic ability or was triggered by a combination of all of those factors, there seems little doubt that paranormal activity really did occur at the little house in Gordon Street back in 1977.

Sources:

Newcastle Sun, (exact date unknown) 1977, reprinted in *Psychic Australian*, Dec 1977.

Newcastle Herald, 6 and 9 Sept 2010.

Paul Cropper, interview with Jan Brown, 18 Sept 2010.

CHAPTER NINE

"The Nice Old Man" of Alice Springs

ALICE SPRINGS, 1989–90. RATING: ★★★½

T'was a month before Christmas, and all through the house, not a creature was stirring … except for a polt.

One evening in late November 1989, 56-year-old Irene Cronin was in her bedroom, enjoying a nice lie-down and watching television. Suddenly all of her family's Christmas presents, stacked beside the TV set, "went up into the air, about four feet, and landed on the ground."

Irene and her family had been living in their rented two-story home in Harvey Street since October. Nothing strange happened for the first few weeks, but after the Christmas presents incident life rarely returned to normal.

Sock shock

Sounds of "thumping and marching" came from the top floor when there was nobody there, lights turned themselves on and off, and the garage door rolled up and down of its own accord. Then something took to pitching rolled-up socks at Irene's youngest daughter, Val, as she walked down the corridor, invariably striking her on the back of the head. Her first reaction was to accuse her mother of playing practical jokes, "but she soon realised it wasn't me or anybody else that was doing it."

Fruit fly

Being hit on the head with a few socks is neither here nor there, but soon heavier objects were taking flight. There were several unusually prolific citrus trees in the back yard, and Irene kept a large bowl stacked full of oranges and grapefruit on a table in the living room. "The fruit would move around", Irene told us, "and hit you in the back of the head". It happened quite frequently and it hurt, but not as badly as one would expect: "it was as if they were just 'bowled' across the room".

A collection of toy devils and clowns (cue spooky music) owned by another daughter, Annie, "were thrown around quite a bit", and a row of dolls in Irene's bedroom took flight: "I was lying in bed again and they flew across me."

A "nice old man"

All very weird, but things became a whole lot weirder: Irene's four-year-old granddaughter, Bonnie Jean, began to talk to a "nice old man" – who wasn't there.

"She screamed the first time", said Irene, "she said a man walked from my room to my son Walter's room". But on later occasions she was discovered chatting away, as if in pleasant conversation with an invisible friend. When asked who it was she would say "this nice man; a lovely man. Look – he's right here!" She described him as old and grey-haired.

Then Irene's 26-year-old son Walter saw him. Noticing a movement in a mirror one day, he glanced up and saw, reflected, just what Bonnie Jean had described: the figure of a man walking from his mother's bedroom, across the corridor to his own. He immediately dashed to his room – but there was nobody there.

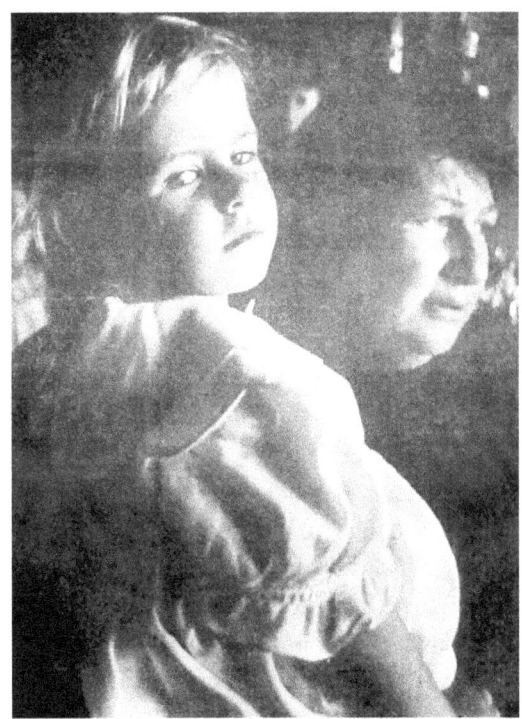

Irene Cronin with Bonnie Jean. (*The Sunday Territorian*, 19 August 1990)

Interestingly, neighbours with whom Irene shared her abundant citrus fruit told her that the original owner, who'd lived there for many years and lovingly tended the fruit trees, had died just a couple of years earlier. Sadly, he'd only just retired and was preparing for a long-anticipated trip around Australia when he collapsed and died on his own front step. Then "the bloke across the road told us that since then he'd heard 'funny things' –

funny noises – coming from the house".

In August 1990, after the Cronins had been living with the "nice old man" and his little tricks for nearly ten months, one of the neighbours tipped off the local paper, the *Sunday Territorian*. Although she initially refused to do an interview, Irene relented when the paper promised to restrict its coverage to just a single article. The result was a good, balanced story by journalist Genny O'Loughlin and a very atmospheric photograph of Irene and young Bonnie Jean.

When we made contact with Irene in 2010 she impressed us as being a gutsy, pragmatic, down-to-earth lady. Clearly, it would have taken more than a bit of flying fruit to upset her.

"I thought it might have been because of us picking fruit and giving it away", she told us. "He might have planted those trees. And we also thought it had something to do with him dying before he could take his holiday … poor old bugger, he wasn't a happy bloke. But I wasn't scared, because he could have really hurt us but he didn't; he didn't seem to want to push us down the stairs or anything."

It seems that during the first couple of months of their occupancy the house was a little crowded: in addition to Walter and Annie, who lived upstairs with Irene, a married daughter, Val, lived downstairs with husband Jeffrey and their three children, including Bonnie Jean. The strange phenomena, however, may not have had anything to do with overcrowding, because it continued at the same intensity after most of the family found alternative accommodation, leaving only Irene, Walter and Annie in the house.

"Souvenir *this*!"

Eventually they, too, found a better place to live and, as they were packing to leave, "the old bloke" saw them off in his own inimitable style: "While we were putting everything into the ute in the back yard he got the shits well and truly. He threw all the grapefruit off the tree at us – not really fast, it was like someone had bowled them – and we were saying, 'Oh, piss off!' The tree was at the side, about twelve feet away. We all got hit. We saw them coming off the branches, off the ground under the tree – there was bloody fruit everywhere! It went on over three or four hours."

After they'd unpacked at the new place, Walter very unwisely returned to Harvey Street to gather bags-full of grapefruit and oranges. He took a mate with him who suggested they also souvenir a couple of the fancy lights that were strung around the swimming pool. Bad move: even though they checked to confirm the power was switched off, Walter suffered a bad shock and a burnt hand.

Rather than cutting their losses and fleeing, the duo rashly loaded their vehicle with forbidden fruit before driving off. On arrival at the new house, Walter walked around the side, only to be knocked half senseless as a gate swung back and hit him in the face. "There was blood everywhere", Irene told us. "He cut his mouth and got a black eye. He said, 'Mum – the thing followed me home!' But that was the end of it: there was nothing after that."

Our comments:

Because Irene Cronin was such an excellent, entirely credible interview subject we have no doubt that events occurred very much as she said they did. Accordingly, we see no reason to doubt that a poltergeist was infesting 15 Harvey Street back in 1989/90. The malfunctioning of electrical appliances, the frequent levitation of objects, even the appearance of the ghostly human figure, all conform very well with activity observed during many other well-documented episodes.

A constantly recurring feature of poltergeist cases, both Australian and foreign, is that people hit by flying objects are not injured in the least – so the Harvey Street polt seems to have been a bit more heavy-handed than most. While Irene recalls that being hit on the back of the head by the grapefruit "hurt, but not as badly as you would expect", young Walter copped a real hammering. Such violence on the part of poltergeists is, thankfully, very rare, but has been recorded from time to time. In this case, where "the old bloke" had given every indication of being very territorial, Walter was, in taking the fruit and attempting to souvenir the pool lights, simply asking for trouble.

The Harvey Street episode is interesting in many ways, not least because it strongly suggests that a deceased person was performing all the paranormal tricks. This, of course, challenges the theory that polt activity has nothing to do with spirits of the dead and is produced entirely by psychokinesis.

Sources:

Sunday Territorian, 19 Aug 1990.

Paul Cropper, interview with Irene Cronin, 28 Sept 2010.

CHAPTER TEN

"The Guyra Ghost"

GUYRA, NSW, 1921. RATING: ★★★½

It was on the first of April
In Nineteen Twenty One
April Fools Day set apart
For people to have fun
Weird noises in the Bowen house!
The rumour raced and ran!
That is how the legend
Of the Guyra Ghost began

From *Minnie Bowen – The Guyra Ghost*, by Colin Newsome, Glen Innes, 1993.

Given the limited number of days in a year, it had to happen: a supposed poltergeist event coinciding with April Fools Day. That unfortunate coincidence (or *was* it a coincidence?) is just one of several awkward factors we have to consider while assessing this many-faceted case.

Until the rampaging spook of Mayanup hit the headlines in the 1950s, the "Guyra Ghost" was Australia's best-known poltergeist. The "Ghost" was a very persistent, wall-bashing stone-thrower that tormented William Bowen, his wife and children – particularly (surprise, surprise) a twelve-year-old daughter, Minnie. The episode lasted for more than a month in the autumn of 1921 and attracted several journalists, crowds of sightseers, Sydney detectives, psychic investigators and even a motion picture crew to the sleepy country town.

What with wall-bashing, stone-throwing, "baffled" police, the fact that the weirdness was focused on a "usual suspect" – an adolescent girl – and because it received an inordinate amount of media coverage at the time, the "Ghost" episode has often been referred to as a major poltergeist case. But while supernatural phenomena almost certainly did occur at Guyra, it seems there was also some hoaxing. This, along with disinformation spread by a dishonest detective, the disappearance of key issues of the *Guyra Argus*, the sheer number of players involved and other complicating factors, makes us reluctant to hail the case as a true classic on a par with, say, the Mayanup or Humpty Doo episodes.

Nevertheless, because it attracted so much attention, nationally and even internationally, because it has often been referred to as one of Australia's greatest mysteries, and despite the fact that it didn't involve a great variety of strange phenomena, we have decided to deal with it in some detail.

The earliest item in our "Ghost" file – an article from the Sydney *Sun*, April 10, 1921 [reprinted from *The Glen Innes Examiner*] – contains a detail that causes us to raise a sceptical eyebrow. Nevertheless, because it sets the scene and covers the events of the first five nights of the episode, it is worth quoting:

BUSH MYSTERY
Will-o'-the-wisp stone-thrower
Armed Searchers Defied
Glen Innes, Saturday.

There have been strange happenings at the residence of William Bower [actually Bowen], *a ganger in the employ of Guyra Shire. The dwelling is a weatherboard cottage of four rooms situated in a rather isolated locality about half a mile east of* [town] *... the occupants include, beside the father and mother, three children, one a girl about 12 years old.*

The mystifying events commenced with the girl alleging that she was pursued by a man ... a quarter of a mile from her home, and who ... attacked her with stones as she was running away ... He disappeared before she reached home.

At night the family was much disturbed by stone-throwing, the missiles striking the walls. The attack was naturally attributed to the individual who molested the girl in the afternoon ... a search [was] *made for the offender, but with no success.*

Constables Stennett and Taylor went to the house the next night. Shortly after their arrival a pane of glass was smashed by what appeared to them to be a pea rifle [.22] *bullet. A search was immediately instituted ... but no trace of the cause could be found.*

POLICEMAN'S CLOSE CALL
The following night Sergeant Ridge, Constables Stennett and Taylor, and four civilians visited the house, and placed themselves in positions inside and outside that would apparently make a visit ... without detection impossible. Stones again assailed the walls at different times ... the party closed in, but nothing could be seen.

The following night the police again visited ... reinforced by ten well-known civilians, several ... armed with guns. The men were placed ... as to make discovery of the cause of the stone-throwing almost a certainty. About 7.30 smash went a window, almost in front of which was Sergeant Ridge.

Less than three minutes later another pane was smashed. The watchers closed in, and torches were turned on, but there was nothing to be seen beyond the two stones, which were found on a bed [in the girl's bedroom].

During the next half-hour fully twenty missiles struck the house … Among [those] *found inside the house was one half the size of a brick.*

[On the fifth night] *there was an increased number of volunteers … Since the mysterious occurrence began the nights have been dark … misty or threatening rain, which … hampered observations. Last night Mr. Burgess … placed at the disposal of the police a powerful motor battery and searchlight, which at intervals was thrown on the house and its surroundings … about thirty sounds, either from stone-throwing or what might have been rappings on the wall were heard, but these stopped when the light was turned on.*

The members of the family are greatly worried by the unaccountable attacks … and are absolutely at a loss to assign any cause for the occurrences.

The Bowen residence in 1921. (*Sunday Times*, Sydney, 17 April 1921)

This article and many others leave little doubt that the Bowens were seriously upset by the attacks, but what concerns us, at this point, is the mysterious, rock-throwing stranger who supposedly pursued young Minnie. That detail doesn't tally with anything in our other Australian cases and seems downright odd. As he was so close to her – literally within a stone's throw – Minnie should have been able to recognise him if he was a local man. And a stranger, one imagines, would have stood out like a sore thumb in a small place like Guyra.

Given the "mysterious stranger" element, it seems odd that after just a couple of nights of stone-throwing, many locals were convinced it was of supernatural origin. It is difficult to imagine how they fitted the "stranger" into that scenario – did they believe he was a ghost?

The smashing of the window by "what appeared … to be" a .22 bullet is also suggestive of human involvement. But as no projectile was recovered the police didn't seem to be entirely sure that the missile was indeed a bullet. Few people, surely, would be stupid or nasty enough to fire a rifle at a small house full of people – including police officers. There is no mention of a gunshot being heard.

It seems that during the first week of strange activity the stones all originated from outside the house and the nights were "dark … misty or threatening rain, which … hampered observations". It is possible, therefore, that despite the presence of three police officers and many apparently trustworthy volunteers, most of the stones were fired by local larrikins lurking in the scrub with their "shanghais" (catapults). While the stone "half the size of a brick" could not have been fired from a shanghai, it could have been hurled by one of the supposedly reputable "well-known citizens" circling the house.

It is worth noting that the first few reports of the case mention only the stone-throwing and "what might have been rappings". The rappings apparently evolved into wall-shaking thumps after the first couple of days.

Between 2 April and early May the Bowens, the police and scores of volunteers tried all manner of stratagems to nab hoaxers or, in the case of those who believed in spiritualism, to deduce the reason for the haunting.

For such a relatively brief and relatively unspectacular polt episode, the "Guyra Ghost" generated a very large amount of press coverage. Frustratingly, although many of those articles contain information first published in the town's local paper, the *Guyra Argus*, all issues of that paper for the key months of April and May have disappeared. Fortunately, the *Glen Innes Examiner* and the *Armidale Express* covered the case in detail (often drawing on *Guyra Argus* articles), and both the Sydney *Telegraph* and the Brisbane *Daily Mail* sent reporters to cover the story.

(*Sunday Times*, Sydney, 17 April 1921)

This is the best summary of the episode that we can come up with, and, as near as we can reconstruct it, the timeline:

Strange days, strange nights

Friday 1 April, afternoon: Minnie claims she was chased by the stone-throwing stranger. Friday 1 April, night: The Bowen house pelted with stones. Saturday 2 April, night: Two policemen visit the house; window smashed, possibly by a .22 bullet (which was, however, not found). Sunday 3 April, night: Three police and four civilians surround the house; several stones hit the building. Monday 4 April, night: Three police and ten volunteers stake out the premises; more than 20 stones pepper the building.

On subsequent nights, up to 80 "vigilants"– many of them armed – were involved. Sergeant Ridge deployed most of them in a wide cordon around the homestead and placed some trusted citizens close to every external wall. He and a few of the most trusted remained inside, to keep an eagle eye on the Bowen family. Despite the "human fences" and other precautions, the stones still flew and the "rapping" continued.

Several observers insisted that the "rapping" was different from the noises made when stones hit the house. Three young men, for instance, who were posted outside Minnie's bedroom, "heard blows on the wall, but declare that no stones afterwards fell to the ground." After the first couple of days, apparently, the rapping became louder and louder, to the point where the mighty thumps were "sufficient to shake the cottage to its foundations and audible to watchers a hundred yards from the house." To those outside, the thumps appeared to come from within the building; to those inside, they seemed to come from outside.

At some stage between the 1st and the 7th of April two other houses were bombarded with stones. One was occupied by a Mr. Hodder – a step-son of Mrs. Bowen from her first marriage – and his young family. The house was situated a few hundred yards from the Bowen cottage, and seems to have been badly damaged, because Mr. Hodder and his family soon abandoned it and moved in with the Bowens for mutual support and protection.

Only one or two newspaper articles mentioned the third damaged house. Apart from the fact that it was owned by a family named McInnes, and the windows were "completely smashed", no other details were supplied.

Right from the beginning, many people suspected young Minnie was the focus of the invisible troublemaker's attacks – or that she was cleverly hoaxing the whole thing. How the attacks on the Hodder and McInnes houses could be reconciled with that notion is not explained, but nevertheless, the suspicion was reinforced when, on Thursday 7th, she was removed from her parents' house. That night, as 70 people surrounded the building, "no stones were thrown and no noises heard" – but as soon as she returned on Friday afternoon, "a stone passed through her bedroom window and landed on the bed." About 30 stone falls and thumpings occurred throughout the night, despite the use, by the police, of a powerful spotlight.

Interestingly, on April 9th – a Saturday night, when one might expect local larrikins to be most active – absolutely nothing happened.

On the night of Sunday 10th, as the stone throwing resumed, something was noted that strongly suggests neither Minnie nor external hoaxers were responsible. As 26 volunteers kept watch outside, four men were directed to guard Minnie in her bedroom, on the south side of the house. Very soon, even though the light was deliberately left off to foil any hoaxer lurking outside, "… the customary sounds of heavy stones striking the wall began. The bombardment continued for some time, and the girl was then quietly removed to the kitchen, which is on the north side. At once, the attacks on the bedroom ceased, and the kitchen came under fire".

An *Armidale Express* journalist who was outside the Bowen house on the night of Monday the 11th noted that the "open nature" of the surrounding area offered virtually no cover for potential hoaxers. He also testified to the violence of the thumps that shook the house that night; they could, he stated, be heard "several hundred yards away."

Dr. Fixit

On Tuesday 12th, Dr. Harris, an outspoken sceptic, set out to prove the "Ghost" activity was simply a hoax.

Like Sergeant Ridge, he organised a large party of volunteers, surrounded the house with an outer cordon of men and placed only his trusted friends close to the building. Stationing other men in every room of the house, he kept a particularly close watch on the family, particularly on Minnie. According to the *Sunday Times*, in fact, he "sprayed the entire walls of the sleeping room with liquorice powder, and had a deep hole cut through the shutter and curtains, all unknown to anyone in the Bowen household."

Nothing happened that night, and in the morning, when one of his supporters suggested he had "chloroformed the 'spook'", the good doctor smugly accepted the plaudit. The fact that nothing had happened on the preceding Thursday and Saturday when he *wasn't* there doesn't seem to have crossed his mind.

May speaks

The terrible loss of so many young lives in the Great War of 1914–18 prompted a big revival of interest in spiritualism in Europe and North America. It was the same in Australia and New Zealand, where many grieving parents, wives and siblings, desperate for (as they say these days) "closure", engaged in séances and various other spiritualist activities. Ben Davey of Uralla, a student of Theosophy, was keenly interested in such things.

So, on Wednesday 13 April, when he visited the Bowen household, he wasn't surprised to learn there had been a recent death in the family. May Hodder, a daughter of Mrs. Bowen by a former marriage, had died on 26 January – about two months before the first apparent polt activity.

> An extremely sad death occurred in Armidale Hospital on Wednesday of last week, when Miss Mary Hodder, daughter of Mrs. W. Bowen, Guyra, passed away at the early age of 21 years. The cause of death was heart trouble, from which the deceased girl had suffered for some considerable time. Very much regret has been expressed by her numerous friends, the family being an old and respected one. The remains were interred in the Church of England Cemetery, Armidale on Thursday morning, Ven. Archdeacon Johnstone officiating at the graveside.

Mary (May) Hodder's death notice. (*Guyra Argus*, 3 February 1921)

According to the *Guyra Argus* of 3 Feb 1921 she died of "heart trouble, from which she had suffered for some considerable time". Sadly, she was only 21 years old, but her death was doubly tragic because of something that was not mentioned in the newspaper: young and unmarried, she was the mother of an eighteen-month-old son, Clifford – and the boy's father had never been publicly identified.

It is hardly surprising that Mr. Davey immediately suspected the stone falls and rapping were by-products of May's spirit trying to communicate with young Minnie (who, at the tender age of twelve, was now largely responsible for the care of the child).

At 9 o'clock on Wednesday night, with Mr. Davey, Constable Taylor, Mr. Richard Pearson, Mr. Hay, Mrs. Bowen and Minnie in the girl's bedroom, and with police and volunteers in every other room and 50 men stationed outside with powerful spotlights, a heavy knock was heard. To those inside, it seemed the outside of the wall had been struck, but the men outside said the noise seemed to come from within.

In an interview with the Sydney *Sunday Times* Mr. Davey described what happened next:

I said to the girl, "If the knock comes again, ask if that's your sister May."

She replied, "I can't speak to my sister – she's dead." I coaxed her, saying, "Speak, dear. Even if your sister can't speak she might knock again."

I hardly spoke the words before the knock came again. I can tell you my hair stood up on end. But I continued to coax the girl, and about five minutes later a third knock came. Then the little girl crossed and blessed herself, put her hands up in supplication, and said, "If that's you, May, speak to me." She was silent a moment and then began to cry.

I asked her, "Did May speak?"

She said, "Yes, May spoke."

I said, "What did she say?"

She said, "I can't tell you. The message is for mother."

She then went over and laid her head on her mother's lap, crying. Her mother said, "Well, tell the gentlemen what she said."

I said, "Well, the crowd might as well hear the message". I then called in the sergeant, who was followed in by all the others …

… The little girl looked up and said the message she received was this: "Tell mother I am perfectly happy where I am, and that your prayers when I was sick brought me where I am, and made me happy. Tell mother not to worry, I'll watch and guard over you all."

By this time the whole of the family was in tears. Otherwise the silence that had come to the whole group of … spectators was most impressive. We waited about the house for about an hour, but there were no more knocks.

What with the trashing of three houses and the whole town in an uproar, it would seem that May had a very strange way of "watching and guarding" over her family. But now that she'd apparently been able to make contact, Mr. Davey hoped the polt activity would come to an end. Sadly, he, the Bowen family, the sleepless constabulary and the stressed-out people of Guyra were to be disappointed. Although the weird activity was suspended for a day or so after the séance, it soon started up again: this time in broad daylight.

A savage attack

On the morning of Friday 15th, while the entire family was working in a nearby paddock, someone – or some *thing* – severely damaged the Bowen house. Windows that "had been stoutly barricaded with wooden shutters and nailed up with battens, were smashed in. The shutters and battens were lying on the ground on the verandah, together with a large stone."

The Bowens were amazed that a vandal – whether human or ghostly – could have carried out such a violent and presumably very noisy attack without attracting their attention. The cottage stood out in the open, only a couple of hundred metres from where they'd been working.

A *Sunday Times* reporter, who visited immediately after the attack, photographed Minnie and her father outside their battered residence.

Minnie and William Bowen. (*Sunday Times*, Sydney, 17 April 1921)

Mr. Moors investigates

One of the people drawn to Guyra by the mystery was Mr. H.J. Moors, who owned plantations and extensive trading interests in Samoa, and who happened to be in Sydney on business. He was a personal friend of Robert Louis Stevenson and also of Sir Arthur Conan Doyle. Like Conan Doyle, he had a strong interest in psychic phenomena.

Arriving in Guyra on Monday 18 April, he requested, and was granted, full access to the Bowen house for a couple of nights. Removing portions of the roof to create lookout posts with good views of the exterior, he and five assistants kept the family under close surveillance and set an elaborate system of traps to detect hoaxers.

Completely undeterred, the "Ghost" continued its maddening mayhem. Moors and his assistants were completely flummoxed: they couldn't even say for sure whether the walnut-sized stones that landed all around them originated from inside or outside the house.

H. J. Moors, 1924. (Alexander Turnbull Library, Wellington, New Zealand)

Moors left after four days, convinced that the "Ghost" episode was a typical demonstration of poltergeist activity. He considered Minnie a normal little girl, and was convinced the strange occurrences were not the result of hoaxing. Because of the "ceaseless vigil" that was maintained "within and without" the house, hoaxers would, he believed, have been easily apprehended. Indeed, given that the house and its vicinity resembled, for a time, "something of an armed camp" anyone lurking in the shadows to throw stones would, he said, have run a real risk of being shot.

Getting nervous

Even before the brazen daylight attack of Friday the 15th, members of the Bowen family had been badly stressed. Early that morning, when a journalist "… adventured through the bush … towards the house, the door opened stealthily, and Hodder, the step-son, polled with a three days' growth of beard, came towards me, a stranger, with his rifle at the ready. Then, as I explained, he caught sight of a rabbit-trapper passing close by. The same suspicious frown came again. The business was badly on the man's nerves."

Whether they believed a polt was responsible or whether they thought a fiendishly clever prowler was at work, many other locals became very jittery. As the *Glen Innes Examiner* put it, the weirdness was "beginning to get on the Guyra people's nerves". It was said that if a hoaxer was identified, he would "come in for a bad time if some of those hefty potato farmers lay hands on him."

Gun fever

At nearby Black Mountain a woman became "so overwrought" by the eerie affair that she purchased a revolver, which one of her little boys promptly got hold of and fired at his sister. The girl didn't die, but was left with a bullet lodged dangerously close to her brain.

Cops and knockers

Alarmed at the increasingly dangerous situation, the State government sent extra police from Glen Innes and a team of detectives from Sydney to sort things out.

Arriving on Wednesday 20th, the detectives rounded up everyone, including every member of the Bowen household, that they considered possible hoaxers, "but after a searching examination dismissed all without obtaining the slightest clue to the mystery".

According to the *Armidale Express* of 19 April, Minnie had already endured protracted interrogation by a local officer, presumably Sergeant Ridge: since the "remarkable séance

"… the little girl has stoutly resisted all attempts to shake her testimony. She was, in one instance, virtually subjected to the third degree. In fact, the examination was so severe as to leave her almost nervously prostrated, and yet she would not deny that she had heard a voice from another world …"

On reading through everything concerning the police investigation, it seems that some, and perhaps all, of the local police believed the weird occurrences really were paranormal. The Brisbane *Daily Mail* reported that Sergeant Ridge was "convinced that there was some supernatural agency at work". Constable Taylor, who'd been involved right from the beginning, told the *Armidale Express* that, given the double cordon outside and the guards inside, it was "a sheer impossibility" for anyone to approach the house undetected at night.

On Saturday the 16th local officers told the Glen Innes *Examiner* that "whatever the origin of the mystery they were perfectly satisfied that Minnie herself was not responsible".

The big-city cops, however, seemed determined to prove the phenomenon a hoax, probably because the NSW Inspector-General of Police, James Mitchell, had made it quite clear that he "regarded the whole affair as a case of larrikinism … and the whole thing should be stamped out." He went on to say that among the police he sent from Sydney was an officer, Constable Hardy, "who has reported that when a youth in Guyra, 15 years ago, there was a similar trouble there. Stones were thrown at a house, and a girl was also concerned in the affair."

Debunkers: Constable Hardy (above) and Inspector Mitchell (below). (*Sunday Times*, Sydney, 1 May 1921)

On Monday 25 April, under the indignant headline, "INSULTS TO THE DISTRICT", the *Guyra Argus* angrily rejected Inspector-General Mitchell's theory and exposed Constable Hardy as a liar:

"The … trouble is, according to the Inspector-General of Police, caused by gangs of larrikins. This is arrant bunkum. To test the genuineness of [Constable Hardy's claim] we wired Sergt. D.J. O'Neill (Moruya) yesterday, who was stationed here at the time, and received the following reply: 'No case of stone-throwing at Guyra 15 years ago. Report incorrect.' Several long-term Guyra residents also debunked the story.

"Misrepresentations like those", continued the *Argus*, "... besides being an insult to the people of the district, are not likely to bring about what is earnestly desired by everyone – an elucidation of the 'mystery'".

But worse insults soon followed. On Tuesday April 26 the Sydney *Sun* scornfully referred to Guyra as "the potato metropolis" and announced that "the mystery has resolved itself into just the sort of prank that bibulous hobbledehoys would indulge in after a spiritual indulgence at their favourite tavern." The article was based on statements issued by Constable Hardy, who had returned to Sydney that morning, having spent only five days at Guyra.

A clever dick

His team, Hardy told the *Sun*, "... arrived at the conclusion that the manifestation was worked by five or six persons, with the object of getting possession of the house." This theory hinged on the fact that rental accommodation was scarce in the district at the time – but it fails to take into account the fact that the Bowen's landlord, Mr. Cox (who must have had to spend a lot of money on repairs) showed no inclination to – and never did – evict the unfortunate family. He was, it might be added, firmly convinced the phenomenon was supernatural.

Hardy, apparently unembarrassed at having already been exposed as a liar by the *Argus*, also claimed to have achieved a major breakthrough. On Saturday the 23rd, he told the *Sun*, he and Sgt. Ridge "took up a position ... on the southern side of the house. A Mr. Starr, a respectable local farmer, watched the northern side and saw the girl throw several stones at the cottage ... the police ... questioned the girl. She at first denied any knowledge of stone throwing ... but when confronted with Mr. Starr ... she admitted throwing stones [and] afterwards admitted that she was responsible for the knocking on the wall, which she effected by striking the inner walls at night time with a stick when people were keeping watch outside. She remarked 'I was always careful that I was not watched or seen by anybody.'"

If we could be confidant that Hardy's account was truthful, Minnie's apparent confession would seem to deal a crippling blow to the idea that supernatural forces were at work. The big city papers certainly seemed to accept the notion: with headlines such as "NO GUYRA GHOST" (*Daily Telegraph*) and "MYSTERY ENDS", (*The Sun*) they pronounced the case closed – solved in large part by clever Constable Hardy – obviously a young man with a bright future.

The mystery unsolved

Citing yet another episode of stone-throwing at the Bowen on 27th April – after Constable Hardy's departure – the *Guyra Argus* of Thursday 28 April rejected his claim to have solved the mystery: "There appears nothing so far, despite reports to the contrary, to indicate that the trouble has been solved, or that Bowen's residence is not still entitled to the weird designation of 'The House of Mystery'".

Mr. Hay's spray

Then, on April 29th, in a statement to the *Sydney Morning Herald*, Mr. Alex Hay, a prominent Guyra businessman, angrily and comprehensively rebutted Hardy's claims. Because of this, and because his statement also gives a valuable first-hand account of vigils at the Bowen house, it is worth quoting at length.

After reminding readers that Hardy's story about an earlier stone-throwing event at Guyra was a fabrication, Mr. Hay said the constable's claim to have solved the case "is of no material value … and is most discrediting to the vigilants … Guyra police and public, who spent night after night for three weeks in the vicinity of the Bowen's house …

"[Constable Hardy] states that [Minnie] was found throwing stones at the house one night. This … is absolutely incorrect. The facts … are as follows: Minnie Bowen, whilst outside the house at midday, [threw] two or three small stones on the iron roof where her sister was washing clothes. Her sister knew at once that it must have been Minnie who threw those particular stones, and, but for the fact that a local farmer was passing at that moment, Minnie would simply have received a severe reprimand for trying to frighten her sister."

An important observation

Mr. Hay then made a very important observation: "Strange to say, throughout the whole episode, no [other] stone has ever hit the iron roof, but [they have] always been directed with unerring aim at either the windows or walls". We will consider the implications of that interesting detail later. "As regards the … knocking … which Constable Hardy has so conveniently credited to Minnie, this is also a small matter … The girl's own version of the matter is that she walked into the room and picked up a piece of wood [used for] propping up the window sash; with this she gave two taps on the wall. She was observed doing so, however, and says she was well aware of the fact …."

The local police, Mr. Hay insisted, "were not of the same mind as Constable Hardy … One night Sergeant Ridge was inside with the whole family, including the girl, whilst Constable Taylor and two trusted civilians sat within a few yards of the wall outside … seven very loud raps came on the wall in quick succession …as the first knock was heard a powerful spotlight was turned on … from a distance of 30 yards. Thus the outside wall was in a blaze of light whilst the knocking was going on … Constable Taylor insisted the knocks came from the inside … Sergeant Ridge … however … insisted that [it] did not … as he was closely watching every person in the room."

On another occasion, with six men "absolutely above suspicion … standing with their backs to the outside wall of a 12-foot room" with Minnie inside, "with a good light burning, and being closely watched by … Constable Taylor, one of our oldest Js.P., and myself … two very loud knocks came on the wall. As usual, the men on the outside insisted that the knocks came from the inside, while the watchers inside believed they came from the outside. I could quote many other cases … where every member of the Bowen family has been under strict observation whilst the knocking went on.

"The whole business, after the first two nights, lost all semblance of being a joke, and had any man … been caught throwing stones … it requires little imagination … to know what sort of a time he would have had at the hands of 50 or 60 determined men."

He went on to point out that several days after Constable Hardy returned to Sydney trumpeting his cleverness, "the mystery is still unsolved, as two stones hit the house last night [Thursday 28th] with tremendous force. Mr. Bowen rushed out … and fired three shots … in the direction from which the stones appeared to come, but without result."

An unfair cop

A Brisbane *Daily Mail* story also casts doubt on Hardy's fairness by showing that his report glossed over at least one incident that didn't fit with his conclusions.

On Thursday 21st a *Mail* journalist had been the only civilian allowed onto the Bowen property. That night, while detectives and uniformed police were inside the house, watching every member of the family, "several very loud knocks were heard." As Constable Hardy rushed outside, a stone struck the wall near him. Despite it being a bright, moonlit night, and several officers being stationed outside, no one who could have made the knocks or thrown the stone was seen lurking anywhere on the property.

During the first week of May, as the thumping and stone falls continued, Minnie's parents, in desperation, sent her 60 kilometres away, to stay with her grandmother, Mrs. Shelton, in Glen Innes. As soon as she left Guyra, all "Ghost" activity ceased.

Whichever way one looks at it, that cessation of hostilities has to be significant. Either the stone-throwing and thumping stopped (1) because Minnie was no longer there to hoax it or to cause it, unintentionally, by psychokinesis, or (2) because the poltergeist needed to "feed off" Minnie's psychic energy to operate. It also has implications for the theory put forward by Constable Hardy and others that most of the stones were thrown by people intent on driving the Bowens from their residence so that they, the vandals, could move in. Why would the vandals cease their attacks just because Minnie had left?

Trouble in the Glen

Minnie's first few days at Glen Innes were entirely peaceful, but if she and her family thought the "Ghost's" shenanigans had come to an end, they were sadly mistaken: on the night of Monday May 9th the weirdness kicked off again, with a shower of gravel on the roof of her grandmother's house. This, the *Armidale Express* reported on 13 May, "was quickly followed by stones of varying sizes and loud knocks on the walls."

Grandma Shelton's house. (Healy/Cropper)

The police were called and one officer, Constable Stewart, briefly attended. While he was walking around the house a stone broke a bedroom window and became entangled in the curtain. He also heard four or five sounds resembling knocks against galvanised iron but (significantly, perhaps) "he was not sure whether they emanated from inside or outside." For some unstated reason, and to the dismay of the Sheltons, he "came to the conclusion the girl was responsible" and promptly decamped.

Further stone-throwing occurred on Tuesday night, when the police were there in force.

On that occasion "a well-known farmer" sounded a sceptical note. He had been having tea with the Sheltons "… when the loud noises on the wall occurred, [and] insisted that he had seen the girl hit the wall with her elbows". This was "stoutly denied by the girl, whose relatives bore out the denial."

As Grandma Shelton's house was situated in town it is quite likely the stones were thrown by local larrikins. The fact that many stones, unlike those at Guyra, were directed at the roof also suggests hoaxing. Despite what the "well-known farmer" thought, however, the wall-shaking thumps were as difficult to explain as ever. A neighbour, Mr. Marsden, said they were like the sound of an axe being struck heavily against the wall. Mr. and Mrs. McKillop, who lived right next door, were so unnerved by the din that they intended to leave their home if the racket continued.

Some thumps were heavy enough to dislodge ornaments on the Shelton's sideboard. When a 200 pound (90kg) man threw his full weight against the wall next to the sideboard the ornaments didn't even shake.

On Wednesday 11 May, though the police cleared the area of all sightseers, a few stones still hit the house and the wall-thumping occurred as usual. That, however, seems to have been the polt's – or the hoaxer's – curtain-call: as far as we know, there was no further "Ghost" activity at Glen Innes or, after Minnie returned home a few days later, at Guyra.

So it seems that in about mid-May 1921, the "ghost" simply faded away.

Minnie moves on

After the polt decided to leave her alone, young Minnie got on with her life. She grew up, married a young dairyman, and, as Mrs. Ince, lived for many years, apparently normally, in Armidale. If she knew more about the "Guyra Ghost" than she let on as a child, there is no record of her telling anyone about it in later life.

A tragic end

In about 1988 or '89, strange, dark-eyed, haunted Minnie, now an elderly, slow-moving lady, was run over and decapitated by a vehicle on the Grafton Road, just outside Armidale.

Our comments:

There are several reasons to suspect a degree of hoaxing was involved at Guyra:

The fact that not only the Bowen residence, but also the Hodder and McInnes houses, were stoned suggests there may have been some substance to the "local vendetta" theory that was occasionally bandied about (but never convincingly argued).

Nearly all of the flying stones seem to have come from outside the houses – there was no rain of stones indoors, as happened at Humpty Doo, Cooyal, Mayanup and other places.

No one remarked on any of the stones falling unnaturally slowly or mentioned that they were unexpectedly warm to the touch.

Most of the stone throwing occurred at night, and some nights during the first week were notably dark and gloomy.

No objects were seen levitating inside or outside the house(s).

The house was located just a short walk from the village. It is therefore not unreasonable to suspect that some, at least, of the stones were thrown – or fired from slingshots – by local hooligans. Some of the many sightseers who came from near and far may also have decided to enliven proceedings by chucking the occasional stone.

Minnie's story about having been followed by the stone-throwing stranger strikes us as very odd. If it was true then perhaps the mystery man threw many of the stones that later hit the house. If we suspect she invented the story, then we must doubt everything else she said, notably her account of the "conversation" with her late sister. But it seems she told her family about the mystery man prior to the first stone falls – and it is difficult to imagine why she should invent such a tale. Those who witnessed her conversation with May seemed convinced of her sincerity.

Several other factors, however, suggest the episode consisted largely of genuine polt phenomena:

The very loud thumps that shook the Bowen and Shelton houses would have been extremely difficult for anyone to fake. Minnie, certainly, couldn't have done so. The thumps were "sufficient to shake the [Bowen] cottage to its foundations" and were audible 100 yards away. Those that occurred at Grandma Shelton's house dislodged ornaments on a sideboard and couldn't be replicated by a 200-pound (90 kg) man. Similar loud, wall-shaking thumps have been reported during many other apparent polt episodes.

We consider it very significant that those posted outside the Bowen house said the thumping seemed to come from within, while those indoors said it seemed to come from outside. Witnesses have reported exactly the same thing during many polt episodes in Australia and abroad.

On some nights, despite bright moonlight and the deployment of torches and a powerful spotlight, stone-falls and wall-banging occurred as intensely as they did on gloomy nights.

Mr. Moors and his crew, despite their good vantage points, couldn't tell whether some stones came from inside or outside the building.

Although several policemen were deployed at Guyra, they never (apart from the trivial incident involving Minnie) caught anyone throwing any of the hundreds of stones – or belting the side of the house with what must have been the grand-daddy of all sledgehammers. While Sydney-based Constable Hardy – a proven liar – wrote the whole episode off to hoaxing, some, if not all, local policemen believed the phenomenon was largely paranormal.

As mentioned earlier, in his angry letter to the *Sydney Morning Herald*, Mr. Hay pointed out that although hundreds of stones hit the house, the only ones that ever landed on the roof were the two thrown playfully by Minnie. We take that as a strong indication that most, if not all, the stones were launched by a poltergeist. Consider this: virtually every stone that hit the house did so at night. If they were all catapulted at long range by hoaxers lurking behind logs and bushes, it stands to reason that many of them – probably about 50% – would have landed on the roof.

The episode that occurred on April 10th, when stones hit the exterior wall of a darkened room in which Minnie was hidden on the south side of the house, and then immediately began hitting the exterior of a north-side room as she was moved there, also strongly suggests polt activity.

The fact that no stone-throwing or wall-banging occurred whenever Minnie was temporarily absent from home, and the total cessation of such events in Guyra after she moved to Glen Innes suggests she really was the focus of a polt's attention. Sceptics might say it simply means she was responsible for some or most of the hoaxing, but even the Sydney detectives didn't believe that – they said that nearly all of the stones must have been thrown not by her but by local hooligans.

If so, one wonders why those hooligans bothered to synchronise their attacks to her absences and, indeed, how they all knew exactly when she was away from home. And why – if their objective was to drive the Bowens away so they themselves could "take possession of the house" – should they have ceased all stone-throwing and wall-banging just because Minnie went to Glen Innes?

Minnie the medium?

Twelve-year-old Minnie appears to have been a poltergeist medium "straight out of Central Casting": the kind of slightly odd, stressed adolescent who seems so often to be the focus of polt attacks.

Given the conditions she had to put up with prior to and during the "Ghost" episode, it would be surprising if she wasn't quite stressed.

For some years she'd been sharing the tiny four-room cottage with a large "blended" family consisting of her mother, father, a couple of younger sisters, her half-sister May Hodder and May's 18-month-old baby, Clifford. The family's age composition was, perhaps, rather unusual: although Minnie's mother was 47 years old in 1921, her father, William Bowen was only 32 – just 11 years older than May (Mrs. Bowen's daughter from a previous marriage).

Mrs. Bowen's step-son from that first marriage, Mr. Hodder junior, was himself married with a young family, so he may well have been almost as old as William Bowen. After his own house was badly damaged he moved his family, for mutual protection, in with the Bowens, whose already rather crowded cottage had, from then on, to accommodate four adults and *nine* little children.

May's tragic death in January 1921 must have caused Minnie enormous anguish. Being lumbered, at the tender age of twelve, with the care of baby Clifford must have been tiring and frustrating. Knowing that the baby's father wouldn't step forward, and that his identity was the cause of much speculation in the little town, must have filled the poor girl with angry and confused emotions.

The unexplained phenomena certainly *seemed* to focus on her, and it *seemed* to follow her to Glen Innes.

Psychic – or just psycho?

Sceptics might suggest that, angry, tired and frustrated, she simply trashed the family home and cleverly let people believe supernatural forces were responsible. But what would a poorly educated country girl know of poltergeist activity? In those days there was no radio or television and, as our files show, apparent poltergeist cases were mentioned only every few years in the press. Besides, as we have seen, many stone falls and wall-shaking thumps occurred while Minnie was under very close observation.

If we judge at least some of the stone falls and wall-thumping to have been genuinely supernatural, two possibilities come to mind: either the polt somehow fed off Minnie's emotional turmoil to produce the phenomena – or she had, in her emotionally upset state, unconsciously produced the strange effects herself through psychokinesis.

"She may possess an occult power"

At least two journalists who met Minnie seemed to think she was psychic. They were also struck by her rather unusual appearance and demeanour.

A *Sunday Times* journalist described her as "tall, thin and dark, with peculiar dark, introspective eyes that never seem to miss any movement in a room. When she speaks to you she never smiles, and seems to look beyond or through you". He went on to say that she had "a rather uncanny aptitude for anticipating questions, almost before they are asked …"

An *Armidale Express* reporter who heard her account of the conversation with her late half-sister wrote that although she was "rather a timid, retiring little girl", she had "wonderfully

"Dark, mystifying eyes" – Minnie. (*Sunday Times*, Sydney, 17 April 1921)

luminous and unfathomable eyes". He suggested she "may possess an occult power which enables her to bridge the great gulf between this life and the next."

Minnie the mover

It seems those journalists were right. We have recently learned that in his later years May's son, Clifford Hodder, occasionally referred to Minnie's psychic powers. His daughter, Diana Brady, told us that according to her dad, "you could sit with Minnie and she could make a piano play, or a chair lift on the other side of the room." He, too, mentioned her "very strange eyes – dark, mystifying eyes."

Clifford very rarely spoke about the "Ghost" episode, and felt very sorry for his half-sister, who had protected him throughout his childhood. A lot of people had, he said, "really picked on poor Minnie … she took the whole blame."

Minnie's half-sister Ellen, the last surviving member of her generation, also told Diana that as an adult Minnie was capable of psychokinesis: she could "move furniture and lift objects without touching them".

We don't know if Minnie had psychic powers from birth or if she developed them because of her exposure to the polt phenomena. There have been other instances of people allegedly becoming psychic – or having their psychic powers enhanced – after being targeted by poltergeists. In Matthew Manning's fascinating book, *The Link*, Dr. A. R. G. Owen tells of a Mme. Mikhailova who became, after being the focus of intense poltergeist activity, capable of producing PK effects at will. In tightly controlled tests she was observed moving small objects by mental power alone.

The ghost the town forgot

The Bowen house still stands, but has been enlarged and renovated. When we visited them in the mid-1990s, the then owners said that though they'd been a little nervous when they first moved in, they hadn't heard so much as a peep out of the "Ghost." Grandma Shelton's house in Glen Innes was demolished just a couple of years ago.

Nowadays it is hard to find any resident of Guyra who admits to knowing much about the story that brought their little town to national, and even international, attention. The episode was, perhaps, the most divisive in their community's history. For some it is still such an embarrassment that they simply refuse to talk about it. We encountered this attitude in 2010, when we attempted to interview Minnie's 97-year-old half-sister Ellen. She hung up on us.

Even the Guyra Historical Society seems to have a strange lack of interest. As mentioned earlier, all the relevant issues of the *Guyra Argus* have mysteriously disappeared, and it seems that some prominent citizens would like the entire "Ghost" story to do a similar vanishing act.

The few who will discuss the episode favour "explanations" which make very little sense. A local historian, the late Colin Newsome, declared that as Minnie was a ventriloquist (we've seen no evidence to back that claim) she somehow used that trick to fake the entire episode – wall banging, stone falls, the lot.

Equally silly theories are bandied about in Glen Innes, where we once heard it suggested the stones that struck grandma Shelton's house were fired from a giant slingshot set up on a very distant hill.

Some years back, when Guyra Shire Council was trying to come up with ideas to attract tourists, one local maverick suggested what seemed (to us, at least) a brilliant idea: the creation of a statue depicting "The Guyra Ghost". Sadly, we'll never know how the sculptor would have gone about such a project (by erecting a plinth with nothing on it, perhaps?) because the proposal was howled down.

The mystery of "The Guyra Ghost Mystery"

In addition to the journalists, psychics and sightseers who visited the town in early 1921, a motion picture crew was drawn to Guyra by the "Ghost" story. But while a film, "The

Guyra Ghost Mystery", was shot, apparently in and around the Bowen house, every copy of it seems to have vanished.

The only relic of the production that we have been able to track down is a print advertisement that was intended to promote it but which may never have been used. It is held by the National Film and Sound Archive in Canberra.

The film was produced and directed by John Cosgrove, a well known theatrical impresario, who persuaded the Bowen family to appear in it as themselves. Fifty-four-year-old Cosgrove, a veteran of many Shakespearean and other stage productions, played the role of "Sherlock Doyle" – a clear reference to Mr. Moors, the psychic investigator who left the area about three weeks earlier.

The "blurb" for the film states that it was "taken at Guyra on the spot, showing the home of the Bowen family, showing the actual stone throwing caught by the camera. Most sensational scenes. Flashlight photographs taken revealing most remarkable results at night, the camera was especially designed for night work by Mr. A. Moolian and after developing the film it showed unexpected results." In fact, according to the *Armidale Express*, the film makers didn't arrive in Guyra until May 11th, by which time Minnie was in Glen Innes. As we know, no polt phenomena occurred after her return to Guyra – so Cosgrove seems to have merely filmed re-enactments.

Since it was, according to *Smith's Weekly*, shot over the course of just three days, "The Guyra Ghost Mystery" is unlikely to have been a very polished production. Although

(Courtesy National Film and Sound Archive)

Impresario: John Cosgrove. (State Library of New South Wales)

Cosgrove told the *Armidale Express* that it would probably be shown there "in a couple of week's time" the film sank without trace. It would, nevertheless, have been fascinating to see those long-lost images of Minnie and her family.

Postscript: A strange coincidence

As mentioned in relation to the Humpty Doo case, odd coincidences sometimes occur when one is involved in fortean research. One such coincidence occurred as we were working on our account of the "Guyra Ghost" episode. It came in the form of a brief news item that a friend noticed in the October 3rd 1922 edition of the *Newcastle News* (Newcastle, Pennsylvania).

We find it quite interesting that young Ella, just like Minnie, became the focus of stone showers immediately after claiming to have been accosted by a mysterious stranger. Like Minnie, Ella couldn't identify the man or even prove he existed.

Perhaps the coincidence is of no particular significance, but, as these are the only two cases we know of that feature attacks by strange men just prior to inexplicable stone falls, it seems worthy of note that they should have occurred on opposite sides of the world, and only eighteen months apart.

Mysterious Stoner Makes Girl Target

SELLERSVILLE, Pa., Oct. 3.— Police and residents here are trying to solve a mystery. Whenever Ella Ruth, 14 years old, a daughter of Mr. and Mrs. Isreal Ruth, of Keystone Point, near Sellersville, goes to the porch or yard of her parents' home, a shower of stones of various sizes fall about her. She has not been hit. This has continued for more than a week.

Every possible place where the thrower of the stones might hide has been searched.

The stone throwing began more than a week ago, one morning after the girl had told of being accosted by a strange man as she was walking toward her home.

Residents have investigated and have seen the stones fall. Chief of Police Sturn, of Sellersville, is at a lost to solve the mystery.

The Ruth girl is of a nervous temperament. There is none who can substantiate the child's assertion that she was attacked along the road and broke away from the man who grabbed her. However, there are a number of residents, including the police chief, who have witnessed the mysterious fall of stones.

Sources:

Much of the material in this chapter originated in the *Guyra Argus*, which was usually the first newspaper to report on developments at the Bowen homestead. However, as previously mentioned, every issue of the *Argus* from April and May 1921 has disappeared – presumably appropriated by an early researcher. Fortunately, the *Argus's* sister paper, the *Armidale Express*, quoted the *Argus* at length throughout the critical weeks, as did many other newspapers.

The Sun (Sydney), 10, 13, 14, 17, 19 and 26 Apr, 1921.

The Miner (Broken Hill), 12 Apr 1921.

Armidale Express, 15, 19, 26, 29 Apr and 3, 10, 13 May 1921.

Sydney Morning Herald, 15, 20, 22, 26, 27, 29, 30 Apr and 11 May 1921.

Glen Innes Examiner, 18 Apr 1921.

Daily Telegraph (Sydney), 18, 23, 26 Apr 1921.

The Argus (Melbourne), 20, 26, 27, Apr and 11 May 1921.

Queensland Times (Ipswich), 11 Aug 1921.

The Newcastle News (Newcastle, Pennsylvania), 3 Oct 1922.

Frank Cusack (ed.), *Australian Ghost Stories*, William Heinemann Ltd., Melbourne, London, 1967. (In his excellent account of the case, Cusack used several quotes from papers he identified as the Brisbane *Daily Mail* and the Brisbane *Sunday Times*. It seems, however, that he made a slight error: the latter was actually the Sydney *Sunday Times*.)

Matthew Manning, *The Link*, Holt, Rinehart and Winston, New York, 1975. (The discussion of Mme. Mikhailova's psychic ability is on p. 150.)

Colin Newsome, *Minnie Bowen – The Guyra Ghost*, Self published, Glen Innes, 1993.

Paul Cropper, interview with Diana Brady, 11 Feb 2010.

CHAPTER ELEVEN

Spookiest of all: The Coalbaggie Bogey

1891–94. Coalbaggie Creek, 35 km north of Dubbo, NSW. Rating: ★★★½

From the *Dubbo Dispatch*, 15 May 1894:

A COALBAGGIE MYSTERY
About three years ago Peter Stein, a hard-headed, practical, frugal German, and his son Jacob took up two areas of 2560 acres each on the ... rather isolated ... Coalbaggie.

[Now spelled Coolbaggie. As well as Mr. Stein, his wife, and Jacob, the family included another adult son, two adult daughters, five younger children, plus a young man named Daley who had been reared by the Steins].

Jacob's selection [had] *an old hut upon it* [and he] *determined to build on the site ... while Peter commenced the erection of a commodious residence on his land, about three miles away. The Steins were, however, no sooner settled down ... than they heard at night strange voices, loud cooeyings, and awful screamings. Thinking that they proceeded from either belated travellers or homeward proceeding selectors, more merry than sensible, they took little notice ... These sounds, however, took place so regularly ... that the idea of noisy roysterers, making night hideous with their noises, was given up.*

About eighteen months ago ... The furniture in Peter Stein's house became as possessed. It jumped about in all directions, and on one occasion the crash of crockery was something decidedly extraordinary and uncanny. Mrs. Stein was baking in the kitchen one day, and after she had her dough prepared ... an invisible hand caught it up and tossed it on the floor. These things, or akin to them, have kept on from then till now, but with the further development that the person responsible – whether spirit of Heaven or goblin damned – has frequently ... had conversations with the several members of the family. Evidently the presence is not of the regular type, for it does not wait till the 'witching hour when graveyards yawn and ghosts troop forth,' but comes along in broad daylight, and talks to a family, who are now somewhat terrified, as may well be imagined.

In reply to a question from Peter Stein, the invisible visitor has said that his name is George William Herbert, and that his mother, who was named Annie, and his sister, who was called Julia, were burned to death ... that his father died in the Cootamundra hospital eighteen years ago – that he (the Speaker) had been hit upon the head and left for dead on the road – that he had been saved – and had subsisted upon herbs and weeds. Upon being asked by the older Stein to show himself he replied that if he did those who saw him would faint, for they had never seen anything like him before.

According to the Steins – and all, from the father to the youngest child, tell the same round unvarnished tale – the visitor sometimes speaks in a gruff manly voice and sometimes as softly as a woman – indeed, it would be difficult to distinguish his voice from a girl's. The dogs ... seem to know when it is coming; although the Steins cannot see it, they appear to have that power, for they bark furiously, and one particular dog goes nearly wild with fear and excitement.

About a fortnight ago things reached a climax, and the invisible one performed all kinds of pranks. It cast tomahawks and knives about with the grace of an Indian juggler, and upset pots, chairs, and other articles of domestic economy. One night while the family were engaged in reciting the Rosary – they are Roman Catholics, and retain the simple devotional acts of the Rhineland – the table round which they knelt was suddenly lifted towards the ceiling and then allowed to come down with a heavy thud. So annoying have been the manifestations that the young fellow who came [to the area] *with the Steins has left the place. Another man named Bowden, employed by them, has also left, saying that if he were given the selection; he would not live there.*

The whole thing is certainly mysterious, but, however the sceptical may be inclined to laugh at it, there is not, our informant states, the slightest doubt that every one of the family thoroughly believes what he tells, and each, from the youngest child to the father of the family, has the same story to tell. Mrs. Stein, who is an English lady, with no tendency to the superstitious, is as convinced as she is of her existence that the place is haunted. A few days ago, at Peter Stein's request, the Very Rev. Father Byrne visited the selection, and though during the night and day he spent there he saw or heard nothing he investigated the affair as far as possible, and is thoroughly satisfied that the Steins are believers and they are being annoyed by a power which can act materially, and talk like a man or woman, all the time being itself invisible.

While this is a fascinating story, it is less than entirely satisfactory in that the *Dispatch's* unnamed informant, though apparently close to the action, was not a member of the Stein family.

On 1 June 1894, however, a follow-up article featured 28-year-old Jacob Stein's own account of the strange episode. He had ridden to Dubbo "with a view to obtain such assistance as would enable a solution to the mystery", and at the *Dispatch* office, "in the presence of several well-known gentlemen", submitted to a lengthy interview.

From the very day the Steins arrived at Coalbaggie Creek, he told them, they heard strange noises in the old hut. "Then when the new place was built it commenced in earnest. It chucked candlesticks, furniture, and everything else about. It hammered the tin dishes, and you could see the dents in the dishes afterwards. It started to talk to us then, but since Father Bolger and Father Moylan were out it has not talked so much. It was quiet for some time afterwards.

"It has often said that its mother and sister were burned to death in the hut. The mother was ironing and her dress caught fire … [and] when she was dying gave [sixty pounds] and a gold watch to an aunt, asking her to keep them for her boy [but] … The uncle … hit him upon the head with the handle of a stock whip and left him for dead on the road.

"… one night, mother and I were sitting … by the fire, and clods were pelted at us as if by some person in the fireplace. We looked and saw a strange figure. It had the body of a child, about five years old, and a most peculiar face, with a whitish beard on it. I went to catch it and it disappeared. On another occasion I saw something like a hand coming over a box, and when I tried to grasp it there was nothing.

"While it talked outside [the house] the furniture and other things would be knocked about inside. [Sometimes] the racket would be going on … in four different places". As it was violently shaking bedsteads, "a few yards away crockery would be smashed at the same time".

Like the Humpty Doo poltergeist and many others, the Coalbaggie spook seemed to have a great aversion to religious paraphernalia: "On one occasion it took up a crucifix … broke it to pieces, and flung the bits in our faces … some blessed candles brought from Dubbo were broken into bits before us and cast at us."

People other than the Steins witnessed the phenomena: "only the other day it attempted to set fire to the house in four different places, and it also set fire to my sister's clothes, and did other things, and this can be testified to by Mr. M'Leod … and a Mr. Dwyer, who with his son was at our place at the time ….

"On Friday and Saturday last it was very bad, and it took us all we could do to prevent it burning down the place. We can smell like fire [sic] before we see it, and the house will be on fire in four different places at once, and the bedclothes and articles of female apparel also burning."

At that point in the interview a *Dispatch* journalist said, "It has been suggested, Mr. Stein, that one of your family is a ventriloquist …"

"Whenever I hear this", Stein replied, "and I have heard it several times – I get real 'narked'. I wish those who offer this solution had the thing tied around their neck. Then they would know if it was a ventriloquist. It is, I assure you, a regular torment to us, and it is driving my father and mother real mad. My opinion is that it is a live spirit, possessed of the devil."

"… on one occasion, it came in the shape of a [koala?] bear, got up on the wall of the kitchen, and when we went to chase it away, it disappeared in a white smoke. On another occasion, a big mouse, about a foot long, came on the roof, and it mysteriously moved about … and another day a wallaby was near the house and it would not shift for my sisters. They tried to put the dogs on it, but [they] came back with their tails between their legs. My brother and myself put two kangaroo dogs on it, and it ran into the creek and disappeared as if into the ground. The dogs came out on the other side looking terribly frightened … that night it talked to us and said … that it was the wallaby we were chasing. It said it could appear as a lizard or a snake or in any shape it liked.

"It told us that it was no use [to] bring out the priests. It said it would haunt us and torment us not only while we were on the Coalbaggie, but would follow us about wherever we went … It talks in two voices, and sometimes speaks sensibly enough, while at others it seems quite mad, and uses language which could not be beaten by the lowest Sydney larrikin. It bids us the time of day, and when I have remonstrated with it for its actions, it says it is only having a bit of fun.

"I once said to it that there was not much fun in breaking crockery … and it told me it couldn't help it, for when its mother caught fire it was taking some crockery out, and the shock was so great that it dropped it. Since then its greatest amusement has been smashing up the crockery. It has done, from first to last, 100 [pounds] worth of damage, and you may be sure that if it was one of ourselves we would not waste money like that.

"Not long since … in the presence of three or four, it took down the frying pan, placed it on the fire, and put six eggs in it … The frying pan could be seen moving [but the poltergeist] was invisible … it is no wonder we are scared … You can hear it talking to [the dogs] and they look in mortal dread, their hair standing up and their eyes bulging out of their heads. It talks in two voices, and sometimes so loudly that it ought to be heard a mile away."

On being asked if the unwelcome tenant ever sang, and if the songs were up to date, Jacob replied that it did, and that "it seems to know all sorts of songs … it seems to be very fond of 'The Banks of the Clyde' [and] 'The Ship that Never Returned'. It sings the last one pretty fair, but it is quite horrible to hear it singing 'The Banks of the Clyde' – it's quite sickening."

Jacob rejected any suggestion that neighbours could have hoaxed the strange events: "No, we are on the best terms with everyone, and the nearest neighbour is living nearly three miles away. … I honestly believe it is a live spirit, possessed by the devil, and having the power of making itself invisible. Why, the night when we were praying, and it lifted up the table towards the ceiling, there were present my father and mother and four of my sisters. Not one of them touched the table, but it went up just the same."

The article concluded with this assessment of Jacob's credibility: "Mr. Stein is a level-headed man, with more than the average intelligence, and he told the above before gentlemen holding the highest positions in the town."

All very reassuring – but there is one slight problem. Given that the story was so mind-bogglingly weird, and that both articles "went viral" – being reprinted in papers as far away as north Queensland – we would have expected a few "follow-up" stories. After hours of microfiche-induced eyestrain, however, all we could find were two very short letters to the editor of the *Dispatch*.

The first, published on 5 June, is a pointless, "humorous" missive from someone who'd evidently never met the Steins. The second, which appeared on 8 June, is of more concern to us "true believers":

SIR, – In your issue of the 1st June Mr. Jacob Stein is reported to have said, "before gentlemen holding the highest positions in town," that "since Father Bolger and Father Moylan were out (at Coalbaggie) it (the alleged 'spook') has not talked so much."

My object, therefore, in writing this letter, is to decline Mr. Stein's compliment and give a most emphatic denial to the statement that I have ever visited the place in question. I am also morally certain that the late Father Bolger did not visit Coalbaggie during the time specified.

Yours sincerely,
J. MOYLAN.
Catholic Presbytery, Wellington,
4th June, 1894.

Uh, oh. Could it be that Jacob, his old dad, and the entire family were compulsive liars?

Jacob had certainly been quoted, on 1 June, as saying "since Father Bolger and Father Moylan were out it has not talked so much", so the story seemed to be on the point of unravelling. But then, in a comment following Fr. Moylan's irate letter, the *Dispatch's* editor cleared things up … sort of:

In justice to Mr. Stein, it must be said he was misunderstood. He did not say the Rev. gentlemen had visited Coalbaggie, but since they were spoken to regarding the manifestations, the "spook" became less talkative. – Ed.

Well – that's a bit of a relief. While it leaves us wondering what else he may have got wrong, it seems the journalist simply recorded Jacob's remark about the priest(s) incorrectly. We note also that in the 15 May article the informant didn't mention Father Bolger or Father Moylan at all – he said, in fact, that it was a *Fr. Byrne* who spent a night and day at the property and left "thoroughly satisfied that the Steins are believers and they are being annoyed by a power which can act materially, and talk like a man or woman, all the time being itself invisible." So there may well have been room for honest misunderstandings on the part of either the Steins or the staff of the *Dispatch*.

Our comments:

Although this story is by far the weirdest in our Australian file, and although everything we know about it comes, essentially, from just two newspaper articles, we are reasonably confident it is largely true. Both articles are lengthy and detailed, and the second one, featuring the interview with Jacob Stein has, we believe, a distinct ring of truth.

If the story was a hoax, every member of the family, plus Mr. Daley and Mr. Bowden, seems to have been party to it. Why on earth would they do such a thing? We find it much easier to believe that they were telling the truth – and that the episode was genuinely paranormal. The fact that Daly and Bowden packed up and left the area – with Bowden saying he that even if he was given the property he wouldn't live there – strongly suggests the strange events really occurred.

The hysterical behaviour of the family's dogs, the spook's violent reaction to religious paraphernalia and the claim that knives and other sharp objects flew around without hurting anyone are all strongly reminiscent of phenomena observed at Humpty Doo, Mayanup and many other poltergeist sites. The gradual escalation of weirdness – starting with strange noises, then progressing through levitation of objects, to disembodied voices, to dire threats, to apparitions and then to fire-starting – conforms to patterns of activity noted during many other well-documented episodes.

Although fire-starting polts are (thankfully) very rare, such behaviour has been recorded during many foreign and a few Australian episodes (e.g. at Cannibal Creek in 1935). The Steins believed the polt was attempting to burn their house down, but as it was apparently capable of doing several things in several different places, day and night, it seems more likely it was simply trying (successfully) to scare the hell out of them. Like the pyromaniac polts of Kota Bharu, Malaysia, Ho Chi Minh City and Cizre, Turkey (see Appendix A) it lit many small fires in rapid succession, but the fires were all quickly found and extinguished.

The kobold

This brings us to Jacob Stein's outrageous assertion that "one night, mother and I were sitting … by the fire, and clods were pelted at us as if by some person in the fireplace. We looked and saw a strange figure. It had the body of a child, about five years old, and a most peculiar face, with a whitish beard on it. I went to catch it and it disappeared."

Since sceptics are already chortling, we might as well give them something else to laugh about – something that may already have occurred to folklorists. In Germany, from as far back as the 13th century, it was widely believed that elf or goblin-like beings called *kobolds* were responsible for a lot of poltergeist phenomena. They were household spirits who, though usually invisible, could take the form of *human-like figures the size of small children*. They were neither boy nor man, but had characteristics of both. They usually lived in the hearth area of a house and sometimes entered and exited *through the chimney*. Sometimes they would follow an individual or family from place to place.

Though they could often be helpful around the house, kobolds were said to be deceivers and flatterers, fond of teasing their mortal housemates. They felt, in fact, that they were master of any house they infested – and woe betide anyone who offended them: then they might throw stones, break windows, and throw pots and pans into the air. It all sounds mighty familiar.

The Coalbaggie polt supposedly boasted that it could transform itself into any animal it chose to, and the Steins claimed that that a couple strange animals – a foot-long mouse and a vanishing bear – did, in fact, appear inside the house. Interestingly, according to German folklore, kobolds were capable of transforming themselves into not only little hominids, but also into various animals.

They could also, it was believed, manifest as fire – which is interesting in the light of the Coalbaggie polt's alleged attempts to burn down the house.

Peter Stein was, as we know, born in Germany, where he may well have absorbed kobold lore, and some of this lore could have rubbed off onto his children. It might be suggested, therefore, that the figure of the little man in the fireplace was nothing but an hallucination prompted by ingrained Old World superstition.

But it seems obvious from the transcript of his interview that young Jacob was Australian born and bred. And as we know, his mother was "an English lady, with no tendency to the superstitious".

Woman with a Kobold. ("La Mythologie Du Rhin", Paris 1862)

If the little man was an hallucination, he was an hallucination that somehow affected mother and son simultaneously.

Then there's Jacob's claim that he "saw something like a hand coming over a box, and when I tried to grasp it there was nothing". (This apparition, older readers will note, is very reminiscent of "Thing"- the disembodied hand that regularly emerged from a box during episodes of "The Addams Family" television series!)

But, strange as it most certainly was, Jacob's claim of seeing the ghostly hand is not the only such report in our files. As mentioned previously, during the Mayanup poltergeist episode three people told of seeing ghostly, glowing hands. Yet another was supposedly spotted during a poltergeist episode at Adelong in 1889 (Case 12, Chapter Twelve).

The creepiest thing about this case – and the thing readers might find most difficult to believe – is the claim that the polt spoke out loud, day and night, engaging in conversation with every member of the family. It is unfortunate that only the family members were specifically mentioned as having heard the voice(s), and if their story was unique we'd have to conclude they were all seriously deluded. But outspoken spooks have, in fact, featured in several foreign poltergeist cases.

The Bell Witch

Perhaps the most dramatic of those foreign cases was the infamous Bell Witch episode of 1817–1821. During those four years the Bell family of Robertson County, Tennessee, was subjected to all of the torments experienced by the Steins – and then some. In that disturbing case the "Witch" spoke out loud, day and night, in the presence of dozens of people. The disembodied voice (or voices) like that of the Stein's spook, were sometimes harsh and manly and sometimes "delicate and feminine". Although sometimes friendly and given to singing popular songs, the "Witch", like the Coalbaggie bogey, frequently upset its audience with nasty, obscene taunts. But unlike the Coalbaggie spook – and unusually for any polt – it was intent on causing serious injury. It delighted in tormenting poor old John Bell – constantly slapping his face, pulling his hair and yanking his shoes off. It hounded him to his death – and then gloated loudly over its work.

What animal is that?

Another interesting parallel is that the "Witch", like the Coalbaggie spook, claimed to be able to assume the form of any animal it chose to. Just before the poltergeist phenomena started, John Bell had seen a peculiar animal in his cornfield. It "looked like a dog, yet it was not", and when he shot at it, it "at once disappeared". The "Witch" later said the animal had been none other than himself (or herself – it was a bit vague about its gender). Like the Steins at Coalbaggie, the Bells subsequently sighted other strange or oddly-behaving animals around the property.

We think it highly unlikely that a family of pioneers in an obscure corner of New South Wales would have had sufficient knowledge of the Bell Witch case to fake such a strikingly similar sequence of events.

The banger of Bingen

It is interesting to note that one of the earliest poltergeist stories on record also features a talkative, fire-starting spook.

In 858 A.D. at Kembdem, near Bingen on the Rhine, a farming family was tormented by an "evil spirit" that began by throwing stones, and then shook the walls of their dwelling, "as though the men of that place were striking them with hammers". Like the Bell Witch, the Bingen bogey focused its malice on the head of the household. It followed him around, burnt his possessions and, developing an audible voice, loudly denounced him for adultery and other sins.

Like the Humpty Doo polt and many others, the Teutonic trickster was unfazed by attempted exorcism: it reacted to the sprinkling of holy water with a contemptuous barrage of stones.

Infernal djinn

It is worth mentioning, also, that throughout the Muslim world the poltergeist-like *djinn* are believed to be capable of stone-throwing, talking, assuming the form of various animals and starting fires (See Appendix A).

A genuine, lying spook

After using the Australian National Library's marvellous "Trove" system to scan many colonial-era newspapers, we have, so far, found not a single reference to the supposedly murdered George William Herbert that the polt talked about, to his dad who supposedly died around 1873 or to his mother and sister who were supposedly burnt to death "on the South Balladoran run".

But while the poltergeist phenomenon contains many unknowns, one thing we *do* know is that most polts are mischievous and "contrary" – and many are liars. So while they may occasionally claim to be spirits of certain deceased persons there is no particular reason to believe them.

In any case, weird and creepy as it certainly was, we see little reason to doubt that the Coalbaggie episode occurred very much as described by the Stein family.

Sources:

Dubbo Dispatch, 15 May, 1, 5 and 8 Jun 1894.

Bathurst Free Press and Mining Journal, 1 Jun 1894.

Light magazine, 8 Sept 1894.

The kobold lore was taken from Carol Rose, *Spirits, Fairies, Leprechauns and Goblins: An Encyclopaedia*, W. W. Norton & Company, New York; 1996, D.L. Ashliman, *Fairy Lore: A Handbook*, Greenwood Press, 2006, both quoted by Wikipedia, and Claude Lecouteux, "The Birth of the Poltergeist", *Fortean Times*, October 2012, pp. 38–41.

The Bell Witch and Bingen cases are both covered in detail in some of the best books about poltergeists, e.g. in *The Story Of The Poltergeist Down The Centuries*, by Hereward Carrington and Nandor Fodor, pp. 23, 31, 137–65 and *Poltergeist!*, by Colin Wilson, pp. 96–97, 100, 108–16, 312.

CHAPTER TWELVE

A Catalogue of Cases, 1845–1998

This chapter contains every case in our Australian files, assembled in chronological order.

If our sole aim was to persuade readers that the poltergeist phenomenon is genuine, we might have been tempted to ignore some "inconvenient truths", sweep the less-than-convincing cases out of sight and present only those that contain strong evidence of paranormal activity.

Our shelves contain quite a few books about unexplained phenomena wherein the authors have resorted to such less-than-honest "cherry-picking" (just as, at the other end of the spectrum, militant debunkers are sometimes guilty of "cherry-picking" only the weaker cases).

No one is entirely unbiased, but we see our poltergeist research as a quest for the truth, pure and simple, and try to stay true to that ethic. Having researched the subject for so many years, and being convinced it is worthy of serious study, we aren't about to sell ourselves, our many generous informants and our readers short.

So, in the interests of completeness, and to assist future researchers, be they polt enthusiasts, disinterested sociologists, folklorists or militant sceptics, the catalogue contains every case, good, bad and indifferent, in our files.

In several instances the reported phenomena was reasonably suspected to be – or actually proven to be – the work of hoaxers. We've included all of those dodgy cases, not only out of fairness to sceptics and to the general reader, but also as a way of reminding our fellow "true believers" that it pays to be cautious.

In some colonial-era cases poltergeists were probably involved but there is too little surviving documentation to be sure. Perhaps other researchers will be able to document those episodes more thoroughly than we have. Some other cases contain sufficient detail to persuade us that polts were probably involved and we are confident that several of the best-documented episodes are completely genuine.

Our rating system begins at zero for apparent or proven hoaxes and ranges from half a star – for questionable or very poorly documented cases – through to five stars for our very best case, the Mayanup episode of 1955–57.

Case 1

October–December 1845. Near Launceston, Tasmania. Rating: ★

This strange little episode isn't one of our stronger cases, but as it is the very earliest in our Australian files and as it might have involved, unusually for Australia, a fire-starting polt, we have decided to cover it in detail.

From *The Launceston Examiner*, 22 Oct 1845:

STRANGE OCCURRENCE
Some of the good folks who inhabit the West Bank of the Tamar have been alarmed by extraordinary occurrences, which, being at present unaccountable, have been ascribed to preternatural agency: at least, the alarm has been such, and the statements so authenticated, that Mr. Midgeley, the chief constable and a subordinate have proceeded to the spot for the purpose of investigating the matter.

The principal scene of the mystery is the residence of Mr. Plummer; but Mr. Hill, a neighbour, has also been similarly annoyed. Anonymous letters of a most indecent description have been thrust through the windows of Mr. Plummer's residence by invisible hands. The house at all hours, both day and night, has been assailed with stones and other offensive missiles. Strict watch has been kept, and yet windows have been broken in broad daylight, in defiance of all caution.

Constables were stationed on the premises, but their vigilance was eluded. Upon one occasion an individual was seen and chased, but, according to all accounts he seemed, when within grasp, to dissipate into air or sink into the earth, like the ghost in the vision of Scrooge.

Mr. Plummer applied to the police magistrate for advice … [he] is a well known and respectable inhabitant; and although no doubt he has been subjected to this annoyance from the ill-feeling of a neighbour, there is something very remarkable in the "Devil and Dr. Faustus" sort of proceeding by which the agent remains invisible whilst working his mischief.

From the *Examiner*, 29 Oct 1845:

THE STONE THROWER
Mr. Plummer and his family are still annoyed constantly by strange proceedings on the part of someone who … appears to be deficient in … mind. The affair becomes more and more remarkable every day, and the family have at times been thrown into a state of great alarm.

Stones are thrown on the roof … and at the windows; letters are found about the premises; and in spite of constant watching, nobody is seen.

Mr. Midgley, the chief constable, proceeded [there] *the other day with six constables, and they all stopped the night. He took the precaution of securing all the people on the farm in one* room. On that night there was no attack. This excited suspicion that one of the family was implicated; but a series of experiments since instituted, have a contrary tendency.

Upon one occasion, a constable was set to watch on top of the house; but was pelted away by stones from the invisible hand. The neighbours … have lent their aid to detect the culprit; but without any … success. "Are there no stones in Heaven?"

From the *Examiner*, 5 Nov 1845:

THE WEST TAMAR MYSTERY:
Another party of constables have been on duty at Mr. Plummer's since our last notice. Mr. Davis and Mr. Midgley have also been exerting themselves to discover the mysterious letter-writer; and although as yet unsuccessful, they seem to agree in fixing upon the same agent as the cause of all the annoyance.

But the motive that could prompt any sane person to such proceedings is now the greatest mystery. The comparatively harmless annoyance of dropping letters and throwing stones has been succeeded by an attempt to destroy the premises by setting fire to a quantity of straw, which, to the astonishment of the household, burst into a sudden blaze whilst they were all on the watch, and a moment afterwards a letter was picked up, the ink of which was scarcely dry; and yet nobody was seen.

Such stubborn facts excited Mr. Davis' suspicions, who, being "a detector" by profession, applied his art to discover the "ghost". By well-directed and constant watching of parties belonging to the establishment, accompanied by hints of prosecution, the preternatural being was quieted, and for two days and nights did not interrupt the repose of the family. Here, for the present, the revelation stops.

From the *Examiner*, 12 Nov 1845:

ATTEMPT AT ARSON:
Another attempt was made a few evenings since, to destroy the premises of Mr. Plummer, on the West Tamar, by setting fire to a quantity of straw in the farm yard. A man was seen near the house, strict watch having been kept for several nights, but he made his escape.

Letters of a most obscene description are found in the vicinity of the dwelling; but the stone-throwing has ceased. The family are still subject to great annoyance, and the fellow … continues to escape detection in a most unaccountable manner.

From the *Examiner*, 26 Nov 1845:

ARSON:
A third attempt was made to set fire to the premises of Mr. Plummer a few evenings since. Constables have been stationed there for some time constantly, but nothing has come to light to fix the parties who are encouraging the extraordinary system of annoyance to which we have several times referred.

From the *Examiner*, 3 Dec 1845:

ARSON:
Another attempt at arson, more serious, and another escape from destruction more fortunate than any of the three proceeding, have occurred at Mr. Plummer's. The reward originally offered has been increased to fifty pounds, and it is expected the Government will contribute an inducement for the discovery of the miscreant.

Constables are continually on watch, but in spite of all their manoeuvring cannot detect the guilty parties. A more cruel and persevering determination to accomplish the ruin of a family we have never heard of in the colony.

Our comments:

Although this case has its weak points, it is worthy of inclusion not only because it is the oldest in our Australian files, but also because some of the reported activity, such as the house being "assailed with stones … both day and night" even while a strict watch was kept, is very reminiscent of phenomena recorded in other, better-documented poltergeist cases.

The incident of the straw, which suddenly burst into flames "whilst they were all on the watch" is reminiscent of the inexplicable fires reported at Granite Creek in 1935 and at other apparently polt-plagued sites.

As unpleasant, scrawled messages have appeared during several better-documented cases, the mention of "letters of a most indecent description" being left by "unseen hands" inside the Plummer residence doesn't, in itself, cause us to suspect a hoax – particularly as the ink was "scarcely dry" on the note that appeared immediately after the mysterious fire.

Scribbling a hasty note is a simple matter today, but to do so – surreptitiously, in a crowded house – in 1845, when a pen and inkwell were needed, would have been a lot more difficult.

On the other hand, the stones "and other offensive missiles" apparently struck only the outside of the house and no levitation of other objects was mentioned, indoors or out. As a suspicious individual (albeit an uncannily elusive individual) was seen and chased it seems likely this episode was the work of a clever hoaxer.

It is interesting to note that the reward offered "for the discovery of the miscreant" was very large indeed; fifty pounds would probably have bought a small house in colonial-era Launceston. Yet despite the hefty reward and the efforts of the police the case was never solved.

Although we have searched many later editions of the *Examiner* we have found no mention of the Plummers and their persecutor later than 3 December 1845. The "miscreant" or – just possibly – the fire-polt seems to have simply tired of the game.

Sources:
The Launceston Examiner, 22 and 29 Oct; 5, 12 and 26 Nov; 3 Dec 1845.
The Observer, Hobart, 28 Oct 1845.

Case 2

September 1866. Goulburn, NSW. Rating: ★

On 20 August 1866 *The Sydney Morning Herald* reprinted the following article from the *Goulburn Argus*:

GHOSTS OR WHAT?
Within the last few days … some extraordinary, and at present wholly unaccounted for, occurrences … have taken place on the premises of Mr. [Charles] *Rogers, cabinet-maker, in Auburn Street.*

Shortly after Mr. Rogers [moved into the premises] *some very strange noises were heard at night in the lower story … as if the furniture were being moved about, doors opened and shut or banged to, and persons walking about … when the outer doors were securely fastened, and none but the regular inmates were inside. On several occasions Mr. Rogers has had friends to stop with him during the night, and these have all heard the same noises, but on their going to the spot from whence they apparently proceeded, nothing more was heard.*

The noises have frequently been heard at intervals for about nine months, and every attempt … to detect the cause of them has been unsuccessful. A young man, a journeyman cabinet-maker, who only came from Sydney a fortnight ago, and who had slept [downstairs] *has … never had but one night's rest. The very first night he slept in the house he was astonished about twelve o'clock by hearing a tremendous crash, as if a chest of drawers had been thrown down stairs and smashed to atoms. He rushed out … but nothing was to be seen except Mr. Rogers who had come down stairs on the same errand.*

On Thursday last the young man was alarmed in the middle of the night by hearing the handles of three doors simultaneously turned, and somebody walk to his bedside, and then walk away again. Since then he has objected to sleep down stairs, and has accordingly been domiciled above. On Saturday night the noises were heard again … and also on Sunday night when sounds similar to the moving of furniture in the shop were distinctly heard by a constable on duty in the street.

On Monday night both Mr. Rogers and his assistant heard footsteps ascending the stairs, and the assistant says he heard a voice addressing him: he tried to call out, but was speechless as if from lockjaw. The same night constables Walker and M'Carthy, who were on the look-out, distinctly heard footsteps inside the shop, and also in the unoccupied premises adjoining; they ran round to the back of the latter, and forcing open the door, rushed in, made a thorough search, but could find nothing. We may state that similar noises were heard as far back as fifteen years ago, and when the house was occupied by the late Mr. Noonan as a public house, and also subsequently by Mr. Joseph Carroll. There is a cellar underneath the shop, and this Mr. Rogers had partially excavated … in the expectation that perhaps something might be discovered to elucidate the mystery; all, however, that was discovered were a couple of spoons and a small mallet bespattered with what looked like blood; on being examined by Dr. Waugh, however, he pronounced the stains to be spirit stains.

The house in question was built between seven and eight and twenty years ago by a butcher named Harrison, and there is a curious tale in reference to the circumstances under which he became dispossessed of it. He has been dead seventeen years. A man named Dick the Sailor was murdered on the premises about six years ago.

Our comments:

Charles Rogers in later life. (Courtesy of the Goulburn Historical Society)

Because the phenomena consisted almost entirely of strange noises, this is far from our strongest case. It is, however, interesting because it is the second-oldest case in our Australian file – and because the remarkably loud and varied sounds continued for nine months – long enough, one supposes, for the bewildered businessman and perplexed police to locate any prosaic cause such as noisy plumbing, hoaxers or rampaging possums.

One thing is certain: Charles Rogers was no weak-minded fool. Within just a few years of going into business in Goulburn at the age of twenty-two, he owned workshops, shops and even a couple of department stores in towns throughout southern New South Wales. He was respected as an entirely self-made man, a community leader, a philanthropist, and as a remarkably good natured, honest person.

We hope that some interested Goulburn resident, on reading this brief account, will be motivated to dig up further details.

Sources:

Sydney Morning Herald, 20 Aug 1866.

The McIvor Times and Rodney Advertiser (Heathcote, Victoria), 31 Aug 1866.

Brisbane Courier, 15 Sept 1866.

Case 3

8–10 June 1867. Adelaide, South Australia.
Rating: ★

From *The South Australian Advertiser*, Thursday 20 June 1867:

THE GHOST STORY
TO THE EDITOR
Sir— I wish to correct a statement which appeared in your issue of the 17th instant, concerning a knocking at the doors of my house. I for one have never believed in ghost stories, but I will give you a true account of what I, with my family, witnessed and heard. On Saturday evening, June 8, at 6 o'clock, there came a rap at the front door, but on going to the door nobody was there. It came again afterwards at the back door—a rap, rap, rap, but no one was to be seen. It then came to the front and passage windows.

I then determined to try and catch the boys, who I thought were causing the disturbance, and got my family to remain at the bottom of the passage while I searched every hiding-place. During my search the knocking continued at the back door, but I could see nobody. This rapping continued until half-past 10 o'clock. It was so loud that it was heard across the road, and by 10 o'clock my house and the next one was surrounded by my neighbours and family, but nobody was to be seen as the cause of the mischief.

We heard no more after half-past 10 o'clock till Sunday morning as we were going to have breakfast. At half-past 7 o'clock, there came two gentle raps at the front door, answered the door, but could see no one. Directly afterwards it came, rap, rap, rap at the back door. This was heard by my neighbours, who ran out to see if it was my door. We then searched the roof and every part of the premises, but nobody was to be seen, and whilst we stood talking at the back the rapping continued at the front door. My little boy said the door half opened in his hand, and there were three heavy raps before our eyes. My next-door neighbour stood under the verandah watching the outside of my door, and he saw the door shake with the knocks. The back door was beaten severely, and I said – "Open the door and see if it will be better", but the rapping still continued, and about 10 o'clock it came to the inner doors, and remained inside the house all day.

There are six inner doors, and each one had three heavy raps. At 1 o'clock the knocking was very severe, and I had eight adult witnesses in the house who saw the doors shake with the rapping. This continued until half-past 4 o'clock. On Monday, the 10th, it returned again about 8 o'clock, and at half-past 4 o'clock a man who had been lodging with me was in the house, and the rapping was so loud that he ran out quite frightened, and was ill next day in consequence.

I know not what is the meaning of all this, but I have given you a full and clear account of what occurred, and I only hope we shall not be troubled with it again. As to my child, which died on the following Tuesday night, I am not going to suppose that the knocking had anything to do with my child's death. I may also mention that a friend of mine, who considered the whole affair complete humbug, was in my house on Monday, and when the rapping commenced on the partition he started, and enquired if that was the noise. On being told that it was he rushed out of the house vowing that he would not live a day in it, and was ill all night from the fright.

I am, Sir, &c., PHILIP HOWELL. Adelaide, June 17.

Our comments:

We have only Mr. Howell's letter to judge it by, but this is quite a good little story. Considering that one of his children lay dying in the house at the time, it seems highly unlikely that he would have hoaxed the events. If anyone else did, they must have been heartless in the extreme. And if Mr. Howell's account is not exaggerated – that is, if the banging continued for many hours, day and night, was so violent that it repeatedly shook eight doors, inside and out, and could be heard across the road – then this may very well have been a genuine poltergeist event.

It is certainly not the only time inexplicable wall-banging has occurred in a house where someone was lying terminally ill.

Case 4

MAY 1872. PINE MOUNTAIN, NORTH-WEST
OF IPSWICH, QLD.
RATING: HALF A STAR

From *The Brisbane Courier* 17 May 1872:

A MOST singular and unaccountable system of stone throwing (says the Queensland Times) has been going on for upwards of a fortnight past at the Pine Mountain, by which a most respectable farmer and his family of the name of Moore, have been subjected to not only very great inconvenience and loss, but have been placed in imminent danger of their lives.

At first the stones appeared come from some of the corners of the paddock, and fell quite close to where these people were working among their cotton. Little notice was taken … until the annoyance became incessant and intolerable, and, strange to say, although a minute search was made no appearance of any person could be discovered, although the nuisance remained unabated.

This state of matters went on for days together, until at last Moore sought the … assistance of the police. Mounted troopers were dispatched to keep a look out … but during their stay nothing occurred, and Moore was allowed to pick his cotton unmolested. But shortly after the constables returned to town the annoyance was renewed, stones weighing from a few ounces up to a pound and a half weight alighting in the field close to where the family were engaged cotton picking. Still no trace of any person could be found near the place nor did Moore suspect anyone to be playing tricks upon him through ill-feeling or from other motives.

The stones appeared to come from a long distance over the tree tops, and some of them were so well aimed that Mrs. Moore was struck on the hat once and on the petticoats on another occasion, and a third stone struck the son on the back and knocked him down, and he was stunned for some time.

As the matter had now become serious, a strict watch was kept, and Moore's son, a very young lad – not more than about fourteen years of age – discovered the whereabouts of the person annoying them. He had taken a gun out to try and frighten the offender from his hiding place, and, in strolling around, he came upon a man hidden in some bushes. He saw what he describes as a very strong crossbow, the bow of which glittered in the sunlight, as if made of steel, fixed on a stock, with a groove along which the missile passed when discharged.

On being challenged the stranger made off, and the lad – boy like – fired after him; the former, exclaiming 'Oh, my hand!' made off at increased speed, and the boy followed as quickly as possible, but missed his game, who took three or four fences in his run as nimbly as a deer.

The matter is in the hands of the police, and we shall doubtless hear more of it anon. We saw some of the stones, any one of which would be sufficient to take the life of a person they might have struck, from the force with which they were delivered. The boy deserves great credit for his courageous conduct – though perhaps he was scarcely justified in firing at the man – and he tells his story in a very intelligent manner. The case at present seems a mysterious affair.

Our comments:

Even though there was an (apparently) natural explanation, this curious case is well worth looking at.

As the only "singular and unaccountable" phenomenon involved was the fall of stones in the great outdoors, it doesn't seem highly likely that a polt was involved. Also, as mentioned previously, it is extremely rare for objects thrown by genuine poltergeists to harm people – so the fact that the boy was knocked down and stunned by a stone may indicate hoaxing.

The fact that the stones didn't fall when mounted troopers were in the area also suggests hoaxing.

We have only the word of the young lad that he saw – and shot – the hoaxer, but as the stones (apparently) ceased falling after the shooting, it seems likely he was telling the truth.

A few odd details, however, make us slightly reluctant to stamp this case entirely "Busted". Firstly, it seems strange that the stones could have flown from various directions, "incessant" and "unabated" in broad daylight for "upwards of a fortnight" before a hoaxer was (allegedly) spotted. It seems unlikely also, that in a sparsely-settled rural area like Pine Mountain a wounded neighbour or stranger would go unnoticed for long.

Also, while we aren't experts on medieval weaponry, and while we are willing to be persuaded otherwise, we think it implausible that stones weighing up to a pound and a half (0.68 kg) could be fired (and fired very accurately, it was said) from a crossbow. In ancient times warriors used slings to hurl small stones and catapults of various sizes to throw larger ones, but we aren't aware of crossbows being used to fire anything other than arrows. In any case, one would expect a late nineteenth century hoaxer to choose a much more concealable and portable device, like the ubiquitous slingshot or "shanghai".

Case 5

August 1872. Bathurst, NSW. Rating: Half a star

EXTRAORDINARY AFFAIR AT BATHURST (*from the Western Independent*)

A most mysterious occurrence happened in Bathurst on Saturday evening and Sunday morning … The windows of the house occupied by Mr. Alderman Halliday, in Russell Street, were completely riddled by stones propelled by hands of persons unknown.

The fusillade, for such it may be termed, commenced at nightfall on Saturday, and was continued as late as midday on Sunday, notwithstanding the presence of a body of police and numerous spectators. Crowds of people visited the scene … on Sunday, and the most startling rumours were afloat as to the cause of it.

Mr. Halliday asserts that several bullets or slugs were fired, but others again maintain that the pieces of lead found had been propelled by a catapult. Yesterday our reporter visited the premises, and found the whole of the windows at the side of the house, and even those of the fanlights over the doors, back and front, smashed or penetrated by stones. Some of the holes made are round, and not much larger than the missile used, showing the force with which it was sent. If all we hear be true, several persons must have been engaged in perpetrating the atrocity, for such it is, considering that seven young children were on the premises at the time. As late as midday on Sunday Mr. Halliday started off to discover the thrower of a stone from the front, when several came from the rear of the premises, one stone whizzing past the ears of the police ; and at times the fall of stones on the roof and verandah was deafening.

The whole affair is enveloped as yet in mystery, as, strange to say, some of the devastation could only have been done from the inside of the house, the fanlights over the doors being out of the reach of any but those immediately close to the back verandah. A very grave suspicion rests upon a person who was resident in the house at the time, and for the sake of our peace and security it is to be hoped that the strictest investigation will be made. Terrible havoc was being made with the windows in the dining-room, at the back, when a young man (who was staying in the house) happened to observe the girl with one of the blinds raised in her band, and having heard a smash, he at once seized her and accused her of having been the cause of the whole affair. She appeared flurried, but almost immediately denied the accusation, and upon being spoken to by Mr. Halliday she again affirmed her innocence, and began crying. After that the stone-throwing ceased.

It is only fair to state that we heard several persons assert that they had seen stones come from the direction of the yard, and strike the glass outside. One or two small leaden bullets were found in the house, and whole heaps of stone. The girl Thompson is not now in the service of Mr. Halliday."

Sources:

Argus (Melbourne), 17 Aug 1872 (reprinted from the *Western Independent*).

Mercury (Hobart), 17 Aug 1872.

Launceston Examiner, 5 Sept 1872.

Our comments:

While it seems likely this episode was the result of hoaxing, we have given it a half-star rating because of the sheer ferocity of the attack and because it continued, day and night, for about 18 hours in the presence of "a body of police and numerous spectators".

While the stone-throwing ceased after "the girl Thompson" was banished from the house, it seems impossible that she could have hoaxed the entire "fusillade" that battered the residence making, at times, a "deafening" racket.

Although she was clearly the prime suspect, and while she may have been able to throw some of the objects that flew from inside the house, she could not have launched the many that came from all sides of the exterior. So if the case was indeed a hoax, it seems that, as the *Western Independent* noted, "several persons must have been engaged [in it]."

Or she may have been an unconscious medium or "focus" of the type so often implicated in polt cases both in Australia and overseas.

The fact that some of the missiles were bullet-like slugs of lead – ideal objects to launch from "shanghais" – seems to indicate that local larrikins were involved. Powerful "shanghais" might well have been be able to shoot such slugs and stones through windows leaving holes "not much larger than the missile used", although, as the journalist pointed out, to do so with seven young children in the house would have been an "atrocity".

The fact that Mr. Halliday was an alderman on the city council may be significant. It is certainly not unknown for snooty bigwigs to become very unpopular with the "Great Unwashed".

So the episode was most probably the work of hoaxers. And yet ... the very fact that the main suspect was, as in so many apparently genuine polt cases throughout the centuries, a young girl (who repeatedly affirmed her innocence) and the fact that no accomplices were ever caught, makes us just slightly reluctant to stamp this case entirely "Busted".

Case 6

July 1873. Ballarat, VIC. Rating: Zero

From the *Ballarat Courier*, 30 June 1873:

STRANGE AFFAIR AT BALLARAT EAST
About 7 or 8 o'clock on Saturday evening a butcher named Penhalluriack, residing in King Street, Melbourne Road, went to the Eastern station and informed Sergeant Larner that all the windows in his house were being smashed in by some mysterious agency, that up to that time 23 panes had been broken and although himself and many of his neighbours had been on the watch they had been unable to discover the perpetrator ... What made the occurrence the more alarming was that his wife lay ill in bed, having been confined only a day or two since. Constable Smith was immediately dispatched to the house where he found matters as described by Penhalluriack. The windows were partly boarded up and blankets hung in front of them, but strange to say even while Smith was in the house, two or three panes were broken. When he went into the front room a pane was broken at the back, when he went to the back another pane was smashed in the front window.

The affair caused a ... sensation in the neighbourhood, and crowds of people surrounded the premises, everybody being on the alert, but nobody able to detect the agency by which the windows were broken before their eyes. Of course there was talk of spirits, ghosts, and similar nonsense, but one reporter, on visiting the place last night with Sergeant Larner, became convinced that the dastardly outrage was the work of some malicious wretch, who seems to have a design upon the life of the poor woman lying helpless in bed. Dr. Dimock, who has been attending Mrs. Penhalluriack, states that something serious, if not fatal, may follow upon the shock to his patient caused by the atrocity. One or two panes were broken yesterday whilst Dr. Dimock was in the house, but strange to say, not a pane was cracked in the window of the bedroom where Mrs. Penhalluriack is lying.

Several stones were found in the house, and these appear to have come from the outside but there is a very strong theory that some of the panes must have been broken from the inside. The backyard is close fenced all round, and a low verandah shades the two back windows, in addition to which blanketing was hung upon the verandah in such a way as to make it next to impossible that a stone could reach the windows from the outside; yet several of the top panes were broken after these precautions had been taken, and one of these panes was certainly struck on the inside as the glass is bulging outwards round the small hole made by a pebble. The only persons who were in the house whilst most of the smashing was going on were Mrs. Thomas, the nurse, and a servant girl named Percifone Jouva. The former was in close attendance on her patient, but the latter, a young woman of about 20, was doing the household work and states that she has several narrow escapes of being struck by the stones, some of which came bouncing into the room just as she was entering it.

> *One or two of the stones, on being picked up were warm, as though they had been carried in some person's pocket.*

Despite the fact that the only strange phenomenon mentioned in this article was stone-throwing – no levitation, rapping, materialisations, etc. – it does contain a couple of details that, if we knew no more of the case, might have seemed significant. Firstly, the fact that a couple of the stones were said to be noticeably warm (in July – the middle of winter) is reminiscent of the warm, even very hot, stones reported in other, stronger cases. Secondly, as several other Australian and foreign cases involve invalids, the fact that a woman was lying, seriously ill, inside the house might have suggested this was a genuine polt episode.

Unfortunately, however, as the *Courier* reported on 1 July, the stone-thrower was all too human:

> *… the perpetrator of the outrage has been discovered … The servant girl, Persifone Jouva … In her absence the dress she wore on the Saturday was searched, and some … small pebbles, similar to those which had done so much mischief, were found in the pockets.*
>
> *On her return … she made a clean breast of it … she smashed the whole of the windows without the aid of an accomplice… She only did it for fun, she said; but … it is evident she is a wilful and dangerous person … She had only been a fortnight in Penhalluriack employ … she was taken to her own home by her mother.*

Sources:

Ballarat Courier, 30 Jun and 1 Jul 1873.

The Argus (Melbourne), 1 and 2 Jul 1873.

The Mercury (Hobart), 8 Jul 1873.

Our comments:

Busted!

Case 7

April 1881. Hugundra, near Berridale, NSW.
Rating: ★★★

Just as this book was about to go to press, Mr. Ian Burke, of Berridale, who is researching the history of his local area, kindly provided us with this very interesting story from the *Goulburn Evening Penny Post*, 26 April 1881 (opposite).

On 27 April a *Manaro Mercury and Cooma and Bombala Advertiser* journalist took a very different tack to the *Penny Post*. Not bothering to visit the site, which was only about 35 kilometres from his office, and offering no evidence to support his opinion, he derided all the eyewitnesses as superstitious fools and suggested that the rapping and other phenomena had been caused by possums, native cats or by hoaxers within the Robinson family.

Ironically, however, though the journalist was so blindly sceptical, he provided us with a couple of additional details that strongly suggest the episode was genuinely paranormal. He mentions that a pair of witnesses standing beside a metal safe inside the house counted "fifty-two raps as if they were given by a saddler's hammer on a hollow case". Another, William Smith, said that as he was sitting on a bed, it "... tilted him up. He called to his companion to strike a light, and while the latter was getting a match ready he was struck rather violently on the nose".

Most tellingly, the sceptical journalist tells us that the girl who seemed to be the focus of the weird phenomena was – like so many other central characters in poltergeist events throughout the centuries – an adolescent: thirteen, going-on-fourteen years of age.

ODDS AND ENDS.

A Cooma exchange is responsible for the following:—It appears that for the past fortnight a selector named Charles Robinson, residing at Hugundra, has been disturbed at night by unearthly noises, and wrappings at the bedroom door of his children's sleeping apartment. He acquainted his neighbors of the unaccountable occurrences, and of course was laughed at by them, they averring that it must be superstitious fancy of his. However, as the man seemed so very earnest and troubled about the matter, Mr. Robt. Evans, of Kiah Lake, together with four other men determined to investigate the affair and consequently repaired to Roberson's house on Wednesday night last, with the determination of having ocular demonstration on the subject. So soon as they entered the haunted chamber, a violent tapping was heard under the bed where a large empty box was placed; the box was of course dragged out and found to contain nothing, and whilst commenting on the strangeness of the knocking a terrible crashing was heard as though some one was hurling bricks at the door of the room; a rush was made by the men in the room at the door and whilst so doing the blankets and bedding were dragged from off the bed, and thrown about the room by an invisible hand in a most mysterious manner. The visitors remained during the night and the noises were continued at intervals until daylight. This is exactly as it was narrated by Mr. Evans himself, who states that he never was a superstitious man or a believer in ghosts, but at the same time he holds this is one of the strangest incidents that has come under his personal experience during his life. Since writing the above we learn from another source that eight of Mr. Roberson's neighbours slept in the house on Thursday night and were all witnesses of the strange phenomena narrated above. The noises are said to resemble the sound of kissing, and loud taps at the wall in all parts of the room and under the floor. The noises can only be heard in the dark, and immediately a light is struck they cease. Every morning everything in the room is found in a state of the utmost confusion. Every effort has been made by the neighbors to unearth the mystery but without avail, the floor boards even having been taken up where the noises were heard, but no clue could be discovered as to the cause of the strange sounds. No the least remarkable part of the matter, however, is that a little girl appears to be the especial victim of the "Ghosts," if such they be, as she is thrown about the room with the bedclothing. The child is said to be nearly deranged by the frights she has received. Several residents of Cooma have gone out to investigate the affair, and a profound sensation has been created in town over the event. The matter sounds very like what might be expected at a Spiritualistic Séance. Surely there are no mediums at Hugundrah.

Ruins of the old house at Hugundra. (Joanne McDonald, *Snowy River Echo*)

Sources:

The Empire (Sydney), 20 Oct 1869.

Goulburn Evening Penny Post, 26 Apr 1881.

Manaro Mercury and Cooma and Bombala Advertiser, 27 Apr 1881.

Ian Burke and Joanne McDonald, "The Devil's Elbow – One of Monaro's Most Mysterious Places", *Snowy River Echo*, Jun 2014.

Our comments:

The range of phenomena reported at the Robinson residence by so many apparently reputable witnesses – the "terrible crashing", the constant, untraceable rapping on walls and under the floor, the dragging and throwing of bedclothes, the tilting of the bed with Mr. Smith upon it, plus the levitation of the unfortunate adolescent girl – makes us strongly inclined to accept the episode as genuinely paranormal.

While it's unfortunate the spook didn't elect to perform its tricks in daylight or while the lamps were burning, we consider the case worthy of a solid three-star rating.

Further research by Ian Burke, the Berridale historian who alerted us to the case, indicates that the series of strange events at Hugundra ceased by June 1881. That, too, may suggest the episode was genuinely paranormal, as our records show that many other well-attested poltergeist cases have petered out after similar periods of time.

Interestingly, Ian has also discovered that a particularly gruesome suicide occurred on the Robinson property twelve years prior to the poltergeist episode. *The Empire* (Sydney) told the tragic story on 20 October 1869:

Last week a magisterial inquiry was held at Hugundra … before Arthur Blomfield, Esq., J.P., touching the death of one Joseph Barnes, a shepherd in the employ … of Mr. C. G. Robinson … it appears that the unfortunate man had for some time previous … been labouring under the delusion that he was constantly pursued by devils, and this so preyed upon his mind that he cut his throat in a most frightful manner, severing the veins and arteries, laying everything bare, even to the vertebrae.

The result of the enquiry was that the deceased committed suicide whilst labouring under temporary insanity. It may be stated that the deceased was not addicted to the use of spirituous liquors, and his mental condition may therefore be attributed to the monotonous life he led as a shepherd.

Ian notes that there is a notorious series of bends on a section of Rocky Plain Road that passes through what was once part of the Robinson property. Known locally as Devil's Elbow, that stretch of road "… has long had a reputation for mystery, and local residents tend to hurry past after dark." He speculates that it may have acquired its ominous name as a result of Joseph Barnes's suicide.

The road at Devil's Elbow today. (Joanne McDonald, *Snowy River Echo*)

We find it interesting that the unfortunate Mr. Barnes was not an alcoholic and was therefore not suffering from delirium tremens. While the magistrate suggested his death was due to "the monotonous life he led as a shepherd", we think it worth noting, given what occurred on the property twelve years later, that many other people who have been plagued by poltergeists throughout the centuries have assumed they were being persecuted by demons.

While investigating the Hugundra story, Ian and local newspaper editor Joanne McDonald (who took the atmospheric photographs that adorn these pages) interviewed 94-year-old Ron Flanagan, whose family has owned parts of the property for many years. Mr. Flanagan recalled that, when he was young, people who travelled the road which at that time crossed the creek near the ruins of the old homestead, often saw a mysterious white object moving from the house towards the old outdoor toilet.

He also said that horses ridden across the creek at that point invariably became agitated and refused to drink. Other old residents of the area, including Ian's late mother, have testified to the truth of that detail.

It may also be worth noting that what became the Robinson property had previously been, apparently, a site of some importance to the Aborigines: the term *Hugundra*, *Hugundree* or *Huegundree*, Ian has discovered, is said to translate as "place of meeting". Encompassing, as it does, a couple of good creeks plus a small lake, it must always have been a desirable spot – so it is possible that dark deeds occurred there when the traditional owners were dispossessed in the early 1800s.

Even today, many locals, including Ian himself, feel there is "something about the place" – something distinctly creepy – around the old Hugundra homestead.

Case 8

1881. Bendigo, VIC. Rating: Half a star

In early 1956, after reading about the intense poltergeist activity at Mayanup, WA, (Chapter Two), Mr. John Sutch wrote to the *Australasian Post* to describe a similar episode he'd witnessed 75 years earlier:

… when I was a youngster and lived in Bridge Street, Bendigo (V.) in 1881 … our house suffered a severe bombardment of stones of all sizes, day by day, for about a week and then stopped as suddenly as it started. Strange to say, the stones always ceased to fall after dark, but resumed at daybreak. My old Dad, like myself, did not believe in the existence of ghosts or poltergeists and enlisted the aid of the police. Directed by a sergeant, they kept strict watch on our house, but failed to find any trace of the culprit. In fact, the stones continued to fall while the police were present. Strange to say, no one was struck by the stones. The Bendigo daily newspapers duly reported and commented on this strange event, but no feasible explanation has ever been given.
John Sutch, 121 King St, Bendigo (V).
Australasian Post, 19 April 1956.

Our comments:

Although Mr. Sutch wrote his letter many years after the event, three aspects of the case suggest it was a genuine polt event: firstly, the "severe bombardment" happened only in broad daylight, secondly the missiles never (in classic polt style) hurt anyone and thirdly, they continued to fall while police were on watch.

On the other hand, the episode consisted only of stones falling outdoors and it occurred in an urban area – which leaves open the possibility that John and his dad were the victims of hoaxers – albeit very determined and resourceful ones with an awful lot of spare time on their hands.

Case 9

MARCH–APRIL 1887. COOYAL, 20 KM NORTH-WEST OF MUDGEE, NSW.
RATING: ★★★★

(The "Ghostly Missiles" case. See Chapter Seven).

Case 10

MARCH–MAY 1887. YANYARRIE, 60 KM NORTH-EAST OF PORT AUGUSTA, SA.
RATING: HALF A STAR

For what was, essentially, a fairly unremarkable case, this episode generated a surprisingly amount of coverage by local and national newspapers. Most of the early articles, such as the one below, seem to have been based on an April 27th report by the Cradock correspondent of *The South Australian Advertiser*.

From the *West Australian*, 10 May 1887:

A STRANGE PHENOMENON
A mysterious ghost story comes from near Yanyarrie, about 17 miles from Cradock, and is creating a sensation here. It appears that at a house of a farmer named Hamdorff during the past several weeks an unaccountable knocking has been heard in various parts of the building. On Monday night Mounted-constable Mitchell, accompanied by Messrs. H. Hayward and A. J. Graham, proceeded to the place, determined to thoroughly investigate the matter. It was a dark and lonely drive, and the party arrived at the house about half-past 8, and found the place a pine-and-pug tenement on the banks of the Boolcunda Creek, about 30 yards from a waterhole.

The proprietor had left for Quorn, taking with him his wife and a little girl about 7 years old, who, they thought, had seemed to attract the knocks, as they stated the noises had almost invariably proceeded from that part of the house in which the child was at the moment. Two boys, aged about fourteen and nine respectively, were keeping house, and the party, in merry incredulity, ate their provisions, let the fire go down, and about 9 p.m. blew out the light, the boys having told them that the "ghost" appeared soon after the light was extinguished.

Within two or three minutes two of the party heard a low distant sound as of a splash from a heavy stone dropped into a pool of water, followed by a footstep, immediately succeeded by a distinct knocking at the outside of the chimney. Two at once went outside, but could see nothing (it was a very dark night), but heard the knocking on the inside. The knocking was as loud and distinct as an ordinary knock at the door. After a few minutes Mr. Mitchell went outside, and Messrs. Hayward and Graham took his place inside, but to each the knocking appeared to proceed from the other side of the wall.

They asked various questions, which were replied to by knocks, and one of the party asked the knocker to 'knock louder', the next shook the building. After nearly an hour's duration the noise ceased about 6 p.m. About 2 a.m., their nerves having become somewhat calmed, they would soon have been asleep, but the same sounds recommenced, and continued till nearly 3 a m., when the supernatural visitant decamped, leaving no trace behind. During the second visit they each went round and round the house in turns, but to no purpose, though the knocking was heard at almost every part, and several times so sharp as to make the building tremble.

Many of the neighbours and residents of Carrieton attest the reality of the sounds. Of course there are incidental rumours afloat of a shepherd drowned near the spot many years ago and of a flitting form having been observed by people out at night horse-hunting, but, whatever may be the cause, I have it on the authority of Trooper Mitchell that the noises as narrated do occur, and that the performance is weird and eerie in the extreme.

So, from our point of view, the story began promisingly enough.

Although she was absent during the events described above, the person who was believed to be the focus of the strange phenomena was seven-year-old Sissy Schulz, who was living with Mr. Hamdorff and his wife.

After leaving the family home, the Hamdorffs took the little girl, firstly, to a hut three miles distant, where Sissy's father joined them. There, in a well-lit room, Mr. A. Mitchell and three other visitors heard tapping coming from the flag stone floor. It seemed to follow Sissy around the room and continued even when they had a firm grip on both of her hands and feet.

Pretty interesting. But then, unfortunately, things got a just a little *too* preposterous, even for the likes of us.

After Sissy was put to bed on a mattress on the floor and appeared to be asleep or in a trance more tapping ensued that was somehow decoded by the witnesses. It purported to come from Sissy's mother Rebecca, who had died five years earlier. Her spirit then supposedly tapped-out a rather implausibly large amount of information, including the place she wanted Sissy to live, the age at which the girl would die, that she should be christened and raised as an Anglican, that she (Rebecca) disliked a particular little boy, and that she would appear to her husband and Mrs. Harmdorff at midnight if everyone else left the house.

Rebecca seems to have reneged on that promise and very soon thereafter young Sissy was visited by Mr. J.A. Jones, a local schoolmaster, who claimed to have caught her in the act of faking some raps and to have proved her trances were feigned. Although the letters to various newspapers in which he detailed his findings are so dense and prolix that they almost defy summary, Jones comes across as such an intelligent and honest investigator that it is difficult to believe he could have been mistaken.

His report triggered a series of heated rebuttals by people who claimed to have heard truly inexplicable rapping while Sissy was being closely observed and, in some cases, to have received electric shocks on touching her forehead. A barrage of very wordy counter-rebuttals and counter-counter-rebuttals followed until, on 5 August, the editor of the *South Australian Register* pronounced that "The discussion must end here". As all the other newspapers followed suit we don't know whether the poltergeist (or perhaps more likely) the hoaxer continued its/her activities after that date.

Our comments:

Although Mr. Jones' sceptical report is quite impressive, and while we can't credit the messages supposedly tapped out by Rebecca Schulz's spirit, we are reluctant to dismiss this story altogether because of the wall-shaking thumps reported by Trooper Mitchell and party.

If the knocking was truly so powerful, at times, that it shook the entire building, and if it was impossible to determine whether it emanated from inside or outside the building it seems likely the events at the original Hamdorff residence, at least, were genuinely paranormal.

Sources:

The Burra Record (South Australia), 3, 20 and 31 May 1887.

West Australian (Perth), 10 May 1887.

Western Mail (Perth), 14 May 1887.

South Australian Register, 19 and 20 May, 16 Jun, 11 and 14 Jul, 5 Aug 1887.

South Australian Advertiser, 19, 20, 24 and 28 May, 1, 7, 10, 16 and 29 Jun 1887.

Case 11

c. 1888. About 100 km east of Hay, NSW.
Rating: ★★½

This unusual incident occurred during a severe drought, as a jackeroo and two stockmen were driving a herd of 130 horses eastwards along the banks of the Murrumbidgee between Hay and Wagga Wagga.

A MYSTERY OF THE BUSH
(By Blue Jacket)

… we passed through Hay, and had got about 60 miles up the river … we had permission from the owner… to camp in a stockyard about 3 miles from the river bank. It was built of good posts and rails, with two large gates, in the centre of a plain, with no trees of any description within a mile.

As the sun was sinking, we rounded the horses up, and put them in the stockyard … fastening the gate securely. We then unsaddled our own beasts, hobbled them … and lit a fire to boil the "billy." By the time we had finished our meal it was quite dark, and we then spread our blankets ready for turning in. As the horses were in a securely fastened paddock, I told the men that there was no need for a watch …. piling more wood on the fire [we] lay down.

I was camped … near the fire, while the two men were lying a few yards away. It must have been about 10 minutes after we had laid down, that, as I was enjoying a smoke and listening to the conversation of the men, I was conscious of a small stick passing over my head and alighting near my feet. Soon after I received a smart tap on the head. I turned round with a start, and asked my companions what they meant by throwing sticks at me? They indignantly replied that they had done nothing of the kind. I remarked that it looked rather funny, and stretched myself out again. A little while after another stick landed on my nose, and this time I told them rather savagely that I would have no more of their foolery. They were most emphatic in their assertions that they had done nothing of the kind. Once more I turned in, but was startled by an exclamation from one of the men, who said that a stick had hit him in the eye.

This time we all sat up, and looked at one another … our saddle and packhorses were running about wildly, while the horses in the yard were snorting and tramping about in a most extraordinary manner. At first we thought they were being let out of the gate … by some person trying to steal them. We went and had a survey of the yard, but found everything secure, and returned to our blankets, talking, and wondering whatever was up. We had not been long turned in again when we could see sticks coming in all directions. I caught one: it was about three inches long. We could not rest with this phenomena unsolved, and so we got up and took a wide circuit round the yard to see if we could find the cause of the mystery. We failed to find anything, but as we were returning a clod of earth whizzed past my head, shattering itself into pieces as it fell to the ground. This was followed by a shower of sticks.

Things were getting rather lively …. We had no firearms, but all the same we shouted out, for the benefit of all whom it might concern, that the first object appearing in view we would put a bullet into it. Valiant words to sing out, no doubt, but at the same time we felt anything but happy. Things remained quiet for a time, and our courage returned; in fact we were laughing over the affair, when, in the middle of a lively grin, with my mouth pretty well open, I just had time to close my jaws on the tail-end of a stick that was disappearing down my throat!

For a few minutes the sticks were at it again, and then quieted down. We were in a deuce of a fright, for we could not make out where they came from. We took another walk around the camp, strained our eyes and listened, but could not see or hear anything. Putting more wood on the fire we patiently waited for the moon to rise, which would be about 12 o'clock. Soon after the horizon in the eastward commenced to lighten up, and the moon soon appeared. Objects now became clearer, and we could see a good distance around. By this time we thought that we could now safely venture to turn in. But no: along came another shower of sticks, little and big, falling around us for the space of two minutes. As we could see pretty well now all around the plain, we felt no fear, and soon after, being tired out, fell asleep.

Byron sang "It is sweet to be awakened by the lark." Nice, no doubt, but it is a different thing to be awakened by a man kicking you with a hard boot. I was aroused this way by one of the men the morning after our nocturnal adventure. While the breakfast was getting cooked I had a look at the horses, counted them, and found them all right. After breakfast, as we were saddling up and, laughing over the events of the night before, one of my men sung out "Look out sir!" and as I turned half round to look up, I was struck with such force on the right cheek by a flying stick, that the blood flowed from the wound, and this in broad day light!

I picked up the missile, and examined it. It was about 4 inches long, shaped like a boomerang and weighed about 4 ounces. The man told me he saw it whizzing along straight for me. A lot of talking was indulged in, and soon afterwards we resumed our journey. When I arrived at our destination I left the horses, paid off the men, and returned homewards alone … As I passed the mysterious stockyard on my return, I took good care that it was in daylight.

Oftentimes since I have wondered where the mystery lay. When I arrived in Hay I was told that this yard was built on an aboriginal burying ground, and what was most curious, several persons have been troubled the same way as I was. About a month afterwards, happening to pass through Hay, a friend told me that a teamster had been found lying insensible near this spot, with his skull split open. As Shakespeare says, "There are more things in Heaven and Earth than are dreamt of in your philosophy."

Source:

The West Australian, 30 Apr 1888.

Our comments:

We like this story because it is a first-hand account and because it is written in the style – dated, yet lucid and engaging – one would expect from a well-educated bushman of the late nineteenth century. We believe it has a distinct ring of truth. It is interesting also, because of its similarity to two other cases where polt phenomena seemed to be confined to particular locations in the bush (Cases 26 and 41).

Several details are quite significant:

The behaviour of the horses – "running about wildly", "snorting and stamping" – recalls the panicky reaction of horses in other cases, e.g. those at Cooyal in 1887 and at Granite Creek in 1935.

The incident occurred on a dead-flat, virtually treeless plain and, although most of the action took place at night, the site was well-illuminated, from midnight on, by moonlight.

The fact that the sticks came from "all directions" suggests that if the events were hoaxed at least a couple of people were involved. It seems certain that, given their unimpeded field of view, "Blue Jacket" and his mates would have seen at least one of the perpetrators.

As at Humpty Doo, there is a suggestion here that the polt eavesdropped on its victims' conversation: during the interlude when the men's "courage returned" and "Blue Jacket" was "laughing over the affair", a stick flew into his mouth and part-way down his throat. In the morning, when he next dared to laugh, he was struck quite violently.

The claim that the haunted stockyard was built on the site of an Aboriginal graveyard is also quite interesting. We have already mentioned the involvement of Aboriginal shamans in the Mayanup case and the possibility that an Aboriginal curse was one of the "triggers" of the Humpty Doo episode.

Case 12

"Spirits" at Adelong.

The following letter, narrating some rather extraordinary proceedings at Adelong, has been handed to us for publication by the lady who received it. It is given *verbatim et literatum*:—

"Main Adelong, Sept. 2nd, 1889.

"Dear sister,—I have strange news for you this time, but don't think I am larking. Last Monday night J. Stanton came running to our house in a great fright, he could not tell mother what was up for a long time. At last he told her someone was throwing stones at his house, and he could not see them. It started Monday night, and kept on until yesterday, just a week. He (Stanton) went for the police, and on Saturday he came for old Dan, and old Dan went up about three o'clock, and the first thing was too big stones feel at his feet. He did not know what to do; he stopped till nine o'clock, and it never stopped while he was there. In the night knocks were heard at all sides of the house, and showers of dry dirt came all over everything in the house. It troubles no one but poor little Nellie, she cannot go anywhere but it is after her. Old Dan ran home. The next day about 10 o'clock I went up, and I never saw such a thing before. The stones came there as soon as I came. I got frightened, and hooked it. They came from all ways over the house, some as big as my two fists, but hurt no one. No one can see them rise. Old Dan saw one rise from the ground when no one was near it. I saw stones, and sticks, and all sorts of rubbish fly from in the house out of the chimney. The stones and sticks came too thick for me to stand it. It only haunts poor little Nellie. I told Fred and Carl, they went up that night and they saw more than they ever want to see again. Nellie can tell them when it is there. We believe she can see it all the time. No one can hear it gathering up the dirt, only the children of the house. On Sunday Hogan, Carter, Mrs. Caspersome, and all the Watsons went up. Stanton had to take Nellie to Carlton's early on Sunday morning, it came too strong, the girl was getting afraid. She had no rest day or night. The last night it came that bad that they put Nellie before the fire to sleep, and Stanton could not hold out any longer; the bed she was lying on rose up from the floor, and nothing but scratching and knocking under her. When the dirt used to come, Stanton used to swear, and it came thicker. When he saw the bed rising he grabbed but got nothing. All this went on all day long, I stopped there about an hour, and I never want to see it any more. While Fred and Carl and Amalong were there it was that bad I could tell you, Nellie said she saw a hand and that is all she saw. Everybody round here were there, and they all say it is a spirit, but no one knows what for. It nearly drove Stanton mad. It is a warning for something. Now, don't you think that I am larking! For all who were there never wish to see or hear the like again. It has no power to hurt anyone. While I was there the stones came all over the chairs among the children, but hit nor hurt no one. They all came that easy, if they hit you, you would not feel them. Next time I will tell you more, but it is rather too frightening now.—Yours truly,

AUGUST EICHHORN."

25–31 AUGUST 1889.
ADELONG, NSW. RATING: ★★★

From *The Bathurst Free Press and Mining Journal*, 24 Sept 1889:

SPIRITS AT ADELONG

The correspondent of the Adelong Argus writes as follows:

Mr. John Stanton, a selector, resides with his family about five miles from [Adelong] ... On Monday night, the 25th of August, about 8 o'clock, the family was much alarmed by stones, dirt, &c., being showered on their residence by some unseen ... agency ... this ... was continued until the following Sunday morning, when Mr. Stanton thought it desirable to take his daughter, a girl about 11 years old, to the residence of Mr. Cottam ... about three miles away. It is somewhat remarkable that all disturbing manifestations ceased as soon as the child was removed.

[The Stanton residence] *stands by itself in an open space ... no other residence near it where any evil-disposed person could hide ... The general impression is that the rappings and stone-throwing are the result of other than human agency. A miner, who was there on Friday, assures me that two stones as big as his fist came over the roof of the cottage, and fell one on each side of him. He went at once to see who had thrown them, and there was no one to be seen.*

On 5 October 1889 the *Ovens and Murray Advertiser* published a first-hand account from a Mr. August Eichorn. As it paints such a vivid picture of the proceedings it is well worth reproducing here in full.

Sources:

The Bathurst Free Press and Mining Journal, 24 Sept 1889.

The Ovens and Murray Advertiser, 5 Oct 1889.

Two Worlds magazine, 31 Jan 1890.

Our comments:

If this episode occurred as described in the *Bathurst Free Press and Mining Journal* and in Mr. Eichorn's vivid account we have little doubt it was a genuine polt event. All of the remarkable ingredients mentioned – the sticks and stones that flew, indoors and out, without ever hurting people; the scratching and knocking; the targeting of "poor little Nellie"; the levitating bed; even the sighting of the ghostly hand – correspond with phenomena observed during several of our best-documented cases.

Case 13

1891–94. Coalbaggie Creek, 35km north of Dubbo, NSW. Rating: ★★★½

("The Coalbaggie Bogey" case. See Chapter Eleven.)

Case 14

July 1892. South Melbourne, VIC. Rating: Zero

This little case illustrates why we should be very hesitant to accept every instance of simple stone-throwing – particularly those that occur in urban areas – as genuine poltergeist events.

All we know about the incident comes from two Melbourne *Argus* articles. Had we seen only the first of them we may have been tempted to give the story the benefit of the doubt and award it a "Half-star" rating. The follow-up article, however, comprehensively skewers the case: it was definitely a hoax.

On Monday 18 July *The Argus* reported that between 4 pm on the previous Thursday and 8 pm on Friday two dozen panes of glass had been broken by flying stones and pieces of coal at 127 and 129 Heather Street, South Melbourne. The occupants could not "explain why the damage should have been done, nor can they imagine from what quarter the stones came."

When the first panes were broken, the tenants "rushed out to ascertain the cause, and had hardly got into the yard when a volley broke in the large panes in the front of the house … several members of the police in plain clothes, and civilians as well, set watch … all round the houses. Even when they watched the stones continued to fly and the glass to crash, and it could not be discovered where they came from."

But on July 20th the *Argus* announced the mystery was over: two policemen had collared 10-year-old Frederick Moncrieff in the act of breaking a window. By that time the little menace had broken a total of fifty. "He then … explained his dexterity … by showing how he jerked the missiles from behind his back even when standing alongside of the police."

In those days corporal punishment was common in homes and schools. While we're glad it is now more or less a thing of the past, we can't help hoping that some of it was vigorously applied to young Frederick's backside!

Source:

The Argus (Melbourne), 18 and 20 Jul 1892.

Case 15

c. August 1892–July 1893. Maclean, NSW.
Rating: Zero

From *The Argus* (Melbourne), 17 Jan 1893:

A STRANGE CASE
Some five or six months ago ... George Hart was drowned ... and ... his childless widow continued to reside in [their] house ... From a few days after his death ... stones and other missiles were, night after night, hurled upon the roof with monotonous regularity, and on one occasion the verandah screen was set on fire ... police and civilians watched regularly ... but without gaining the slightest clue.

Sometimes stones would strike the roof in almost opposite directions; then knocking would be heard underneath the house, and although those on the look-out would rush off in the direction whence it ... had come, no sign of anyone could be seen. [Many] windows have been smashed to atoms, and the iron roof ... damaged.

Mrs. Hart has now become insane, and she has been removed to the Grafton Gaol for medical treatment. A few of the residents have offered a reward for the conviction of the offender, but so far not the slightest clue has been obtained.

This episode, which featured in many other newspaper articles between January and July 1893, is further good ammunition for sceptics. Although it featured two or three hallmarks of polt activity, plus repeated suggestions that it was a supernatural event, and although it remained unsolved for at least six months, it was finally revealed as a cruel hoax.

The stone-throwing resumed as soon as poor Mrs. Hart was released after two weeks in the asylum. It continued for 16 days until, on the night of 13 February, the police caught a neighbour, William Bateman, and his son Denis "red-handed". While the despicable duo were in the lock-up three more stones were thrown, and police arrested two more of William's sons.

Despite the arrest and speedy conviction of the Batemans the stone-throwing continued

The Maclean Mystery.
A HAUNTED HOUSE.

(*Australian Town and Country Journal*, 11 March 1893)

for at least a further ten nights. Although Bateman senior and his three sons were reportedly still in jail during that period, it is possible that other members of the vicious clan were still at large and in the mood for mischief – or that unrelated hooligans decided to "copy-cat" the nasty behaviour.

Sceptics will be heartened to learn that despite the apprehension and successful conviction of the Batemans, a Sydney spiritualist, C. Haviland, was, as late as 18 April, calling for their release on the grounds that the stone-throwing was clearly the work of a polt.

A creepy sleeper

The final item in our file, from the *Sydney Morning Herald*, 15 July 1893, provides a suitably odd postscript: on the night of 12 July the long-suffering Mrs. Hart had her nerves further tested when she discovered William Bateman (Junior) "… snugly curled up underneath the bedclothes in her room." William, who the police stated had "… for some time past been showing signs of insanity", stated that "… he got through the window, and only wanted to have a sleep."

Young Willie's creepy sleepover seems to have been the last straw for the honest folk of Maclean. The article goes on to report that immediately after that incident, "some unknown persons showered a number of stones on a house [the Bateman's, one assumes] near Mrs. Hart's, and sent the occupier a threatening letter to the effect that if stone-throwing was not discontinued … their house would be blown up by dynamite". After that, "not a single stone has been thrown on Mrs. Hart's premises."

So, another promising story bites the dust. Again we are reminded why we should never assume that all episodes consisting almost entirely of stone-throwing – however difficult the perpetrators may be to catch – involve polt activity – particularly when they occur in built-up areas.

On the other hand, this case did not consist *entirely* of stone-throwing. As we have seen, our earliest source – the 17 Jan 1893 Melbourne *Argus* article – mentioned, very briefly, that during the stone-falls, "knocking would be heard underneath the house". That small detail isn't much for die-hard "true believers" to cling onto, but it would be remiss of us not to mention it.

Sources:

Argus (Melbourne), 17 Jan, 14 and 22 Feb 1893.

Brisbane Courier, 17 Jan and 2 Feb 1893.

West Australian, 3 and 23 Feb 1893.

Maitland Mercury and Hunter River General Advertiser, 14, 16 and 23 Feb, 30 Mar, 13 Apr, 18 Jul 1893.

Sydney Morning Herald, 4 and 17 Feb, 5 and 19 Apr, 15 Jul 1893.

Case 16

January 1893. Gulgong, NSW. Rating: ★★

From the *Maitland Mercury & Hunter River General Advertiser*, 31 January 1893:

The Western Post says:-
A mysterious affair is reported from Three Mile, near Gulgong. It is declared that the old residence of Mr. B. Naughton (now occupied by a man named Deane) is haunted. For some nights past stones have been hurled with monotonous regularity against the walls and on to the roof of the house, and, although a crowd of people are on watch, they have been unable to discover from whence the missiles proceed. Strange noises were heard above the ceiling, and, thinking an opossum or some other animal was the cause of the rustling, the calico was torn down, but no sign of anything could be seen, and the noises still continue. A few nights since a huge boulder, which was apparently too large to come through the chimney without being forced, dropped into the fire-place.

A peculiarity of the whole affair is that the stones, which apparently strike against the walls with considerable velocity, leave no mark. Great excitement prevails in the locality, and at night the place is crowded with curious visitors, all of whom try in vain to solve the mystery. The particulars of the Three Mile mystery are collateral with those of the Cooyal case some few years ago, and which has not been solved up to the present.

Our comments:

Three elements of this case suggest hoaxing:
 Firstly, because the stones fell (apparently) only at night, it is impossible to rule out the possibility that they were launched by practical jokers armed with easily-concealable "shanghais"; secondly, although many struck the exterior, there is no mention of stones (other than the "huge boulder") falling inside the house.
 The fact that this episode began soon after the widely-reported Maclean case, might suggest it was the work of a "copy cat" hoaxer.
 On the other hand, three other factors strongly suggest genuine polt activity:
 Firstly, even after the calico ceiling was entirely removed, the source of the "strange noises" in the loft could not be found; secondly because the stones, which struck the walls "with considerable velocity" *left no mark* (like those at Humpty Doo and other polt sites), and finally because the "boulder" that dropped into the fireplace was apparently too large to have come down the chimney without being forced. As we have seen, this is not the only time that objects too large for any available aperture have found their way into houses (and tents and cars, for that matter).

Case 17

FEBRUARY 1893. STANMORE NSW.
RATING: HALF A STAR

From *The Maitland Mercury & Hunter River General Advertiser*, 16 February 1893:

MYSTERIOUS STONE THROWING.
There appears to be what may be called an epidemic of stone throwing and producing noise in the mysterious manner which we have noted of late as prevalent at the Maclean, in Melbourne, and other places. The Echo says During the past week several of the residents of Stanmore, and more particularly one family residing in Marshall Street, have been subjected to considerable annoyance and inconvenience owing to the actions of some mysterious person, who persists in throwing stones on the roofs of the houses, and attempting to open the doors. The disturbances began in Marshall Street early in the week, and, with one or two exceptions, have continued every night since, and, although strenuous efforts have been made to capture the author of them, all the attempts have signally failed.

The performances started with regularity at about a quarter past 7 each evening, and were kept up with very little intermission till very late in the night, or rather, early in the morning. During the whole of the time the inhabitants of the house mentioned were in a state of terror and dismay, which was intensified one evening when a large stone crashed through one of the windows, and did considerable damage. During lulls in the stone-throwing, the unfortunate people in the house could hear persons trying the outer doors of the dwelling, but no one ever entered the place. One of the plans adopted for the capture of the unwelcome visitor was to leave one of the outer doors unlocked.

One of the young men of the house posted himself at the door with his hand on the knob ready to fling the door open directly he heard anyone at it from the outside. Presently there was silence, as if the stone-thrower were resting, and in a few seconds more someone was heard outside trying to open the door. The young man inside opened the door immediately, but there was no one about, and in a minute or two more stones fell on the roof.

On one evening a watch was kept by some neighbours, and they stated that although they distinctly heard someone walking about in the garden in front of the house while the stones were being thrown, yet they could not see anyone. Another neighbour stated that on one evening as he was crossing over to the house, he saw a man jump over the fence into the garden, and when he looked in there was no one to be seen. On one evening one of the young men of the house fired the contents of a revolver into some vines growing in the garden, but there was no result. The matter was reported to the police, and a constable in plain clothes was stationed in the garden for one evening, but, as no stranger appeared, he was not sent to the house again.

Other residents in the vicinity have been treated in a somewhat similar manner, with the exception that no stones have been thrown on the roofs. The continual annoyance to which the residents in the house in Marshall Street have been subjected have told on them very much, and some of them are almost worn out for the want of sleep.

Our comments:

There's not much for true believers to pin their hopes on here: the stones fell only at night in, it seems, a residential area, so hoaxing can't be ruled out. The apparent attempts to open doors might also have been cleverly hoaxed. To cap it all off, a prowler – albeit an uncannily elusive one – was actually seen on the property.

The article mentions that there seemed to be "an epidemic" of stone-throwing in various places following the much-publicised Maclean case. So this could well have been the work of copy-cats.

Case 18

May 1894. Enmore, Sydney, NSW.
Rating: Half a star

From the 4th to the 19th of May 1894 three terrace houses in Charles Street, Enmore, were subjected to intense barrages of stones. Most of the "volleys" occurred in broad daylight: at 7 am, 3 pm and 7 pm, each lasting for up to an hour. All the windows in two of the dwellings were smashed or holed and – strangely – further missiles were able to pass very accurately through the original holes.

One house was occupied by a policeman, Senior Constable Bennett, another by the Hurcombe family and the third by a railway porter named McCann.

Even though uniformed police were stationed in a cordon around the block and "several plain clothes officers [were] daily stationed at various elevated positions commanding a full view of the whole of the surroundings" they were unable to spot the perpetrators. So many missiles were gathered from the premises that they soon constituted a large heap in one of the yards. Most were between the size of a pebble and half a brick, but some weighed up to five pounds (2.25 kg). The heaviest, it was said, could not have been thrown further than 30 yards.

At 3 pm one day a three-inch diameter rock flew through the McCanns' kitchen door "when police were secretly stationed in … different positions possessing a full view of the only direction from which the missile could come".

The officer in charge, Sergeant Bradley, noted that although the dining room window of the McCann house was a favourite target of the stone thrower(s), "a more difficult target could not have been chosen" as it was protected and almost hidden from view by two trees. Even when the whole window apart from the top quarter was blocked with a sheet of iron, and the remaining space screened with bags, many stones managed to get through.

One detective, who'd been stationed in a room directly over the window, with a perfect view of the surrounding yards, houses and back lane, expressed his frustration to a *Daily Telegraph* journalist: "I was never so taken aback in my life to have to acknowledge that I cannot see a person who must be within a few yards heave a brick at me. It's preposterous. A few minutes ago, as I was straining my eyes out here, with not a soul in sight and not a leaf stirring on the trees, without the least warning crash came another brick through that ill-fated window."

No polt – just a precocious perp?

Eventually ten-year-old (some reports said twelve-year-old) Eva Grieves was caught red-handed throwing two stones. She had been living with Mr. and Mrs. McCann for three years and most reports referred to her as their adopted daughter.

On the moonlit evening of 17 May Mrs. Hurcome saw Eva throw a stone towards the McCann house. She then picked it up, "conveyed it to her mistress, and informed her that another stone had been thrown". Six days later at 7 am, Senior Constable Meares watched from Mrs. Hurcome's bathroom window as Eva accompanied Mrs. McCann's sister to the outdoor washhouse. In due course, while the adult was occupied with her chores, Eva stepped outside and threw a stone onto the roof.

Eva brick

When confronted by Constable Meares, the girl at first denied the offence, but later "confessed to all". Her *modus operandi*, she said, had been to creep out of the house and throw the stones from under a large castor oil tree that grew in the centre of the yard.

That was the end of Eva's "adoption". It seems, in fact, that she hadn't been adopted at all: she'd been, as the *Barrier Miner* put it, "apprenticed out" to Mrs. McCann by the State Children's Department. Although she'd supposedly been well cared for, it could be that she was being used as cheap or even unpaid labour. Being "a sharp, intelligent child" she may well have been resentful. Be that as it may, after her confession Mrs. McCann refused "to allow the uncanny creature to remain in the house" and she was sent back to the "Industrial School" from whence she came.

So ... the case appears to be a cut-and-dried hoax – another "wake-up call", sceptics might well say, for us "true believers". Fair enough.

End of story? Well, yes ... but ...

Sceptics will, no doubt, roll their eyes at this: but while we accept that a hoaxer was caught fair and square, her confession obviously falls well short of accounting for everything that happened.

It seem very unlikely, for instance, that a ten-year-old girl could have kept up such an intense fusillade of stones – terms such as "volleys" and "bombardment" were repeatedly used – almost entirely in broad daylight, with police in the house, in the yard, and all around for almost two weeks before she was noticed.

At least some of the missiles could not have been thrown from the place where Eva said she hid: on May 10th for instance, stones hit the McCann house "from two different directions" – while police were actually standing in the back yard.

There is no mention, in all of the many reports, of any stones other than the final one thrown by Eva landing on a roof – all of the others, apparently, hit doors and windows with remarkable accuracy.

Some of the stones were so heavy – up to five pounds (2.25 kg) – that the police "expressed astonishment that a girl of [her] age could cause such large stones to reach the window", which was 20 yards (19 metres) from the spot where she supposedly launched them.

As a *Herald* journalist put it, "the strangest part of the affair is the absolute precision of the aim in wielding the stones". After windows had been smashed, further missiles "were able to accurately pass through the original holes." This detail has been noted during many apparently genuine polt cases, including the Humpty Doo episode.

A dream of djinni?

Finally, there is another decidedly strange detail that must be mentioned: during her confession, Eva claimed "that she was told in a dream to throw the stones and was unaware that she was doing wrong: she was simply obeying dreamland commands"!

While that exceptionally weird claim might simply indicate the poor girl was barking mad, it might – just possibly – have other significance. We'd be remiss if we didn't point out that some poltergeist researchers have suggested that on rare occasions polts actually possess people, causing them to do things they would not normally do. (In Muslim lore, too, the polt-like *djinni* is said to occasionally possess unwitting mortals).

Sceptics may well say we are simply grasping at straws. Perhaps that's the case. The stony bombardment, after all, *did* cease when Eva left the neighbourhood, and it must be admitted that the episode featured only two hallmarks of poltergeist involvement: showers of stones from outside the houses, and stones flying with remarkable accuracy through small apertures. There was nothing else: no stones falling indoors, no stones falling unnaturally slowly, no unnaturally warm stones, no wall-banging, no levitation, no materialisation of objects, no weird messages, etc.

Although it seems impossible that Eva threw all, or even most of the stones, we should bear in mind that the events attracted large crowds – on one evening in early May approximately 1000 people assembled outside the house. Local youths hidden among the throng may have decided to enliven the evening sessions, at least, by throwing or catapulting a few extra stones.

So, Eva's weird dreams notwithstanding, we can award this case just half a star.

Sources:

Brisbane Courier, 10, 19 and 23 May 1894.

South Australian Register, 10 May 1894.

The Sydney Morning Herald, 11, 12 May 1894.

The West Australian, 11 May 1894.

The Argus (Melbourne), 12 and 19 May 1894.

The Barrier Miner, 19 May 1894.

The Bay of Plenty Times, 1 Jun 1894.

Case 19

EARLY 1895. SIX-MILE FLAT, NORTH OF BRAIDWOOD, NSW.

RATING: ★★★

From the *Brisbane Courier*, 3 May 1895:

NOCTURNAL BOMBARDMENTS
For some few weeks past considerable excitement has prevailed amongst residents of Six-mile Flat, Warri-Bombay, and Colombo (writes the "Braidwood Dispatch") by a series of extraordinary occurrences, the origin of which is still as deep and impenetrable as ever, notwithstanding the most careful and rigid inquiry, although there are people who refuse to believe anything else than that they are the result of supernatural agency.

It appears that a miner named Cunningham and a mate lived in a hut belonging to Mr. Terence M'Grath, of Colombo, which is situated close to the Shoalhaven River. They had occupied the place for some time, when all of a sudden one night the building was bombarded with clods from an ant bed which had been [dug up] by Cunningham, and which is situated about 100 yards from the hut. The pieces of hard mud penetrated the cracks between the slabs, although how some of them could get through it puzzled them, since they were larger than the opening. They naturally looked about to find the author of the throwing, but without success.

When they went outside, they aver – and their testimony is since corroborated by a number of other witnesses – the clods hit the inside of the building. On the following night a repetition of the business occurred, and the men became somewhat alarmed. They told some others of it, at the same time expressing their belief that the throwing was the work of a ghost. These persons visited the scene, and found the facts exactly as stated by Cunningham and his mate.

The story spread, and others, viewing the matter as a joke, likewise visited the place with the assurance that they at least would discover the origin of these peculiar occurrences. They left in the same happy condition of mystification as those who had preceded them, although they went with guns, which they fired in the direction from where the throwing proceeded. And here we may remark that the clods thrown strike the hut in almost exactly the same place every time between two slabs near the window.

On several occasions no less than eighteen people have been on the lookout at the same time, forming a sort of semi-circle round the side of the hut where the throwing occurs. They fired their guns, loaded with shot, into the bushes of the trees surrounding the place, with such good effect that there is not a tree or log within a couple of hundred yards of the hut that is not riddled with shot.

To make sure that the clods came from the ant bed, a number of them were marked with charcoal, and these have been subsequently found inside the hut, perfectly unbroken. Although the spot is plainly within view of the watchers, and any one visiting it could easily be detected, and to make assurance doubly sure the watchers have actually placed cotton thread on small stakes right round the bed, but this line was not broken or touched, showing that there is no possibility of any one sneaking up to the bed, throwing the clods, and running away.

The most peculiar thing about the matter is that the clod-throwing started simultaneous with the disturbing of the ant bed by Cunningham. And what is still more peculiar, the presence of this man in the hut is absolutely necessary to produce the "manifestations." Without him there is no clod-throwing.

Many sensible, level-headed men have visited the spot, and although loath to believe that the throwing is done by any supernatural agency, they are absolutely unable to account for the proceedings. The throwing usually commences at about half-past 10 o'clock at night, and continues sometimes till daybreak, although as a rule it only lasts for a couple or three hours.

Source:

Brisbane Courier, 3 May 1895, quoting the *Braidwood Dispatch*.

Our comments:

As the property in question is only a few miles north of Braidwood, and as the *Dispatch* journalist seems to have been pretty close to the action, we're reasonably confident that the events unfolded more or less as reported.

Several details strongly suggest polt activity:
- The clods of ant bed repeatedly struck the same spot on the hut's exterior wall.
- On many occasions the "pieces of hard mud penetrated the cracks between the slabs, although … they were larger than the opening." This detail is reminiscent of the "boulder" that found its way into the fireplace in Gulgong in 1893 (Case 16) and of apparent teleportation in many other polt-plagued houses.
- The ant bed was clearly visible from the hut.
- Many eyewitnesses observed the phenomenon.
- Systematic, logical measures were taken to prove or disprove hoaxing: creating a cordon of observers, marking the ant bed with charcoal, erecting a string barrier around it, etc.
- Any hoaxer would have been in dire danger of being shot.
- As in many other polt episodes one person, in this case Cunningham, was the focus of the polt's attention.
- As in a few other cases (e.g. the Mayanup episode, which began after many trees were bulldozed) the activity started immediately after a feature of the landscape was disturbed.

Case 20

Feb 1900. Watsons Bay, Sydney, NSW. Rating: ★

From *The Advertiser* (Adelaide), 7 February 1900:

MYSTERIOUS STONE-THROWING
A stone-throwing mystery is exercising the attention of the police and residents at Watson's Bay. Since Thursday night [1 Feb] the residence of Captain Creer, master of the pilot steamer Captain Cook, has been regularly bombarded with stones. The proceedings opened ... by a large stone flying through the window of the captain's bedroom. After that stones kept dropping on the roof at short intervals, and then other windows were smashed. The same thing occurred on Friday, Saturday, Sunday, and Monday nights, and not a whole window now remains in the house. Several of the occupants ... had narrow escapes. Every effort has been made to discover the attacking party. On Monday evening stones commenced to fall at 7 o'clock, when it was still quite light, and though fully 20 people, including detectives, were watching all round the house from 7 o'clock up to 11 o'clock the bombardment continued, several of the watchers being hit, but the guilty party remained undetected.

The bombardment continued for at least a month, sometimes lasting all night and continuing into broad daylight with detectives and volunteers still on watch.

While a *Warwick Examiner and Times* journalist wrote that "there are large trees and scrub on three sides", all the other reporters agreed that there was "no bush worth speaking of in the vicinity of the house nor any other apparent means for effective concealment".

A journalist acquainted with Captain Creer's family reported that several times, as the detectives kept watch, "stones came with very great force through the windows; instantly [they] rushed out, but ... made no discovery."

On one occasion, he continued, "a young lady friend of mine was in the dining room [with] several members of the family and two policemen ... The moon was shining brightly. Suddenly a stone came through the door ... and passed through the window. The force with which it had been propelled was so strong that it cut through a swinging calico blind that hung in front of the window. The usual rush outside took place, but nobody was visible." As some of the stones weighed all of two pounds (907g) this was clearly a very dangerous situation.

Before long the mystery site began to attract sightseers: "passengers from the ferry boats come and stare at [the] house, and listen to the stones falling, but without seeing whence they come. Of course, Captain Creer, who has lived quite quietly for 20 years at Watsons Bay, doesn't like this notoriety that has been thrust upon him."

Although the bombardment continued for at least a month, we have no record of perpetrators being arrested. Newspaper references to the case ceased in early March, so it seems the episode simply petered out, with the mystery unsolved.

Sources:

Advertiser (Adelaide), 7 Feb 1900.

Mercury (Hobart), 10 Feb 1900.

Warwick Examiner and Times, 14 Feb 1900.

Clarence and Richmond Examiner, 17 Feb 1900.

Kalgoorlie Western Argus, 1 Mar 1900.

Our comments:

As this episode featured no strange phenomena other than outdoor stone-throwing it would be rash to declare it a genuine poltergeist case. On the other hand, the bombardment continued for at least a month, and some of the details mentioned may indicate it was more than just the handiwork of hoaxers:

* Although most of the stones flew at night, several flew "when it was still quite light".

* The fusillades lasted for several hours at a stretch, even as two detectives and up to 20 men kept watch.

* While there are devices capable of propelling a stone with such force that it would enter a door and pass out through a window, cutting a swinging calico blind on the way, it is difficult to imagine how such a device could have been deployed in a setting where there was said to be "no bush worth speaking of in the vicinity of the house nor any other apparent means for effective concealment".

* There appeared to be no motive for the potentially lethal attacks: Captain Creer, it was said, was "very popular at the Bay, where he has resided for over twenty years".

* One newspaper mentioned that "one of the occupants of the house is sick". This could be significant, as invalids have featured in many other poltergeist cases both here and abroad.

Case 21

SEPTEMBER–OCTOBER 1900. NARRABRI, NSW.
RATING: ★★★

From the *Bathurst Free Press and Mining Journal*, 19 October 1900:

A STONE-THROWING MYSTERY
NARRABRI PEOPLE PUZZLED
Narrabri, Thursday.

Parties of police and civilians have been proceeding out nightly to … Stoney Creek. There is a selectors homestead in the vicinity, and stones appear to come upon it from every direction. Strategic movements were arranged; the selector's family remaining indoors, while others surrounded the premises, which were unlit. Almost immediately young Guest … was struck on the cheek. Several have been struck every night. The throwing has been going on for over a month nightly from about dark, continuing several hours.

The stone-throwing took place mostly in open daylight, while a party of police and civilians were watching and some mounted men were scouring around to a distance of 200 yds, The most extraordinary thing is that there are no stones in the vicinity, the soil being a level plain, and the nearest neighbour's house is over a mile away, with scrub intervening. To dispel suspicion all the party submitted to a search, and no stones were found on any of them. The first stones were thrown about half-past 5 o'clock, continuing at intervals till 9 o'clock.

Some unimpeachable residents near, one being a J.P., declare positively that a similar occurrence took place not many miles off some years ago, and that it has never been cleared up. They were engaged tank sinking, and every evening for some weeks clods of earth larger than a man's fist were thrown into their camp, which could not have been projected even with slings without being seen on the open plain.

The *Advertiser* (Adelaide) of 22 October repeated most of the above, but added an intriguing detail:

The stone-throwing mystery … remains unsolved. Mr. Avery's daughter fainted upon being struck with a stone on the foot, but was not seriously hurt. The stone when picked up was found to be quite hot.

The story was continued in the *Singleton Argus* of 23 October:

The theory which was advanced by the police that Avery's daughter was the performer is discounted by the fact that the daughter is now in town, having been brought in for medical treatment. Yet the trouble is as great as before, or rather more so, as the lengthening days do not appear to affect the time of starting the bombardment. There are more stones thrown in daylight now, but the throwing still finishes about the same hour.

Mr. Avery... whose house is the subject of the battery, is a very old resident of the district, and has a large family, all grown up; several sons and daughters residing at the selection.

A family named Stalk, who resided some five miles from Avery's, removed into town some six weeks ago, and it has transpired that they were subjected to almost precisely similar treatment for more than a month. So it may reasonably be surmised that the same cause was operating in their case. Avery, the present subject, is not a man likely to be driven to desert his home, nor are his family weak-nerved.

Avery's sons state that the stones come from two different directions, north-east and south-west. Young Avery and his brother-in-law went in each directions and fired shots. As each shot was fired a stone was returned as if in answer and resembling an echo.

One night James Avery, the eldest son, remained at home by himself, the rest ... being in Narrabri. The stones came as usual.

Sources:

Bathurst Free Press and Mining Journal, 19 Oct 1900.

Singleton Argus, 20 and 23 Oct 1900.

Advertiser (Adelaide), 22 Oct 1900.

Northern Star (Lismore), 24 Oct 1900.

Mercury, (Hobart), 25 Oct 1900.

Warwick Examiner and Times, 27 Oct 1900.

Australian Town and Country Journal, 27 Oct 1900.

Poverty Bay Herald, 31 Oct 1900.

Our comments:

How could we not like this case? Not only does it contain a couple of hallmarks of polt activity, plus some interesting, unique features, but its location couldn't have been more appropriate: a stone-throwing sensation at Stoney Creek!

Several details strongly suggest it was a genuine polt event:

Although the stone showers didn't occur indoors, as at Humpty Doo and other places, they were extremely persistent and well-attested. The bombardment came from different directions for hours on end, day and night, and persisted for over a month. The property was situated on a level plain and the nearest neighbour lived over a mile away.

We find it very significant that the stone-throwing continued "in open daylight" while police and civilians surrounded the house and "mounted men were scouring around to a distance of 200 yards", and that the investigators were so thorough: everyone in the party was frisked for stones.

It is also interesting that the polt must have transported (or should we say teleported?) its ammunition for some distance because there were, despite the presumably ironic place-name, "no stones in the immediate area."

At least one stone (like many at Humpty Doo, Mayanup and other well-documented polt sites) "was found to be quite hot". It is interesting that that particular stone – the only one said to be hot – hit Mr. Avery's daughter – the person the police suspected, until that theory was disproved, of being the "performer". We wouldn't mind betting she was going through adolescence at the time. And as she was "brought into [town] for medical treatment" she may have had a nervous temperament.

In light of what we know of the migratory habits of some poltergeists, it is very interesting that only a month before the stones began to fly at the Avery property, the Stalk family, who lived five miles away, had been subjected to "precisely similar treatment" from the stone-throwing phantom.

The other episode during which, according to "unimpeachable" witnesses, "every evening for some weeks clods of earth larger than a man's fist were thrown into their camp", on an open plain not far from Narrabri, might have been the work of the same wandering polt.

Finally, the way that "a stone was returned, as if in answer" to each gunshot fired by the Averys is reminiscent of some of the games played by mischievous phantoms during other well-attested polt episodes.

Case 22

1901. Leichhardt, Sydney NSW. Rating: ★★

Although the following story has only a single source – a letter sent to a newspaper by an anonymous correspondent – we believe it has a distinct ring of truth. We'd be surprised if most readers, on perusing the entire, unedited text, do not agree.

THE UNEXPLAINABLE.

WILL you publish the enclosed true account of my experiences at Leichhardt? It may, perhaps, induce others to relate similar occurrences. I can solemnly vouch for the truth of every word I have written, and much more, as I have merely given the chief part, without the many minor details.

I have been much interested of late by the reports given by your representative of Mr. Charles Bailey's seances in Melbourne, and the phenomena which is alleged to occur thereat; and though these reports are by many ridiculed as the most arrant absurdity, I, for one, am inclined to the belief that, absurd as they appear, they are genuine, and that they occur according to natural law, though that law may be unknown to us at present. And my reason for believing this is that my own experiences have been nearly as marvellous as those of Mr. Bailey's. I lived for eighteen months in a cottage in Leichhardt, Sydney (the number and the street I will suppress, for obvious reasons) without being subjected to any annoyance, when, without any warning, stones commenced to fall with a tremendous crash on the roof, in the evening about sundown, but whilst it was light enough for me to see perfectly. Then they came through the back door, which faced a large open green, some three or four acres in extent, which precluded the idea of anyone in hiding being responsible for the occurrence. This lasted continuously for some days, and then the stones commenced to fall from the inside. I have watched them leave the ceiling, as it were, and fall on to the table, when laid for meals, and on to the sideboard, covered with glasses, &c., into jugs, butter dishes, &c., yet break nothing. Sometimes they would fall into a vessel containing water, when you would see the water splash up, yet on emptying the receptacle you would find nothing to account for it. One day I lifted a large stone from the bath, where it had fallen, and placed it on a table, and next moment I saw it fly back into the bath, no person in the room at the time but myself. On another day, while writing, I was annoyed and frightened by no less than eighteen or twenty pieces falling on the table during the time I was writing a letter. Among these pieces of stone was one which attracted my attention, as being different from the rest, and it seemed to me that I had gathered and thrown it out of the house before. So, to make sure, I put it with some other pieces, into the tea cosy, which was on the table, and placed the cosy in a chiffonier, and continued my writing. In a few moments what appeared to be the stone fell upon the table again. I rose, went to the chiffonier, which had been closed all the time, took the tea-cosy out, and found it empty, none of the stones and found it empty, none of the stones which I had placed there only a few minutes before remaining. If this is not a case of "matter passing through matter," I would like someone to explain what it is, as there could be no possibility of any fraud or trickery. This stone-throwing continued for about three weeks, always in the daytime, commencing in the morning and ceasing at 3 or 4 in the afternoon, but the mystery was not confined to stone-throwing. The hall would be covered in loose dirt or soil as soon as I washed it. The tiled verandah would also be thick with this loose garden dirt, though there was only a grass plot for a garden; and, more mysterious still, would be cleaned off again in a few minutes, as clean as if washed out. These occurrences can be testified to by my husband, brother-in-law, and others who witnessed many of these particularised, and to the truth of which I am willing to make a sworn declaration. It had such a disastrous effect on my nerves that there were days upon which I fled the house, and would not return till evening. On no occasion did any of these things take place at night, and although we lived nearly two years after in the same house, we were never troubled again. This happened in 1901. If any of your readers can explain these occurrences away to my satisfaction I should like to hear their explanation, and I should like to hear whether any other tenants of this house have had any similar experiences. Anyone doubting the truth of the above, or wishing further details, can have the same by calling at my address, which I forward to the editor. I have no object in making this public, other than a wish to discover the cause of this apparently supernatural phenomena. But I know that the term supernatural is a misnomer, as there is nothing above nature, but there are many of nature's laws as yet undiscovered by us, and occurrences such as I have related, absurd though they may appear, are well worthy of investigation by scientific men. Trusting you will pardon the trespass on your space.—"MYSTERY."

Source:

The Sunday Times (Sydney), 24 Feb 1907.

Case 23

February 1901. Ballarat, VIC. Rating: Zero

By 25 February, the *Melbourne Argus* reported, "an extraordinary case of window-smashing" had been going on in Scotts Parade, Ballarat, for several days. Stones had been thrown "at all hours in a most mysterious manner. The fusillade was maintained even when the police were on the spot, but the stone-thrower escaped detection". One dwelling "was reduced to a state of siege, and windows were broken at the adjoining houses …"

It was not until 50 panes of glass had been shattered that a Detective Rogerson collared 14-year-old Margaret Eddy, a member of the family whose house was most damaged. He caught her in the act of throwing a stone and, after initially maintaining her innocence, she confessed to "the whole of the damage".

Her long-suffering father undertook to pay for the damage, no legal action was taken and, as far as we know, no further stone-throwing occurred.

Sources:

The Argus (Melbourne), 25, 26 and 28 Feb 1901.

Advertiser (Adelaide), 27 Feb 1901.

Our comments:

This episode is quite similar to the notorious Enmore case of 1894, but while we entertain some hope that the earlier case was more than just a hoax, we are under no illusions about this one.

As at Enmore, the Ballarat girl was caught red-handed and confessed, but unlike Enmore, this episode lasted for only a few days and the flying stones weren't said to be as heavy or to display the quite uncanny accuracy of those in the earlier case.

It turned out, furthermore, that Margaret Eddy had "form": according to the *Argus* of 28 February, "… she was formerly in domestic service at the house of a city chemist, and while there umbrellas, boots, hats, and other articles … frequently found their way into the kitchen fire. A child was blamed for the pranks, but the girl Eddy, who has since been taxed with them, now admits that she alone was to blame."

There's no denying that the episode serves to remind us that not only mischievous boys but also, occasionally, seemingly innocent young girls, engage in inexplicable rampages of destruction – and manage to cleverly evade detection for a time.

Case 24

August–September 1901. Glenbarra, near Manilla, NSW.
Rating: ★

"For some time", the *Barrier Miner* reported on 31 August, there had been "queer tapping" on the outer wall of a slab house occupied by a boundary rider, Andrew Michie, his wife and daughters. The dwelling had also been "bombarded" every night with stones, and despite "careful search and diligent watch" by Mr. Michie and two friends, "the author of the stone-throwing could not be found".

The house, which was "situated on a grassy plain, in a lonely spot", and "fronted by a small watercourse, fringed with clustering oak trees", was "gradually being disfigured by the stones, some of which are of unusual size. The door has been smashed off its hinges, windows broken, the iron roof dented, and the slabs splintered.

"On one occasion a missile shot through the front door, striking one of the ... daughters on the head, and inflicting a nasty abrasion. All the efforts of the police and black-trackers ... have been unavailing.

"A pair of trousers and a comb were left outside ... The following morning half the trousers and half the comb were missing, and ... a few evenings later ... descended on the roof attached to a large stone.

"Michie offers a reward for the elucidation of the mystery ... supplemented to the extent [of 20 pounds] by the owner of the station."

So far, so good for "true believers". On 19 September, however, the *Advertiser* mentioned a couple of things that will gladden the hearts of sceptics:

"The stone-throwing continues. Fourteen were thrown this afternoon ... Senior-Constable Sewell and three volunteers arrived shortly [afterwards] ... and an examination of the stones showed they bore many figures and curious hieroglyphics in lead pencil. Two were numbered '70080' and '70800'. The constable then proceeded to examine the family in figure making. A girl of 17 years wrote, under direction, the numbers appearing on the stones, and the ... figures bore such a startling resemblance ... that the officer immediately concluded that she knew something about the stone-throwing business ... [he] attributes the mysterious rappings ... to the actions of the girls, who ... sleep near the wall ... [he] says the girl acknowledges throwing some of the stones, and that a younger sister threw the others."

Score one for the sceptics ... or maybe not: because the journalist rounded-off the article by stating that the girl later denied confessing to anything.

By 24 September, however, the *Advertiser* had the girls back in the "frame":

A MISCHIEVOUS GIRL

The ... mystery ... has been cleared up beyond doubt. A girl now states that she was the author of the annoyance, but gives no reason for her conduct ... she explains that she and her sister used to carry stones into their bedroom during the day. At night they would open the window to toss stones on the roof. The rappings were created by striking the wall when in bed with her heels.

Sources:

Advertiser (Adelaide), 31 Aug, 19 and 24 Sept 1901.

The Barrier Miner (Broken Hill), 31 Aug 1901.

Poverty Bay Herald (New Zealand), 9 Sept 1901.

Mercury (Hobart), 23 Sept 1901.

Queanbeyan Age, 25 Sept 1901.

Our comments:

If the *Advertiser's* final report is correct then this odd case should surely be stamped "Busted".

But there have been several instances (e.g. at Humpty Doo and Guyra) of investigators, under pressure to solve such cases, claiming to have heard confessions, which were later emphatically denied. Could the Michie girls have been "fitted-up"?

It is, in fact, very difficult to imagine how the girls could have caused all the mayhem detailed in the earlier articles. The dwelling had become "disfigured by the stones ... [a door was] smashed off its hinges, windows broken, the iron roof dented, and the slabs splintered."

A boundary rider's slab cottage would have consisted of only a single storey, and would in all likelihood have been a simple rectangle – so how could the girls have thrown stones onto the roof from within their bedroom – let alone rocks massive enough to dent galvanised iron? And to splinter a typical rustic slab wall, as reported, would have required blows from a sledge hammer – if not a battering ram.

The episode lasted for at least a month. How could their parents and other investigators not have noticed that nearly all the stone-throwing and wall-rapping occurred when the girls were in their bedroom? Some of the stones were of such an "unusual size" that they would have been difficult, one imagines, for the girls to conceal. And what of the stone that "... shot through the front door", striking one of the girls and inflicting "a nasty abrasion"?

It seems unlikely that anything scrawled on an uncut stone in pencil would be neat enough to compare to any figures later written on paper. And why would the girl, if guilty, not alter her "figure-making" so that it differed from what was on the stones? Why, indeed, would she throw inscribed stones around on a day the police were expected to visit?

At the risk of being considered naïve, we retain one star's worth of hope that this was more than just a hoax.

Case 25

1904. The Hundred of Foster, near Mannum, SA.
Rating: ★

Fourteen years after the event, an Adelaide *Register* journalist interviewed 78-year-old Henry Hayward about strange events that occurred on his property in the Hundred of Foster, half a mile east of the Murray River, in about 1904.

For two weeks, day and night, stones, sticks and clods of earth fell, sometimes in veritable "showers" on that "nice little block in the Mallee scrub". Despite constant vigilance and thorough searches no hoaxers were ever discovered. Guns were repeatedly fired, without effect, in the direction from which stones came.

One witness "swore that he saw … a big stone … rise out of the ground" before it fell between his feet. Various neighbours, including an outspoken sceptic, observed the stone falls and left convinced that "the trouble was not the work of a human being".

After two weeks or so, Mr. Hayward, worried that someone would be seriously injured, wrote to Police Trooper Gibbons in Mannum, but on the day he posted the letter the stone showers abruptly ceased.

At the conclusion of his *Register* interview the old man mentioned one more strange thing: "during the whole of the time the stones were falling no one was hit by any of them."

Source:

The Register, Adelaide, 27 Mar 1918.

Our comments:

Although the *Register* article, summarised above, is our only source for this story, it contains a lot of interesting detail and Mr. Hayward's account has, to our sympathetic ears at least, a distinct ring of truth. Having kept quiet about it for fourteen years, he decided to approach the newspaper with his story only after reading of recent events, possibly involving a poltergeist, at Gawler (Case 30).

It is significant that many of the falls occurred in broad daylight, that one witness said he saw a stone "rise out of the ground" and that none of the (apparently) hundreds of falling objects ever hit anyone.

Apart from the fact that Mr. Hayward and his wife had several sons ranging in age from twelve to twenty-three, and at least one daughter, there is not much in this case for sceptics to seize upon.

Case 26

November 1906. Mitchellstown (15 km South-West of Nagambie), Vic.
Rating: ★

On 9 November 1906 *The Broadford Courier and Reedy Creek Times* reprinted this article from the *Nagambie Times*:

SPOOKS AT MITCHELLSTOWN
It appears that three woodcutters camped about a mile from Vearings paddock in a lonely part of the forest have during the past week or so been the medium of some fantastic and mysterious manifestations on the part of "spooks".

It is said that while standing or sitting near the camp fire chips and small stones strike them, not with any force, but descending on them like leaves from the trees. To lend variety … the occasional jam tin arrives. At first each of the campers thought the other was doing it, and remonstrated with each other, but [when] *they found they were thrown by some invisible hand or hands they became alarmed.*

The following night they got a couple more [witnesses] *down but still the mysterious throwing went on, and the same occurred the third night. On the fourth night they had 8 or 10 watching and they … built camp fires all around so that it would be impossible for any throwing to take place without the culprit being seen …but it still went on, and the chips and stones still fell gently on them.*

One facetious and incredulous individual who did not believe in the supernatural came to scoff, but after the ghostly chips and stones arrived, one of which struck him behind the ear, he retired to the tent, and subsequent events interested him no more.

On the fifth night the spooks must have been in a frolicsome humour, for as [indecipherable] *jam tins arrived in their midst one of the party, still unconvinced, put one kerosene tin on top of the other … inviting the spook to knock it over and in the same mysterious way it was forthwith knocked over, although all were sitting around watching. "I do not know what it can be", said one of the party afterwards, "but it ain't no human being."*

It is said that at this particular spot some years ago a murder had been committed, but if such is the case, and the spirit of the murdered individual is now trying to wander around he must be a humorous and playful kind of cuss.

Our comments:

If the details of this odd little story are correct, it seems likely a polt really was out there in the scrub, messing with the minds of the bemused bushmen.

Stones descending gently "like leaves falling from trees" and striking people without force have been noted during many well-attested poltergeist episodes. The fact that the falls continued even when the area was well-lit by several extra fires is also reminiscent of other polt cases, as is the "spook's" apparent response when challenged to knock over the kerosene tins.

On the other hand, all we know about the incident comes from a single article in the *Broadford Courier* – a second-hand story at that. We've been unable to locate the *Nagambie Times* to check the original version and to see if there was any follow-up.

Case 27

MAY 1908. BRUNSWICK, MELBOURNE, VIC.
RATING: HALF A STAR

Mysterious noises occurred over the course of several weeks at the premises of Mr. William Stein of 41 Albert Street, East Brunswick. The noises included a great deal of tapping on windows, "just as if someone were rapping his knuckles against it", followed by very loud noises "resembling muffled explosions" or "as if someone had run a battering ram against the wall". Walls and ceilings were shaken and badly cracked. For some days "the opening of the back door at night was the signal for a volley of stones from the darkness". Crowds besieged the house as word spread of the strange events. Sixteen policemen took turns standing guard and several stayed overnight, some even concealing themselves in the loft where many of the noises appeared to come from. They could not, initially at least, solve the mystery.

The police eventually brought in an expert plumber who opined that the "explosions" were caused by "gases in the water or sewerage mains". He had had "an exactly similar experience at a large factory in Melbourne." The house, however, was not connected to the sewer mains, and the theory did nothing to explain the fusillades of stones. So the Steins remained convinced the phenomena was the work of "some malicious persons who wished to annoy them".

There is no mention of the episode coming to an end; indeed, the final article in our file states that "So intolerable has the nuisance become that the family contemplate vacating the house, although until a few months ago they had lived there in comfort for more than thirteen years."

Sources:

Argus (Melbourne), 23, 25 and 26 May 1908.

Advertiser (Adelaide), 23–25 May 1908.

Mercury (Hobart), 26 and 28 May 1908.

Kalgoorlie Western Argus, 2 Jun 1908.

Our comments:

Given that they occurred in an urban area, and only after nightfall, the phenomena don't seem all that remarkable. The "muffled explosions" could have been caused by a build-up of gas in the water mains, though why adjoining houses weren't affected is not explained.

The window-tapping and stone-throwing might have been the work of hoaxers, though it seems odd that the window-tapping always immediately preceded the "explosions" and that the police could never nab the tappers, who must have been virtually within arm's reach.

It seems quite odd, too, that the police, despite maintaining a constant watch, didn't so much as glimpse a suspect, although, to be fair, the crowds of sightseers that were drawn to the site in the final weeks wouldn't have made their investigation any easier.

Case 28

NOVEMBER–DECEMBER 1910. PORT MELBOURNE, VIC.
RATING: HALF A STAR

For at least six weeks three houses in Princes Street suffered an "almost continuous bombardment" by stones, brick pieces and iron piping. Woodwork was splintered and every window on the northern, eastern and southern walls was broken; crockery and furniture was smashed and damaged. Residents could think of no reason for the attack.

The bombardments began after midnight and, as they continued until 7 am – broad daylight at that time of year – several objects were seen in flight. The *Argus* reported that police, who had "watched day and night … have actually seen a brick speeding on its way to one of the houses. When they traced the missile to its apparent source they found … no sign of anybody having been there or in the vicinity."

The stony bombardments were potentially lethal: a Mrs. Sievers and a Mr. Loy suffered severe cuts and abrasions and police were also struck. On one occasion, as Mrs. Loy was bathing, half a brick came through the window and struck her on the back.

The occupants of all three houses found that the only way "to enjoy comparative peace" was to keep all doors shut and to stay away from windows. For their own safety, children had to be "kept as prisoners" inside the residences.

Sources:

The Argus (Melbourne), 15 Dec 1910.

The Advertiser (Adelaide), 15 Dec 1910.

Our comments:

There appears to have been no newspaper coverage of the episode after 15 December, so perhaps it simply petered out. If police had solved the mystery we would have expected a follow-up article.

As the "almost continuous bombardment" went on, day and night, for several weeks, and remained unsolved despite a continuous police stake-out, it might possibly have been the work of a poltergeist. On the other hand none of the police or victims seems to have considered a supernatural explanation. None of them, at least, mentioned the supernatural to journalists.

No objects fell, materialised or levitated indoors, and, contrary to what usually happens in polt cases, people were repeatedly struck and injured. Two of the victims, in fact, suffered severe cuts and abrasions, which suggests the houses were targeted by extremely nasty and elusive vandals.

The episode occurred, after all, in an old and probably densely-populated inner-city suburb, and no information is provided as to foliage, hedges or walls that might have provided cover for hooligans.

Case 29

MARCH 1911. BURNLEY, MELBOURNE, VIC.
RATING: ZERO

According to the Melbourne *Argus* of 21 March 1911 "showers" of stones had been falling "for some time" on the roof of the Cunningham residence, at 85 Edinburgh St, Burnley. Windows were broken and "at dead of night weird sounds of knocking have proceeded from the walls". Several neighbours were called in and a close watch was kept, but to no avail. This, said the *Argus*, led the searchers to conclude that the house was haunted. William Cunningham and his family began vacating the place at night and sleeping at a neighbour's house.

On the evening of 13 March, while a police sergeant and constables were on the premises, a window was smashed, "but the cause was not apparent … an intruder could not have possibly have made his escape without observation … the police were puzzled … the noises continued."

Finally, on the 18th, a constable twice observed the Cunningham's eight-year-old adopted son, Arthur, throwing stones onto the roof. The little rogue "admitted he was the culprit, and said in explanation that 'he threw a stone on the roof one day, and it caused so much fun that he kept it going.' The police were not completely satisfied that young Arthur was wholly responsible for the noises heard at late hours of the night … they plied him with questions, but he persisted that 'he did the lot.'"

Sources:

The Argus (Melbourne), 21 Mar 1911.

Sydney Morning Herald, 21 Mar 1911.

Our comments:

So it was a hoax. And yet, the police were not convinced that Arthur was responsible for the weird knocking heard late at night while he was supposedly in bed. Perhaps he had an accomplice; although she was quickly cleared of the charge, a neighbour, Miss Neylan, had been accused, on 14 March, of throwing some of the stones.

Case 30

FEBRUARY 1918. GAWLER, SA. RATING: ★½

Our only source for this story is the following article from the Adelaide *Register*, which was reprinted by the *Border Watch* (Mount Gambier) on 12 February and by the *Barrier Miner* (Broken Hill) on 16 February 1918:

"GHOSTS" AT GAWLER
MYSTERIOUS OCCURRENCES

Mysterious occurrences have caused much curiosity here, and are almost the sole topic of local conversation (writes the Gawler correspondent of the "Register"). Near to midnight on one occasion recently, a certain parent sat up in bed upon hearing screams coming from the room of one of his children. Speedily he ran to the comfort of the little one, who was sobbing hysterically, and speaking in broken phrases of dancing lights and funny noises.

Pityingly he picked up the youngster to soothe it and carry it to his room, when he heard slow and distinct knocking on the wall. Then a bright light and all was still. Questioning his senses, he made his way to his room. Seated on the bed and now thoroughly awake, he pondered over the peculiar illusion, when there it was again. The electric lights flashed up and went back into darkness. "What could it be?"

Frightened and trembling he awaited the next phenomenon. It was not long in coming. A flower stand started on a peregrination of the hall, the bed heaved, and soon he and others were precipitated on the floor. Next night there was a similar occurrence, and a continuance for almost a fortnight.

After a few nights' experience, the husband told friends who scoffed at the idea as ridiculous, and offered to take their turn in the watch. Four men seated on the bed challenged the knocking and received answers to their requests. Startled, they waited for more. Soon the lights appeared, and shortly afterwards they were bundled unceremoniously on to the floor. They did not linger for further developments, but hurried out of the house, satisfied that something uncanny had possession.

The police were informed, and made investigations, and it is said that one of the constables experienced the indignity of a tumble from the bed. Hundreds of people visited the scene and declare that they have witnessed the flashing lights and phosphorescent streaks appearing on the doors and windows. In spite of the number of spectators the antics continue, and the happenings are creating consternation in that neighbourhood. The double bed is the main source of mystery. Its behaviour is eccentric and cantankerous. It may tip on one side only, and next time topple right over; it may take, a quick sliding motion from the wall, and with the velocity attained precipitate its occupant on to the floor, and then as speedily slide back again. The "spirit" knockings are numerous and accommodating, for as many knocks asked for will be given on the walls. A strong idea is current that spiritualistic influence is being practised in the neighbourhood, while other folk declare in favour of mechanical contrivances.

Our comments:

If everything happened as reported above, then a poltergeist was certainly pestering the unnamed family at Gawler.

The "slow and distinct knocking" that sometimes responded to questions, the flashing lights and phosphorescent streaks, the levitating flower stand and the bed that repeatedly slid around and tipped people onto the floor all correspond with phenomena observed at other polt-plagued locations in Australia and elsewhere.

The fact that the correspondent decided not to identify the people involved detracts somewhat from the story, as does the apparent absence of follow-up articles. Although it seems likely he did, we can't even be entirely sure that the correspondent actually visited the troubled residence.

Reports of this episode prompted Henry Hayward to go public with his account of the 1904 episode near Mannum, South Australia (Case 25).

Case 31

1919. Broken Hill, NSW. Rating: ★★

Warning: While dyed-in-the-wool poltergeist enthusiasts (and, indeed, dyed-in-the-wool sceptics) will find plenty in this case to interest them, it may contain a little too much detail for readers with just a casual interest in the subject.

The case presented an unusual problem for us: although it is not particularly strong in terms of poltergeist phenomena, journalists from the *Barrier Miner* covered it in such detail, and included so many interesting quotes in their reports, that we were reluctant to drastically edit their good work.

So, as we're not particularly pressed for space, we've decided to reprint two quite lengthy *Miner* articles, with just a little editing, and to summarise the others while attempting to preserve their original flavour.

THE BARRIER MINER, 16 APRIL 1919:
MYSTERIOUS KNOCKINGS REPORTED IN RAILWAY TOWN
POLICEMAN'S LONG VIGIL

The house occupied by Mr. William Richard Roberts, in Gaffney Street, Railway Town, has become an object of much attention … because of a story …. that frequent mysterious knockings have been heard by the inmates.

[The noises] have not caused the inmates any concern [but] the fact that hundreds of people [want to enter] the house in the hope of hearing the mysterious knockings led to Mr. Roberts making a complaint to the Police.

Last night about 200 people congregated in the precincts [and] a police officer waited in the house from an early hour … until 11 pm without hearing anything [and was] satisfied that there was nothing in the report, or that it was a trick, …

THE MINER, 19 APRIL 1919:
BED DANCING IN MID AIR IN RAILWAY TOWN HOUSE
STRANGE KNOCKINGS HEARD
QUESTIONS ANSWERED BY TAPS
TENANT TELLS THE STORY

On Thursday a "Miner" reporter interviewed Mrs. Roberts at her … four-roomed wood and iron house. [Her] story is a remarkable one, and more remarkable still is the belief of some of the Roberts family that the knockings are caused by the spirit [a departed relative]. Although the knockings have been heard for the past three weeks, nothing has yet been found … which gives any clue as to the method by which [they] are produced. There is nothing imaginative about the knockings at all. They have been so loud at times to attract the attention of people who live many hundreds of yards away …. Many theories have been advanced … but they are all said to have been tested and still the knockings go on when the "spirit" is in the mood.

Mrs. Roberts said: "I suppose you have heard … that there is something to be seen. Well, there is not anything to be seen. I only wish there was something which we could see that would give us a clue to the agency which is causing us so much annoyance. I will begin from the first we know of the mystery. About three weeks ago, on a Sunday night after I and my husband had gone to bed, one of my sons, who had just previously arrived home from the city, called out and asked me if I was walking about the house. I replied that I had been in bed since he came home. My son then said 'Well, there's someone walking along the passage'.

My husband got out of bed and had a look round but could see nothing. My son was ahead of him. Very suddenly there came a violent knocking from the back bedroom. We all entered the room, and the knocking continued, and gradually became louder. My husband said that there must be an iguana or something of the sort inside the wall. He pulled the woodwork to pieces but found nothing. He even went to the length of pulling down the whole of the wall … but without finding anything that would explain the noise. My own opinion was that there was a battery of some kind concealed in the wall, but my husband could find no trace of any wires or anything one would expect … if some electrical appliance was being used."

Lovely To Talk To

One of the Miss Roberts here interjected: "It is so funny. The knocking comes for four nights running, and then goes away for four nights. It is lovely to talk to. It will answer by knocking any question you like to put to it."

"That is providing that the question you ask is one that can be answered by knocking", said the reporter, and Miss Roberts replied: "Well, you see, we only ask it questions that can be answered by knocks, such as the ages of persons, and such things."

[Her mother] continued the story: "We have had all the boards down in the room, and can find nothing … Only one really startling thing has occurred during the time we have been annoyed by this knocking. One of my sons was on a stretcher in the room while the knocking was going on, and he was thrown off it three times. Then another dreadful thing happened last Sunday night. We were all in bed, and when it was nearly midnight we heard a terrible crash in the room where we had before heard all the knocking. My husband said, 'That's the side of the house knocked in', and that is just what it sounded like. We ran into the room. We saw the bed on which my son had been sleeping dancing about in mid-air, and then by some unseen agency it was hurled to the other side of the room, a distance of about 12ft, The bedding and blankets were underneath, and the bed was upside down. My son was not hurt, as he got off the bed before it was taken up in the air".

Spirit Gets Angry

Miss Roberts again interrupted to say: "When it first comes it makes a scratching noise, and *then a gentle tapping begins to attract attention. If we do not take any notice of it, it appears to get very angry, and beats the wall terribly hard. We ask it all kinds of questions, and it answers them correctly. We have had total strangers with us in the house, and it has told them their ages and answered other questions that can be answered by knocking. It also [gives] two knocks for 'No' and three for 'Yes'. It will tell anyone anything they want to know. It is lovely talking to it. If it is a trick, as the policeman who came says, then it is a very clever one. If they came here any night that the knocking is going on they will not find any wires."*

"Has anyone suggested that wires are being used to produce the knocking?" the reporter asked.

"They have suggested all kinds of things", replied Mrs. Roberts, "but none of the things suggested have cleared up the mystery. It is a complete mystery to us, and a jolly annoying and distressing one. We cannot get any sleep at night for the knocking".

"Have you any theory, Mrs. Roberts?" ventured the reporter.

"Yes I have but I am not going to discuss it anymore."

"Then your theory is no ordinary one?"

"Yes, it is a very ordinary one. There will be a warm time in store for the person or persons responsible. I think it is someone using a very strong battery and trying to frighten us. If they are trying to frighten me they can knock on. I was never frightened as a girl and I am not going to be frightened now. None of us are frightened of the knocking or the ghost that cannot be seen, if you like to call it such."

Effect on Health

"The only thing that worries me", Mrs. Roberts added, "is that my baby boy, who was a fine big boy, is getting so thin with the frights he is getting. The noise it makes is cruel, and even the neighbours are not able to sleep for it."

Miss Roberts said: "People say it is rot, but it is not. It could not know all the things it knows if it was not some extraordinarily wonderful thing. It knows everything about people who came here and were absolute strangers to us. If it is a human being I would like to meet him as he must be a walking encyclopaedia."

"Are you a believer in spiritualism, Mrs. Roberts?" asked the reporter.

"No. indeed I am not," replied Mrs. Roberts. "There is nothing on God's earth that will make me believe in spirits coming back and all that rot. My husband says it is the spirit of my dead mother, and the girls think the same; but I am not having any of that. I am going to stick it out until I find out what it is. Some nights, when the knocking is going on I go in and sing about the spirits in Heaven and all the rest of it, and 'throw off' at the knocking. The knocks then get louder and louder, as if it is wild at me making fun of it. I am not frightened, and have not felt frightened at any time."

"When was the last time you heard the knocking?"

"It was dreadfully bad on Sunday night last, and we had another lot of knocking on Tuesday night."

Onkaparinga. Winners Known.

"Yes", cut in Miss Roberts, "on Tuesday night Dad was asking it for the winners of the Onkaparinga races. It told him all the winners. It cannot talk, and instead of giving the names of the horses it knocked off the racing numbers of them. One morning it told us we were going to have six deaths in our family. That was at 6 o'clock in the morning and at 10 o'clock we got a wire telling us of one relative's death. We have had three of these deaths since it told us this. If it is a trick I will congratulate him on his cleverness."

Mrs. Roberts continued: "We would have said nothing to the police only that so many people were wanting to come into the house at night. They became more annoying to us than the knocking. The noise is always in the same place. If we do not take any notice of it, it gets terribly wild and nearly knocks the wall down. When we sit down and talk to it, it becomes very quiet and the knocking is just like the knocking of a gentle hand."

Miss Roberts continued: "I believe it is a spirit, so does father and another sister. If it is a trick, I hope whoever is responsible is found out. I do not believe it is a trick, but a spirit."

By 23 April, one of the *Miner* journalists was becoming distinctly sceptical:

THE RAILWAY TOWN 'SPOOK' AGAIN TAPS OUT ITS ANSWERS BUT STOPS WHEN POLICE PAY A VISIT LAST NIGHT

It is a disappointing "ghost" in more ways than one. [It] responds to such vulgarly familiar styles of address as "Come along, old chappie, shake it up" and "tap away old fellow, we are all waiting" [but] shows a discrimination which is so unghostlike ... a discrimination which is so really human ... "It" does not like policemen [and] will not tap within the hearing of a policeman.

[One policeman] stated, in a very loud voice, in the very room ... that "it's a fraud." Consequently, the "ghost" refuses to answer any questions put by the policeman.

Last night ... three visitors, a "Miner" reporter and two friends called at the house, and were admitted.

The father has a theory

Mr. Roberts substantiated and enlarged upon the story told by his wife. "I can't explain it any more than anyone else can", he said, "but I have a theory". After some pressure [he] expounded his theory.

"It's the lad there", he said, pointing with the stem of his pipe towards a tired-looking boy about 14 years of age ... [adding] that, except for one instance the "tapping" occurred only when the boy was about. "There seems to be an affinity between it and Vic ... [he] got a bit scared about sleeping in that room and last night we moved him. Then the tapping came to the wall of the room we had moved him into."

Son Willie, who works the night shift ... was resting in [Vic's new room] in the morning and heard "two loud claps". Vic and his mother ... were in town at the time.

[So Mr. Roberts] *says that he is convinced that Vic has something to do with "it", but without being able to help it, and that it is something of a phenomenal character.*

Ghostly errors

Mr. Roberts told the journalist that on the previous evening the dining room table had moved about the room despite the family's best efforts to restrain it, and that a bench had done the same a few nights earlier.

Mr. Roberts and guests then attempted to "call up" the "ghost", but didn't succeed in doing so until Vic went into his dimly-lit bedroom, from whence there soon issued tapping that the journalist thought could have been made by "a finger capped by a thimble". The "ghost's" subsequent inability to correctly answer questions did nothing to assuage his scepticism.

If young Vic was faking the taps, then his older brother Willie was also in on the hoax, as he sat in Vic's room during part of the proceedings.

Enter the law

Shortly thereafter, a policeman walked in and the tapping suddenly ceased. He then walked straight into Vic's bedroom and demanded, "Now tap". On receiving no response he continued: "No, you never will tap when I'm about ... It's all a fraud, and I've found you out." He pulled Vic's bed away from the wall, saying "Ye'll hear no more tapping now ... I've got it all sized up."

"Well", said Mrs. Roberts, "if you know so much about it, why don't you tell us. We want to know, I can assure you. It is no pleasure to us to have our nights disturbed and people crowding round the place every night."

"You know all about it, and so do I", said the policeman. "Tell us", shouted a chorus, "You're bluffing."

The family suggested that the policeman step outside for a time, and they would endeavour to get "it" to converse again. He consented, but "it" would not converse. Not a single tap was heard, despite imploring appeals, such as "Come along old chap ... let's hear from you". Even telling "it" that the policeman had gone had no effect.

"We'll put the bed against the wall again", said son Willie. *He did this, but before doing it he went between the bed and the wall, which did not seem necessary, and appeared as well as could be dimly observed ... to fumble with something on the wall ... however, ... the "ghost" still refrained from tapping.*

Letters – one supporting the unnamed policeman and two supporting the Roberts family, appeared in the *Miner* on 25 and 28 April. One correspondent accused the sceptical *Miner* reporter of inaccuracy and the unnamed policeman of outright dishonesty:

The report stated that the knocking has never been heard while the police were present. That … is absolutely incorrect, as I have been there in the house with the police while the knocking was going on.

Does the policeman forget hearing two knocks when his age was asked for? Also when the question was asked, "Are you afraid to knock when the police are here? Does he not remember hearing two more knocks, and pulling a board off the wall to see where the knocking came from, and finding nothing? And yet the policeman declares he knows all about it. Well, if he does, why does he not let us all into the know?

I do not think it is a right thing for a representative of the law to blame the inmates of the house when he knows perfectly well it is untrue … the knocking is going on as usual … if the mystery cannot be cleared up by stating the truth concerning it, I am sure it never will be solved by bluff.

I am, etc.,
ONE WHO WAS THERE

After publishing a final letter of support on 30 April, the *Miner* ceased its coverage of the Gaffney Street episode, so it seems unlikely that the "ghost", or the hoaxers, continued tapping and banging much beyond that date.

Source:

Barrier Miner (Broken Hill), 16,19, 22, 23, 25, 28 and 30 Apr 1919.

Our comments:

If this episode happened as claimed by the Roberts family then it was almost certainly a genuine polt event.

There appears to be no doubt that the rapping and banging really occurred and that it was, at times, extremely loud – too loud, one imagines, to have been caused by a 14-year-old boy surreptitiously tapping on his wall with a thimble. As the *Miner* reported on 19 April, "There is nothing imaginative about the knockings at all. They have been so loud at times to attract the attention of people who live many hundreds of yards away." During one particularly violent event Mr. Roberts thought the wall had actually fallen down: "That's the side of the house knocked in."

If the entire episode was a hoax it seems certain that most if not all of the family members were involved. Yet the quotes attributed to them in the lengthy article of April 19th give the strong impression that Mr. and Mrs. Roberts and their daughter were genuinely mystified.

We also find it interesting that the trio had such divergent theories. If they'd conspired to fake the rapping we wouldn't have expected them to publically disagree on its cause.

The mother was particularly forceful in her belief that it was the work of malicious hoaxers and that someone was "using a very strong battery and trying to frighten us". While gizmo-savvy denizens of the 21st century may find her theory rather potty, it is important to remember that in 1919, in remote towns like Broken Hill, electric light and electrical appliances were still amazing novelties.

After at first assuming a goanna was trapped in the wall, Mr. Roberts thought for a time that the rapping was caused by the spirit of his late mother-in-law. Eventually, however, he evolved a theory more in line with the thinking of many present-day polt researchers: that there seemed to be "an affinity" between "it" and 14-year-old Vic, and that, although the boy wasn't a willing or witting participant, he had something to do with the strange events: the rapping was "something of a phenomenal character".

So it seems Mr. Roberts' thoughts were running along the lines of recurrent spontaneous psychokinesis – even though that term had yet to be coined (by parapsychologist William Roll, in 1958).

But young Miss Roberts – and, apparently, her sisters – believed that the knocking was "caused by the spirits of deceased relatives."

Mrs. Roberts said that her baby, "who was a fine big boy, is getting so thin with the frights he is getting. The noise it makes is cruel …" If the rapping was a hoax, Mrs. Roberts must have been party to it. Would she deliberately compromise the health of her infant? Or would she lie about the state of his health? We think not.

The types of strange phenomena that supposedly occurred – the phantom footsteps, the "scratching noise" that built up to a gentle tapping and sometimes to a terrible banging, the levitating bed, table and bench, the "ghost's" violent reaction to hymn-singing – all conform to the range of phenomena noted at well-documented poltergeist cases throughout the centuries.

The Gaffney Street "ghost" isn't the first invisible resident to have supposedly conversed with its mortal housemates via wall-tapping, and Miss Roberts' assertion that it correctly predicted several things, including a series of deaths in the family, is interesting.

We do, however, find it difficult to imagine how it could have conveyed such complex information via simple knocking. And in any case, when put to the test on 22 April it proved to be somewhat less than omniscient. Its inability to correctly answer questions on that occasion is just one of many reasons we are a little sceptical about the "ghost".

While the neighbour interviewed on 19 April confirmed that the wall-banging was sometimes so loud that "it keeps me awake. It can be heard hundreds of yards away", he also said that he was present in the house when Vic was said to have fallen out of bed, but that "The bed did not move on that occasion at all." The behaviour of Vic and Willie on the evening of 22 April, as reported by the *Miner* journalist, also seems indicative of clumsy hoaxing.

The journalist discovered what was, in his judgment, another reason for scepticism:

Members of the family stated that a dog was kept, but that the animal was not in the least disturbed by the noises or the "ghostly" tapping. It barked not, nor did it whine … when the uncanny approaches, dogs … whine and crawl on their bellies.

Dogs, however, don't always react to the presence of a polt. During the remarkable Mayanup episode (Chapter Two) dogs went berserk when the first stone falls occurred but soon calmed down and, for the following two years, as noisy, weird events occurred all around them, never reacted at all.

The journalist also seems to hint that the Roberts might have faked the "ghostly" phenomena to scare off people interested in buying the residence:

The house ... is up for sale. The landlord had ... received an offer, but would give [Mrs. Roberts] *the first chance to purchase.*

It is unfortunate that the otherwise quite thorough *Miner* journalists didn't detail the exact makeup of the family, although it seems there was at least one adult son, at least three daughters of indeterminate age, 14-year-old Vic, and a baby boy.

It could be said that the duration of the episode – one month – is a fairly typical life-span for a poltergeist episode, but perhaps a month is also about the maximum time hoaxers can maintain interest in their pranks. As no one outside of the Roberts family witnessed the supposed levitation of furniture, as the other phenomena consisted only of tapping and banging – albeit remarkably loud banging – and as there are plenty of grounds for scepticism, we don't rate this case all that highly.

Still and all, when we read again the statements of feisty Mrs. Roberts, her thoughtful husband, and her wide-eyed daughter, we can't shake the feeling that they seem to be genuinely mystified by the "ghostly" events, and that they really sound like they're telling the truth …

What the heck – let's call it a two-star case.

Case 32

April–May 1921. Guyra, NSW. Rating: ★★★½

Prior to the Mayanup episode of the 1950s the "Guyra Ghost" was Australia's most notorious poltergeist. (See Chapter Ten).

Case 33

MAY 1921. KINGSTOWN (65 KM SOUTH-WEST OF GUYRA) NSW. RATING: ZERO

From the *Glen Innes Examiner*, 2 May 1921:

GHOST AT KINGSTOWN. PEACE OF HOMESTEAD BROKEN.

Almost before the echoes of the Guyra "mystery" have died away there springs up another similar affair at Kingstown. The preliminaries of the Guyra campaign have been adopted, and it remains to be seen whether the other features will follow. It appears that the scene of operations is Mr. C.A. Greenland's peaceful homestead. He has done nothing to raise the ire of the Guyra or any other "ghost", and he is at a complete loss to understand why his residence should be singled out for this unpleasant notoriety.

The first evidence of anything amiss occurred on Wednesday evening, when suddenly out of the silence of the night came a smart fusillade of stones. The missiles rattled on the roof and a number went through the windows. Some of the stones were of a heavy calibre and quite obviously could not have been thrown from a greater distance than 15 or 20 yards. A hurried but exhaustive investigation followed, but as was the case with the Guyra affair nothing was discovered nor was anyone to be seen. The family again retired for the night and about 3 am there came another attack – if anything more severe than before. A search was again fruitless.

At daylight assistance was sought, and a number of men in vain sought an explanation. About 11 o'clock yesterday morning, when one of Mr. F. Mitchell's employees was close to the house, three more stones came suddenly and seemingly from nowhere, two landing on the wall and on the roof. The direction from which they came was quite evident, but the most vigorous scouring of the neighbourhood revealed nothing. The Bundarra police were then sent for and a thorough investigation was at once entered upon.

Our comments:

This may well have been a hoax inspired by the events at nearby Guyra. Although the two intense "fusillades" occurred at night, only three stones, apparently, flew in broad daylight, and all of them fell outdoors: there was no levitation of objects indoors, no wall-thumping or other activity that might indicate polt involvement.

In cases such as this, though, one wonders why there is no mention of the dogs – sheep dogs, cattle dogs or hunting dogs – that were to be found on virtually every Australian farm. Did they not bark? Didn't the property owners "sic" them onto the supposed hoaxers? If not, why not?

Case 34

February 1922. Darling Point, Sydney NSW.
Rating: Half a star

This is a murky, complicated episode. Although it was almost certainly a case of arson, it wasn't a *simple* case of arson. Because there have been several apparently genuine polt cases that also involved fire, because there was speculation at the time that the outbreak was of supernatural origin, and because there are a few rather odd aspects to the case, we are reluctant to simply "bin" it. Another reason for our interest is that one of us (Paul) recently investigated three rather similar episodes in Malaysia, Vietnam and Turkey (see Appendix A).

Over the course of three days, beginning on the afternoon of Monday 6 February, a series of fires broke out in an old, two-story house owned by an organ builder, W.G. Rendell, J.P., and his family. Fire Brigade officers and police were on the premises throughout almost the entire episode.

The occupants felt that "something extraordinary" was causing the blazes, and the firemen soon saw why they were so concerned: shortly after they arrived three very unusual fires broke out in the house and in an adjacent shed. In view of this, the Chief Fire Officer ordered his men to stay on the premises. On the following day there were four similar blazes: "A flame would suddenly shoot up into the air, and lick up any surrounding inflammable material. First curtains caught alight, then bed draperies, bedding and furniture. One fireman … while keeping watch … sat down on a chair, deeply contemplating the mystery [when] the chair suddenly burst into flames. Following upon this … while the chief officer (Mr. Jackson) was in the house some curtains became ignited with the same weird suddenness …."

Mr. Jackson, however, had the presence of mind to smother the fire with cloth rather than dousing it with water. He then "wiped the burnt material across his lips. Shortly afterwards his lips swelled and smarted, then blistered." He "expressed the belief that phosphorous or some other chemical … had been dissolved and sprayed about the house" and a subsequent report by Thomas Cooksey, the Government analyst, seemed to support his theory. A light fabric so sprayed, said Cooksey, "would ignite much more rapidly than a heavy one."

Four detectives were assigned to the case, and after three days, during which 19 fires occurred, Detective Leary said they were "convinced as to the originators of the outbreaks" and that they had a prima-facie case to submit to the coroner. By the 7th of March, however, all the coroner was prepared to say was "that the fires had been maliciously caused, but by whom he was not in a position to state."

Then, on 13 March, after a hiatus of six days, three more fires broke out. Although by this time the house no longer actually belonged to Mr. Rendell – in the interim he'd sold it to a Mr. Herbert Solomos – all three fires occurred in the work shed which still housed some of Mr. Rendell's property, notably a valuable church organ.

On 15 March one of Mr. Rendell's daughters, 38-year-old Evangelina Reynolds, and 20-year-old William Thomas were arrested and charged with arson. They appear to have been the prime suspects for two reasons: firstly because they said they were the only people on the premises when the second series of fires occurred and secondly because Evangelina's husband had allegedly threatened her father on several occasions. The old man had, in fact, banished him from the house.

Although Evangelina stated that she and Thomas had been in the house all day and that it would have been impossible for anyone else to have sneaked in, she adamantly denied lighting the fires and pointed out that she was always the first to detect and extinguish them. She agreed that "someone is trying to burn us out", but whoever it was "must be a lunatic, for each [fire] was started where it could easily be extinguished."

It seems the police didn't really have much of a case, because on 10 April the Coroner threw out the charges, saying he could see no evidence to justify any action against the duo.

So Evangelina and Thomas were in the clear; the blazes of 13 March were apparently the last of the series, and the fiery mystery, as far as we know, was never solved.

Sources:

Daily Telegraph (Sydney), 9 Feb 1922.

Sydney Morning Herald, 10 Feb, 14 Mar, 1, 7 and 11 Apr 1922.

Argus (Melbourne), 10 and 11 Feb, 3, 7, 14, 15 and 31 Mar, 7 Apr 1922.

Western Argus (Kalgoorlie), 14 Feb 1922.

Brisbane Courier, 7 and 31 Mar, 1 Apr 1922.

Our comments:

While the fires were genuinely quite mysterious, this episode featured nothing else suggestive of poltergeist activity – no stone falls, levitation or teleportation of objects, etc. – and there are reasonable grounds to suspect that one or more very human arsonists were involved.

Mr. Rendell seemed to have had a talent for annoying people. As well as his alienated son-in-law, it was said that "there were many people in his trade who were his bitter enemies". Vera, another of his daughters, said she could think of half a dozen who might wish to damage his business.

There seems little doubt that fires can be started in the way suggested by the police. During a demonstration in the Coroner's Court, pieces of cloth burst into flames two minutes after being smeared with phosphorous solution.

On the other hand, while loose cloth ignited on cue, there doesn't seem to have been any attempt to induce a bookcase full of books or the top of a couch to go up in flames – as had happened at Rendell's house. It seems, also, that if such a fluid was used at Rendell's house it had remained "dormant", in several instances, for much longer than just two minutes.

In any case, an arsonist using such a method would have been taking an insane risk: Chief Fire Officer Jackson told of one Sydney fireman being burnt to death and others having their clothes set alight while handling the notoriously volatile chemical.

Accustomed as we are to hearing of unhappy adolescents being in the proximity of apparent poltergeist phenomena, we couldn't fail to notice that on 14 March the *Sydney Morning Herald* mentioned a third person being on the premises when the second series of fires occurred: Evangelina's 12-year-old son John.

Given the poisonous relationship between his father and grandfather, it seems likely the boy was quite stressed at the time. Was he present during the earlier outbreak of fires? He probably was, but we can't be sure: all of the journalists were frustratingly vague about exactly who was living at the house prior to 13 March. Apparently the police didn't consider the lad a suspect, presumably because purchasing, dissolving and applying the highly dangerous chemical would have been beyond the capabilities of a twelve-year-old. But could he have been, like the anguished adolescents in so many other cases, an unwitting catalyst for genuine fire-polt activity? Well … maybe.

It seems unlikely that Evangelina and Thomas would have started the final three fires and then frankly state that they were the only people in the house at the time – an admission that had the immediate result of making them prime suspects. Evangelina's claim to have always been the first to detect and extinguish the fires doesn't sound particularly suspicious and her observation that whoever was starting the fires "must be a lunatic, for each [fire] was started where it could easily be extinguished" seems very reasonable.

While some of the detectives seemed determined to pin the fires on the duo, a Constable Bull, who'd been present during several outbreaks of fire, said he saw nothing suspicious in the actions of them or of any of the other occupants.

Case 35

June 1922. Balmain, Sydney NSW. Rating: Zero

From *The West Australian*, 28 June 1922:

A BALMAIN MYSTERY.
HOUSES BOMBARDED. SYDNEY, JUNE 27

For four successive nights two small houses in a back street in Balmain have been bombarded methodically and continuously by brick bats, small boulders and other missiles in a mysterious manner. The furniture in one of the houses has been overturned, chairs have been broken and clothes torn from the beds. On Monday more windows were smashed in the two houses, and a fusillade of bottles followed. Detectives are watching the houses, but the mystery has not been cleared up.

Sources:

The West Australian (Perth), 28 Jun 1922.

The Mercury (Hobart), 28 Jun 1922.

The Cairns Post, 28 Jun 1922.

Our comments:

Balmain is a densely populated inner-city suburb, and the "fusillades" of "brickbats, small boulders" and bottles all, apparently, occurred outdoors and at night – so hoaxing cannot be ruled out.

But not everything happened outside: clothes were torn from beds – a favourite poltergeist trick – and furniture overturned and broken. If the episode was a hoax, there would seem to have been at least two people involved, including a resident of one of the houses. Newspaper coverage seems to have been pretty sparse, so it is difficult to figure out exactly what transpired.

Case 36

September 1922. Murwillumbah, NSW. Rating: Zero

VILLAGERS ALARMED.
MYSTERIOUS LIGHTS AND SOUNDS.

Sydney, Tuesday:- Memories of the Guyra "ghost" are revived by reports of strange happenings at Murwillumbah, where women and children are in a state of terror over mysterious lights and noises in an empty house on the river. The house was recently vacated by Mr. T. Williams. It is asserted that the lights appear and disappear, and then the whole house is brilliantly lit up. All the time noises are heard, like a number of people arguing and talking at once, though listeners are unable to distinguish one word. Then follows something like the sound of an object falling, and then being dragged across a room, and hammered on the wall. Two businessmen kept watch on Sunday night, but when they rushed up the house was in darkness, and the noises ceased. Men in the village have determined to solve the mystery, and intend to surround the house.

Sources:

The Argus (Melbourne), 20 Sept 1922.

The Northern Star (Lismore), 22 Sept 1922.

Our comments:

Apart from the hammering on the wall, this might better be categorised as more of an "ordinary" ghost story than a poltergeist episode – unless, of course, it was just a hoax. Perhaps the hoaxers were speedily apprehended. Perhaps, also, this was some sort of "spin-off" from the much-publicised "Guyra Ghost" episode of 1921.

Case 37

JANUARY 1924. ROUND MOUNTAIN, NEAR MURWILLUMBAH, NSW.

RATING: HALF A STAR

STONE THROWING MURWILLUMBAH MYSTERY

A mysterious case of stone throwing at Round Mountain is engaging the attention of the police while women and children are in a state of fear and will not venture out of doors at night.

A few nights ago stones were thrown on the roof of Mr. H.J. Walker's residence. The members of the family ran outside only to be struck by stones. Next day some of the family were cutting grass at the foot of a hill when they were bombarded with stones. They ran up the hill and the fusillade increased in vigour as they approached the brow but they were unable to see any one.

The next day stones came through the doors and windows and also on the veranda, and at night the house was again bombarded, but although Constables Macarthy and O'Donoghue were on the scene nobody could be seen. The male residents are joining forces with the police in an endeavour to solve the mystery.

Source:

Brisbane Courier, 22 Jan 1924.

Our comments:

This incident, which occurred about eighteen months after the other Murwillumbah episode, consisted entirely of stone falls – no levitating objects, rapping noises, etc. – and the flying stones were restricted to the outdoors – no materialisation of stones inside the house.

Although many of the stones fell at night, many also fell in broad daylight, on two successive days, in conditions where it should have been fairly easy to spot hoaxers. Police were present for a while, but only, apparently, after dark. Not a bad story – but it rests on just one short newspaper article.

Case 38

March 1925. Clifton, 30 km south of Toowoomba, QLD.
Rating: Zero

"For some considerable time" a family was disturbed by mysterious knocking above the ceiling of their home and "the wife of the occupant finally insisted that the house be vacated". Police investigated and "verified the existence of the noise, for which there was no normal explanation."

For three days "a watch was kept by some hundreds of people, and it is stated they heard a noise resembling the beating of a drum, the sound gradually lessening in volume. It is understood the services of two well-known spiritualists are to be obtained, and to use a divining rod to prove the existence of a supposed underground stream beneath the house."

Some were convinced the noise emanated "from some supernatural agency" and it was claimed that whatever was making the knocks could be communicated with, by way of "two, three or four knocks being given in response to a request". Others thought the sounds came from the cracking of rafters and warping of a galvanised iron wall due to gradual subsidence of the building.

Source:

Townsville Daily Bulletin, 25 Mar 1925.

Our comments:

This occurred shortly after the First World War when there was a strong resurgence of interest in spiritualism. It seems, also, that the "well-known" spiritualists may have read of ghostly activity supposedly occurring above underground streams in the UK.

As there was no mention of strange phenomena other than the knocking/drumming and, apparently, no further newspaper coverage, it is hard to say whether or not this was a genuine poltergeist episode.

Case 39

MAY 1932. LAUNCESTON, TASMANIA.
RATING: HALF A STAR

MYSTERIOUS STONE-THROWING

Residents of South Launceston, particularly in the neighbourhood of Garfield Street, are being caused a lot of uneasiness of late by mysterious stone-throwing. Windows are the chief targets, pieces of metal also dropping on the roofs of houses, and persons have received injuries, but, fortunately, so far of a minor nature. Plainclothes police and civilians are keeping watch, but the attacker has not been detected.

Throughout Monday and Tuesday the sniping was particularly severe. A woman was on a lawn at the back of her home when a stone more than an inch in thickness whizzed past her head. It is said that even when a detective and a civilian were making an investigation a piece of metal dropped almost at their feet, the missile being so large, and thrown with such swiftness, as to give the impression that a powerful catapult was being used. Where they come from is a mystery, the sniper directing aim from various angles.

Source:

The Mercury (Hobart), 5 May 1932.

Our comments:

The missiles apparently flew day and night from various directions, even when police were present. But they only flew outdoors, and no other phenomena suggestive of poltergeist involvement were reported.

As the incidents occurred in a built-up area, hoaxing seems likely. But one piece of metal was so large, and flew so fast that a detective thought "a powerful catapult was being used" – so if hoaxers were involved they were risking people's lives.

Case 40

MARCH 1935. CANNIBAL CREEK, 100 KM SOUTH-WEST
OF COOKTOWN, QLD.
RATING: ★★★½

(A particularly interesting fire-polt case. See Chapter Five.)

Case 41

1941. Parabeena Creek, south-west QLD.
Rating: ★★

When J. B. Heggarty was employed on a huge cattle station (which he referred to only as "X" Downs) in far south-western Queensland, a group of stockmen, who'd been out mustering, returned to the homestead with a strange tale to tell.

Having decided to rest up for a couple of days, they'd camped in a long-abandoned hut on Parabeena Creek. Half-ruined, it had a tin roof but just two remaining walls. All was well until dusk, when Fred, the head stockman, ventured outside to fill the billy can and was startled by a big stone landing nearby. Assuming he was the victim of a joke, he shouted, "Cut it out!"

His mates, however, all denied involvement, and, even as they spoke, another stone fell even closer. Then a third stone upturned a boiling billy. Although no one saw where it came from, various men were accused of throwing it, but when "a veritable hail of stones [landed] on the corrugated iron roof, creating a terrific din", and it was realised every man was inside the hut, their squabbles abruptly ceased.

As a hurried search revealed no strangers lurking outside, and as the hut was "many miles from the nearest habitation, in the midst of a vast expanse of wild scrubland", the mystery deepened.

Intermittent stone showers continued all night, making such a din that the men, huddled in their bedrolls, found it very difficult to sleep. At sunrise, although a much more thorough search was made, and although the ground had been softened by rain, not a single suspicious track was found.

The day passed without incident, but at nightfall, when another stockmen arrived and scoffed loudly on being told of the "ghost", "… a big stone, apparently coming from nowhere, knocked over a jam tin he was about to pick up."

Further missiles fell here and there, "apparently materialising out of thin air, for nobody could detect from which direction they came – and … showers of smaller stones peppered the roof."

Later, a large campfire, in full view outside the hut, "suddenly scattered [as if] violently kicked apart". Several six-foot-long logs, several inches thick, were "flung aside by some invisible force."

That night the men were again kept awake, not only by the stone showers, but also by "a weird sound, resembling a wheezy organ", that seemed to emanate from above.

With daylight peace returned once more, but at nightfall the stone showers resumed, robbing the men of yet another night's rest.

At daybreak Fred sent a rider to the homestead thirty miles away to fetch the station manager, who duly arrived that afternoon, accompanied by the local police sergeant, who questioned all the men separately without detecting any discrepancies.

On the final night, all was peaceful.

Source:

J. B. Heggarty, "The Old Hut", *The Wide World Magazine*, Jan 1951, reprinted in Frank Cusack, *Australian Ghost Stories*, pp. 130–134.

Our comments:

Mr. Heggarty, an intelligent, educated man, seems to have done a pretty good job of investigating and documenting the episode. He "knew [all of the participants] intimately, from living and working with them … having listened to their statements very carefully, I came to the conclusion they were speaking nothing but the truth."

The stockmen, he reminds us, "were hard-bitten, level-headed bushmen of long experience. Accustomed to a tough life and camping in all sorts of places, they were not at all likely to fall easy victims to superstitious terrors or to give way to hysteria."

Six weeks later, Heggarty "camped at the old hut myself, where I saw numbers of stones still lying on the roof, mute evidence as to the bombardment. Fortunately for my peace of mind, no uncanny manifestations occurred. I worked cattle around the same locality for about three years, but never heard of any further trouble."

Sceptics might ask why a poltergeist should cease its activities just because the policeman and manager were in attendance. Apart from that mildly suspicious detail, however, we see little reason to doubt that something truly uncanny occurred out there at Parabeena Creek.

Case 42

1946. Wilcannia, NSW. Rating: ★★★

This case, which contains unusual details that might throw new light on the nature of the poltergeist phenomenon, is covered in detail in Appendix C.

Case 43

JANUARY 1949–JANUARY 1950. TARCUTTA, NSW.
RATING: ★★★★

(A very interesting and unusual case. See Chapter Three, "A Ghost in the Machine".)

Case 44

9–10 June 1949. Mortdale, Sydney, NSW.
Rating: ★½

During the afternoon and evening of 10 June the Green residence in Villiers Street, Mortdale, was subjected to continuous, sometimes deafeningly loud, knocking. As Mr. Green, a fireman, was on duty at the time, his wife, her three young children and a female friend endured the racket for an hour until Mr. B.B. Smith, who heard the noise from next door, came to their assistance.

The knocking continued, at times developing "hammer force" and seeming to come from the roof, the walls and under the floor. Windows rattled and glass panels were dislodged. Mr. Smith and other neighbours looked through the whole house, even underneath the floor, but could find nothing. They rang the police.

The din became even louder when the police arrived, accompanied by Mr. Green, who they'd fetched from the fire station. Constables Townsend and Gibb, and Detectives Wedlock and Robertson searched the house and even climbed into the roof cavity. Constable Gibb said that, although it sounded silly, he could offer no explanation except that a ghost was at work. "We would rush into the room from which the noise came", he said, "and then there would be a crash in the room we had just left."

Although the banging came from the floor, roof, and walls it centred mainly on the children's bedroom. "But", one policeman said, "it was a physical impossibility for the children to make the din".

The disturbance, which had begun about 5 pm, continued with varying intensity till 1 am, then faded away. Mrs. Green and the children, who'd spent the night with neighbours, returned home in the morning, accompanied by a friend.

According to one report, the rapping resumed on the following night, after which, it seems, it wasn't heard again. Not surprisingly, perhaps, the police finally came up with a "logical explanation": the knocking must have been caused by high water pressure.

Sources:

Sydney Morning Herald, 11 and 13 Jun 1949.

Morning Bulletin (Rockhampton), 13 Jun 1949.

Our comments:

Although no strange phenomena, other than the very loud and persistent knocking, was reported, this may well have been a genuine poltergeist episode.

The way the knocking moved around, seemingly playing games with the investigators, is very reminiscent of "trickster" behaviour noted during poltergeist episodes throughout the centuries.

The policeman's observation that the rapping was centred mainly on the children's bedroom may also be significant. We wouldn't mind betting one of the kids was a troubled adolescent.

But as we have only a couple of short newspaper articles to go by, and as the episode seems to have come to an end after a couple of days, it's impossible to say for sure whether anything truly supernatural was going on.

Case 45

1955–2002. Mayanup, Pumphrey and Boyup Brook, WA.
Rating: ★★★★★

(The most remarkable case of all. See Chapter Two.)

Case 46

1956. Baradine, 45 km north-west of Coonabarabran, NSW.
Rating: ★

A family of itinerant rural workers, including a ten-year-old boy and an 18-year-old married woman, rented a house in Baradine in early 1956. Soon after they moved in, stones, wood, metal objects and dried mud were thrown at the outside walls; then the sound of "dancing feet" was heard inside.

Baradine locals were said to be convinced that supernatural forces were at work, and an "experienced Sydney journalist" who visited the property said that "he not only saw sticks and stones hurtling through the air, but he himself was struck (but not hurt) three times by wood or metal while standing outside the house. He was certain the missiles were not thrown by human hand."

The weird activity continued for some weeks before it "went away".

Source:

Eric Bell-Smith, "Spooks with spirit", *People* magazine, 17 Sept 1958.

Our comments:

It's unfortunate that our sole source for the story – the *People* magazine article – doesn't include key details such as the exact date of the incident or whether the bombardment occurred in daylight or only after dark. It also fails to identify either the affected family or the Sydney journalist.

On the other hand, the lengthy article is a general review of poltergeist cases in Australia and elsewhere, and it is evident that the journalist, Eric Bell-Smith, either had a very good knowledge of the subject to begin with or did his homework thoroughly before putting pen to paper. As all the other material in his story seems correct, it seems likely that his brief account of what happened at Baradine is also correct.

The Sydney journalist's assertion that he wasn't injured after being struck repeatedly by flying objects is reminiscent of testimony recorded during other, better documented, polt episodes. On the strength of that – and of a general gut feeling about the case – we feel it's worth a one-star rating.

Case 47

c. 1957. Borden, WA. Rating: ★

Cyril Penny and his nephew Aden Eades, who'd both been involved in the amazing series of events at Mayanup and Pumphrey (Chapter Two), experienced a brief reprise of the uncanny action near Borden, 160 kilometres east of Mayanup.

They told Helen Hack that one rainy night, while sheltering under a tarp, they'd suddenly been pelted with sandalwood nuts which were, they noted, bone-dry. When they threw a handful out into the darkness with the challenge, "Here – have another go", a "shovel full" was hurled back at them.

We don't know exactly when this occurred – it could have been any time after 21 March 1957, when the men were known to be en route to Borden.

Source:

Helen Hack, *The Mystery of the Mayanup Poltergeist*, p. 65.

Our comments:

The fact that, despite the downpour, the nuts were bone dry strongly suggests this was a genuine polt event, as does the invisible assailant's immediate reaction to the men's challenge.

As the story comes from an excellent source – Helen Hack, who wrote the definitive account of the Mayanup/Pumphrey/Boyup Brook events and who knew both men well – we are strongly inclined to believe it is true.

Case 48

1977. NEWCASTLE, NSW. RATING: ★★★

("The Gordon Street Poltergeist". See Chapter Eight.)

Case 49

NOVEMBER 1986. SAN REMO, NSW. RATING: ★★★½

(A particularly interesting case. See Chapter Six.)

Case 50

1990. ALICE SPRINGS, NT. RATING: ★★★

("The Nice Old Man" case. See Chapter Nine.)

Case 51

1994–1996. CANBERRA, ACT. RATING: ★★★★

("The Caressa" case. See Chapter Four.)

Case 52

FEBRUARY–MAY 1998. HUMPTY DOO, NT. RATING: ★★★★½

(See Chapter One.)

CHAPTER THIRTEEN

Rapping it up

Once, while reflecting on the maelstrom of weirdness that enveloped his Mayanup property back in 1955–57, Doug Hack remarked: "If this poltergeist was trying to tell you something, you couldn't work it out – there was no sense to it."

Four years ago, when we penned the first draft of this chapter, we confidently titled it "Conclusions". But now, having worked and re-worked the manuscript, having visited several additional polt sites in Europe and Asia, having read much more widely and having consulted with other researchers, we feel obliged to admit that we're almost as mystified now, about the true nature of poltergeists, as we were when we blundered into the world of weirdness at Humpty Doo back in 1998.

So, while still enjoying our research and occasional attempts at on-the-spot polt busting, we fully empathise with Mr. Hack's expression of frustrated curiosity.

That having been said, we certainly haven't wasted our time. We've rescued many interesting, long forgotten cases from obscurity and have established that patterns of polt activity in Australia conform very closely to those recorded throughout the centuries in Europe, the Americas, Africa, Asia and the Middle East.

While the most commonly reported phenomena – rapping, levitation and teleportation of objects, stone falls, etc. – are interesting enough in themselves, throughout this book we've pointed out several instances where very odd, seemingly "one-off" effects reported during some of our cases have been found to match incidents recorded during very obscure episodes that occurred in different parts of the country many decades earlier. The fist-sized black object that Brett Styles saw flying under the patio roof at Humpty Doo, for instance, matches the "black object" that two women saw "come through one angle of the house and go right through the opposite angle" at Cooyal 111 years earlier.

Sometimes the match was found in obscure foreign cases. The detail of the bottle opener disappearing from the Humpty Doo house and returning brightly polished, for instance, corresponds to events reported during an 1849–50 episode in the Navidad region of Texas, where a heavy log chain and a saw disappeared and returned, "… polished as bright as a looking glass". The bullets that kept finding their way back into the Humpty Doo house correspond to musket balls that did the same thing during the "Belledoon Mysteries" episode near Wallaceburg, Ontario, in 1829–30.

While these coincidences don't constitute proof of the reality of the polt phenomenon, we think most readers will agree it is extremely improbable that different people, so separated by distance and time, would have simply imagined or invented the same crazy little details.

Even if we hadn't witnessed poltergeist activity ourselves, the obvious sincerity of the many people who told us of similar experiences would have convinced us of the reality of the phenomenon. Some were severely shaken by their ordeals.

One woman in particular was still so traumatised when we interviewed her, many years after the event, that she begged us to keep all key details – her name, state of residence, and even the year in which the incidents occurred – confidential. Her distress was palpable – it was impossible not to believe her.

That episode, which featured rapping, pockets of intense cold, the levitation and flight of many extremely dangerous objects that somehow never caused injury, and violent reactions to religious ritual – was one of the most remarkable in our files: right up there with the Humpty Doo and other "four-star" cases. A retired police officer and ministers from various religious denominations were among the many who saw the objects fly. Like the Mayanup polt and others, the spook was mobile: it followed the poor woman and her family from residence to residence.

Hot shots

While the mountains of good testimonial evidence and our own experiences have convinced us that poltergeist events really do occur, we have run across only one piece of good, empirical evidence during our Australian researches: the infra-red photography of Brendan Gowdie. As detailed in Chapter One, Mr. Gowdie, using a sophisticated thermal imagining camera, filmed many of the objects that flew and fell inside the house at Humpty Doo in 1998.

While the camera revealed that objects tossed by his colleagues displayed warm spots and streaks corresponding to fingerprints, the objects that "seemed to come from nowhere" were *uniformly warm all over*. To fake that effect, a hoaxer would have to heat the objects in a microwave, then remove and throw them using tongs – a tricky procedure that would have been impossible to manage time and again, under the circumstances. Besides, as Brendan points out, the tenants had no idea what kind of camera he was using.

RSPK or, occasionally, "wild talents"?

The late parapsychologist D. Scott Rogo strongly believed that disembodied spirits have nothing to do with poltergeist effects. He argued that they are, instead, the result of recurrent spontaneous psychokinesis (RSPK) generated by people: "… poltergeists focus on families, which tend to repress and sublimate large amounts of … inner aggression [which builds up] within the unconscious mind of one of the family members, until it explodes in the form of the poltergeist".[96]

Rogo was far from alone in that belief and it is certainly true that troubled adolescents *were* at the epicentre of the action in a significant proportion of our Australian cases. It is worth noting, also, that adolescent girls were present at all three of the polt-plagued locations – in Malaysia, Vietnam and Turkey – that Paul visited in 2011–13 (see Appendix A).

While Rogo's theory involves psychokinesis produced unwittingly, one of our cases features a person who may have been able to produce such effects at will. Family members stated that in later life Minnie Bowen, the girl at the centre of the "Guyra Ghost" episode, could move objects simply by looking at them. It is not known whether she had that ability at the time of the "Ghost" episode, or whether she developed it as a result of being the focus of the polt's attention.

There is no suggestion that anyone else in our assembled cases was capable of intentionally producing and consciously controlling psychokinesis, but we do have three odd stories which, though too poorly documented to be included in the main body of the book, are nevertheless too intriguing to simply throw away. They feature individuals whose supposed psychokinetic powers would put Mandrake the Magician to shame. (See Appendix B, "Wild Talents").

Creepy places?

While a significant proportion of Australian cases do feature stressed adolescents, as per Rogo's theory, many others don't involve families or children at all. There are a few episodes, in fact, where the phenomena seemed linked to specific *locations* well away from human habitation, rather than to a person.

The 1888 incident reported by the drover "Blue Jacket", for instance, took place "in the centre of a plain, with no trees of any description within a mile" at the site of, it was suggested, an Aboriginal burial ground. Similarly, the ruined hut at Parabeena Creek, where the stockmen were peppered with stones in 1941, was "many miles from the nearest habitation, in the midst of a vast expanse of wild scrubland".

---

96   Interview with D. Scott Rogo, in Michael Clarkson, *The Poltergeist Phenomenon.*

The dear departed

In some cases also, there are indications that spirits of the dead might have been involved. The 1990 Alice Springs case, where the "nice old man" appeared, is the best example of that. The San Remo case of 1986, where another "old bloke" died in the affected house while knocking forlornly on the wall, is another. It doesn't seem unreasonable to suspect, also, that the fires at Cannibal Creek in 1935 were orchestrated by the restless spirit of the old Chinese leper.

A couple of things ...

Because this is intended to be, primarily, a source book for other polt researchers, as well as an interesting (we hope) glimpse into to the weird world of Australian poltergeistery for the general reader, we won't go too deeply into the various theories about the true nature of polts or about where (if anywhere) they hang out when they're not pestering us hapless mortals. Greater minds than ours have wrestled with the problem and have had to admit defeat.

We would, however, like to mention a couple of things that might throw a little bit of extra light on the mystery.

Knock, knock – what's there?

We know of nothing similar having been done in Australia, but in 2009 Dr. Barrie Colvin, building on the work of others, notably J. L. Whitton, acoustically analysed recordings of rapping from ten different poltergeist sites and came up with some very interesting results.

He found that when normally-produced rapping is analysed the loudest part of the sound is invariably at the very beginning, after which the sound gradually decays. Polt-produced raps, however, begin relatively quietly before building up to their maximum volume.

The peculiar acoustical pattern of the poltergeist rapping, in fact, indicated that the sounds arose from *within* the structure of the material rather than from its surface. This accords with the testimony of the many Australian witnesses who have insisted that rapping seems to have come from inside the walls of their polt-plagued dwellings.[97]

It is important to note that the ten recordings tested by Dr. Colvin were collected at various sites around the world, on different types of apparatus between 1960 and 2000 – *yet they all exhibited the same anomalous acoustic profile.* As ghost-hunter Alan Murdie

---

[97] Barrie Colin, "The Acoustic Properties of Unexplained Rapping Sounds", *Journal of the Society for Psychical Research*, Vol 73.2 No. 899, April 2010.

has pointed out, hoaxers of the 1960s and '70s could not have had the advanced knowledge to create an effect "detectable only by instrumental analysis, and only identified [decades] later."[98]

Neither here nor there

Those who find it difficult to credit the seemingly impossible things – objects materialising, dematerialising, passing though solid walls, etc. – that are reported so often during poltergeist episodes, might usefully reflect on what scientists have discovered in the realm of quantum physics.

Difficult as it is for most of us to get our minds around, some sub-atomic particles, the boffins tell us, can be in two places at the same time. Others change their behaviour simply because they are being observed.

The strangest particles of all are neutrinos. So utterly mysterious that they are sometimes referred to as having "ghost-like" qualities, they pass right through solid matter, including human bodies, without touching anything, leaving no trace. Physicist Frank Close goes so far as to suggest that *they may exist partly in extra dimensions and be able to travel back in time.*[99]

The weird little neutrino, although postulated by Wolfgang Pauli twenty years earlier, remained undetected until the 1950s, when it was proven to exist during a series of experiments amusingly – and perhaps significantly – titled "The Poltergeist Project".

A mind-bender

In light of what had recently been discovered about neutrinos, Professor Hans Bender, who investigated a remarkable poltergeist episode in Rosenheim, Germany, in 1967–68, suggested that polt researchers should consider "the hypothesis of higher space, or a fourth dimension ... Clearly, no room is closed if an object can take a trajectory in higher space. It will, in addition, appear or disappear instantaneously".

In recent decades, many mainstream scientists have speculated about, and run calculations on, other dimensions and even parallel universes. In February 1998, for instance, *Scientific American* published a theory that in addition to "our" ten-dimensional universe there is a ten-dimensional parallel universe.

Mind-boggling stuff, but, as Professor Bender suggested back in the '60s, it certainly could explain a lot about the games poltergeists play.

---

98 Alan Murdie, "Enfield and the 'skeptics'", *Fortean Times*, No. 288, Special issue, 2012.
99 Frank Close, *Neutrino*, Oxford University Press, 2010.

The final rap

While the authors greatly enjoy working together, and agree on most matters, we don't always come to exactly the same conclusions about the many and various mysteries we investigate. So now, as we prepare to wrap up (or should we say "rap up") this compendium of Australian poltergeistery, we aren't surprised to find that we have a slightly different "take" on some aspects of the phenomenon.

Whereas, for instance, Paul, like D. Scott Rogo and many others, inclines to the view that most, if not all, polt phenomena is caused by psychokinesis generated unwittingly by people at the centre of the activity, Tony, like Colin Wilson and others, favours the idea that disembodied spirits are often involved.

Paul feels that the dozens of case histories and our many comments throughout the book have given readers quite enough to think about, and that little else needs to be added.

Tony, on the other hand, who likes to engage in speculation – some might say wild speculation – about possible connections between the poltergeist phenomenon and other fortean phenomena, would like to comment further. He has therefore been allocated space, in Appendix C, to explore those ideas.

Our opinions may differ slightly on some aspects of the mystery, but, having seen the paranormal activity at Humpty Doo with our own eyes, having researched so many similar cases and having interviewed so many credible eyewitnesses, we entirely agree on this: that poltergeist activity *does* occur – and occur quite frequently – here in the wonderful land of Oz.

APPENDIX A – THREE ASIAN FIRE POLTS

By Paul Cropper

In late 2010 I read that intense poltergeist activity was allegedly occurring at a house near Kota Bharu, Malaysia. The episode was particularly interesting because, like the 1922 Darling Point and the 1935 Cannibal Creek incidents (Cases 34 and 40) it featured supposedly inexplicable outbreaks of fire. In February 2011 I visited the site and, on returning to Australia, wrote the following report. It was published in *Fortean Times* No. 281, November 2011.

The Fire Djinn

Between May and December 2010 a series of strange incidents occurred in the home of a seventy-three-year-old widow, Zainab Sulaiman, in a kampong near Kota Bharu. Objects disappeared and reappeared, clothes were found cut to shreds, food scraps were strewn across beds and large quantities of salt and smelly fish sauce were dumped into cooking pots.

It was all decidedly annoying, but Zainab and her family – a widowed daughter-in-law and two granddaughters – didn't find it particularly frightening. They were merely being pestered, they assumed, by a mildly mischievous spirit. Even when a pair of pants, missing for three days, reappeared inside the refrigerator, they remained calm, hoping the imp would tire of its tricks.

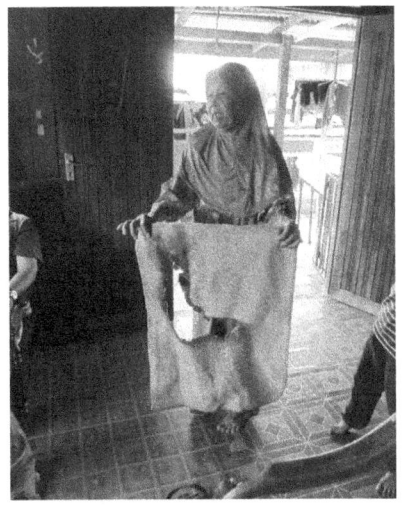

Zainab Sulaiman. (Healy/Cropper)

But in mid-December the weirdness escalated dangerously: over the next ten weeks dozens of small fires broke out on clothes, rugs, linoleum and mattresses throughout the residence. Sometimes several occurred within a few minutes; on one hectic day there were no fewer than 78.

Although all were quickly extinguished and surprisingly little damage was done, Zainab didn't get a lot of sleep during those weird weeks. Her flimsy wooden dwelling, elevated on stumps and packed with clothes and bolts of cloth, was a veritable tinder box. She didn't dare leave it unattended.

Stop that infernal djinn!

News of the weirdness spread quickly, and on January 4 a group of Muslim holy men arrived and declared the house was infested by invisible entities known as *djinn*. (*Djinn* is the plural; the masculine singular is *djinni* – or genie).

Djinn have featured prominently in Middle Eastern folklore since time immemorial and Mohammed, under the direction of the angel Gabriel, incorporated them into Muslim theology. Many of the tricks they reputedly play are highly reminiscent of those often attributed, in other cultures, to poltergeists.

The holy men concentrated their chanting on a set of ancient swords, knives, and brassware that they thought the djinn had "possessed". Perhaps, they suggested, Zainab's parents, to whom the objects had originally belonged, had flirted with black magic. Be that as it may, their "cleansing" ceremony, far from defusing the situation, seemed merely to annoy the fire-starter(s): on the very next day 46 blazes broke out.

But while their exorcism failed, something recorded by photographer Zulhanifa Sidek might indicate the holy men were correct in identifying the hot-fingered imps as djinn.

A mysterious fire in Zainab Sulaimain's house, captured by Zulhanifa Sidek. (Zulhanifa Sidek)

Zulhanifa witnessed two fires. One flame, licking up from a stack of clothing in a cupboard, struck him as being unusually bright and well-defined. Even more remarkable was the fact that, as his photographs show, it was completely smokeless. Perhaps significantly, The Koran (55:15) states, "And the djinn did he create from a smokeless flame of fire".

Several other ghost busters tried to douse the djinn. Ong Q. Leng, a photogenic, flamboyantly-dressed "miracle-working doctor", performed kung fu-like motions to expel the spooks and "lock" the house. "I could sense an evil presence the moment I stepped [in]", she said. "There are little djinns under the house [and] big ones outside …" While claiming to have chased them away, she left herself with a small "out": "there is a 50–50 chance they will return."

Of all the journalists who covered her story, Zainab considered Syed Azhar, of the Kuala Lumpur *Star*, the most accurate and sympathetic. She took to phoning him when the invisible arsonist was most active, and during five visits to her house he interviewing all those involved and witnessed some of the attempted exorcisms.

When I met Syed in Kota Bharu in February 2011 he was still wavering between accepting the episode as supernatural and dismissing it as a hoax. He'd witnessed several fires but hadn't actually seen them start, nor had he witnessed objects teleporting. He had, however, interviewed people other than Zainab's family who *had* seen such things, including one who'd seen a fire burning, impossibly, on a wet towel. He was sure Zainab was sane and honest, and found it difficult to believe the daughter-in-law or granddaughters could have started so many fires without being caught.

Wan Nurfatifa and Zainab Sulaiman. (Healy/Cropper)

He did, nevertheless, note that 13-year-old Wan Nurfatifa seemed to "know" when fires were starting and was usually the first to find and extinguish them. She said she "smelled them".

Because he knew that poltergeist activity is often focused on adolescent girls, Syed didn't think that Wan's fire-spotting talent necessarily meant she was hoaxing. Similarly, her revelation that her sweater had caught fire on a school bus, rather than suggesting she was a hoaxer, might have indicated she was the unwitting catalyst for a polt's paranormal pranks.

When Syed took me to the house on February 19, I was favourably impressed by the energetic, motherly Zainab, who obviously had a loving relationship with her quietly-spoken daughter-in-law and well-behaved grandkids. But I was dismayed to learn that all had been quiet, on the djinn front, for the previous ten days – the longest period of peace thus far experienced.

I needn't have worried: that evening the djinn – or somebody – obliged by starting two fires in quick succession. The first began at about 9.15 pm while Syed and I were in the living room and the entire family were out of sight in the kitchen. We didn't become aware of it until Zainab walked calmly up the corridor carrying a smouldering cushion. The semi-circular burnt patch was pretty impressive but, call me an old sceptic, on entering the kitchen I noted that the circular gas ring was burning.

Five minutes later I noticed 11-year-old Nur Fatili pointing excitedly into a bedroom. On entering, we found a nylon blouse smouldering. Again, not very dramatic; but as the blouse was one of many hanging very close together, it did seem rather odd that the fire hadn't spread.

Although both events might have been genuinely paranormal, neither would have … ahem … set a sceptic's world on fire. As the fires were the first to have occurred in ten days, I found the family's calm, even happy, demeanour rather surprising. Perhaps it was a "cultural thing", but there was certainly nothing like the level of excitement I'd observed – and experienced – during the Humpty Doo polt episode of 1998. I also thought I detected an element of "show" when the cushion was brought out. Even so, I found it very difficult to think ill of kindly Zainab. Perhaps, I mused, she'd faked things "just this once" so as not to disappoint one who'd travelled so far to visit.

On the other hand, it had previously been noted at Kota Bharu that (as at other reputed polt sites) the arrival of strangers triggered brief upsurges of weird activity.

A hell of a note?

Then I examined a bank note that had supposedly appeared inside the house some months earlier. A message scrawled on it translated as "Goodbye, everyone". Because I'd encountered similar, rather inane, polt-jottings at Humpty Doo, the note-on-the-note didn't, in itself, induce scepticism. That came later, when I noticed that the djinn's handwriting was quite similar to that of 13-year-old Wan.

Because of the exotic location, because of the overlay of djinn folklore and because fire-starting polts are (thankfully) relatively rare, I found the Zainab case particularly interesting. But as I didn't see objects levitating or appearing out of nowhere, or actually observe fires as they ignited, I simply can't say whether or not the episode was genuinely paranormal. Had it also featured, as many of our Aussie cases have, showers of stones observed by scores of witnesses, it would, of course, have been much easier to decide.

So by the time I left the house I was, like Syed, wavering between scepticism and belief – and I'm still wavering.

Some aspects of the case strongly suggest the episode was genuinely paranormal:
- Zainab never sought to profit from the episode. It had, in fact, cost her dearly. Many of her possessions were destroyed, and she'd paid the Muslim priests 1000 Ringgits for their failed exorcism.
- She seemed completely honest, and it would have been virtually impossible for any of the family to start the fires without her noticing. No outsider could have lit them.

- No family member had an obvious motive to hoax the affair.
- Independent witnesses saw objects move and disappear.
- The steady escalation of weirdness: beginning with objects moving and disappearing, progressing to the slashing of clothes, then to the weird message, and finally to the fires – conforms to patterns of polt behaviour noted elsewhere.
- The very fact that more than 200 fires occurred without at least one of them doing serious damage – or for that matter completely consuming the flimsy dwelling – does seem almost miraculous. Uncannily localised fires have been noted at other polt sites.
- The unusually bright, smokeless character of the flame photographed by Zulhanifa Sidek corresponds remarkably well with what the Koran says about the genesis of the djinn.
- The surges in weird activity that occurred when strangers arrived corresponds with known polt behaviour.
- The presence of adolescent girls is sometimes seen as a veritable hallmark of a genuine polt case.
- The djinn's rather pointless message was reminiscent of others found at polt sites.
- After the holy men tried to "cleanse" the house, the rate of fire-starting sharply increased. Similar sudden escalations of activity after attempted exorcisms have been noted at many other polt sites.

On the other hand, a few things suggest the episode was bogus:
- Although none had occurred for ten days, two fires broke out on the very day I visited. Some might see that as a little too fortuitous.
- The family seemed strangely unexcited by the fires.
- At one stage so many of the girl's uniforms were damaged that they had to stay home from school. Could that have been a motive for hoaxing?
- Most suspicious of all was the similarity of Wan's handwriting to that on the 10-Ringgit note.

But regardless of whether or not they were genuinely supernatural, the fires I observed at Kota Bharu were the last to occur. The djinn, or the hoaxer(s), have called it quits, and Zainab can sleep soundly once again.

Djinn and poltergeists

Middle Eastern folklore and Muslim theology are full of stories about djinn and their amazing powers. Not all of their behaviour corresponds with poltergeist phenomena observed in "the West", but a significant amount of it does:
- They take possession of buildings or locales and "persecute terribly any person who goes [to live there]".
- Throw stones at people.
- Travel great distances at blinding speed.
- Sometimes possess humans and hijack their vocal chords to speak.
- Are usually invisible and benefit from their invisibility to frighten people.
- Are "fearful … by nature, but can feel emotions [such as] anger or sadness … djinn benefit from these states, being better able to cause fear in [humans] … when they sense your fear, they will attack."
- Can take the form of humans, black dogs, black cats and other animals.
- Can be good or neutrally benevolent but are generally "ignorant, oppressive and treacherous."
- Levitate objects.
- Mimic the voices of deceased humans.

Fiery phenomena in Vietnam

The house in Ho Chi Minh City. (Healy/Cropper)

In early 2012 I noticed various internet articles about another family – this time Vietnamese – that was allegedly being terrorised by mysterious outbreaks of fire. The similarity to the Kota Bharu episode was so striking that I decided, once again, to make an on-the-spot investigation.

After flying into Ho Chi Minh City on 25 May 2012, I arranged, with the kind assistance of Mr. Trung and Mr. Anh of Tuoi Tres News Agency, to meet the family in question.

This time, the affected residence proved to be a large, three-storey house on a very pleasant tree-lined street, and the family, which consisted of Mr. Viet Pham Quoc, an employee of Air Vietnam, his wife and four children, was considered to be quite wealthy.

Although very hospitable, Mr. Pham Quoc and his wife were rather reserved at first. While happy to detail the sequence of events, they didn't want any further media attention and insisted, quite reasonably, that I not make audio tapes or photograph any of the children.

Both parents and all of their polite, well-educated offspring spoke very good English, and, during the three and a half hours I spent with them, told their remarkable stories in what was quite evidently an honest and unaffected manner.

The sheer number and frequency of the reported fires was quite astounding: in the two months since it all began, they said, there had been several blazes a day; more than a hundred in all – until five days prior to my visit, when they'd suddenly ceased.

Just prior to the first fires all of their electrical "breaker" switches had inexplicably tripped, not just once, but several times. Although electricians who repeatedly examined the wiring found nothing amiss, many of the subsequent blazes affected light switches throughout the house. One particular switch caught fire *ten times in one day*. Mr. Pham Quoc showed me a quite impressive film clip he'd taken during one incident: a light switch surrounded by very intense flames. I later noticed a bag full of damaged switches standing in the hallway.

Scorched fan. (Healy/Cropper)

Two electric fans, some clothes, a mattress, a toilet seat, a bucket and other objects had also been burned or scorched, but the worst incident occurred on 12 May, when an entire room was virtually destroyed.

A poltergeist girl

As in so many other episodes, the strange phenomena were sharply focused on an adolescent child – in this case eleven-year-old Thuy. But although the fires occurred only when she was nearby, and never when she was asleep, her parents insisted she would not, and in fact *could not*, have started them. On several occasions, they pointed out, fires had started in cupboards upstairs when everyone, including Thuy, was dining downstairs.

Once, when she was with her father in the living room, a T-shirt hanging on a rail suddenly ignited. Soon afterwards, in similar circumstances, a telephone handset caught fire.

I was mildly surprised to find that, far from being a tormented soul, Thuy seemed to be, like everyone else in the family, happy and well-adjusted. Very intelligent and, thanks to the International School she attended, very fluent in English, she told her strange story in an unaffected and articulate manner. I could detect no trace of mischief in her demeanour, no "showing off" or pride in being the centre of attention.

Although she never sensed, beforehand, that the fires were about to occur, she said that she sometimes "felt electricity" when they were happening and felt quite tired afterwards.

Once, while playing on an iPad with her sister, the younger girl's T-shirt had begun smouldering. I was shown a picture of a T-shirt with a one-inch diameter hole burnt in it.

If there was not already sufficient evidence that the phenomenon was somehow linked to her presence, the fires followed Thuy to her Uncle's house when her parents sent her there for a few days.

The major fire of May 12, which destroyed an upstairs bedroom, and which required the Fire Brigade to extinguish, started on the floor beside a bed. Thuy had fetched something from the room a few minutes earlier. Sceptics may gleefully pounce upon that detail, but her parents remained convinced of her innocence. While in no doubt that the phenomenon was somehow reliant on, or triggered by her presence, they were adamant that she wouldn't deliberately endanger the family and that, in any case, she couldn't possibly have started so many fires without being caught in the act. I couldn't detect the slightest suspicion on their part, and was, in fact, quite touched by their loving and protective attitude.

Paul Cropper in the damaged bedroom. (Healy/Cropper)

Although most of the burnt objects I was shown would have been within reach of a child, some, like a fan near the toilet, were high enough to have caused difficulty. I thought it very improbable, also, that a child – or an adult for that matter – could have repeatedly sprayed accelerant onto live light switches and ignited it without electrocuting themselves or shorting-out the entire system.

Another thing that strongly inclined me to accept the case as genuinely paranormal was the open, candid demeanour of the family. Intelligent, polite, calm and reasonable, they had no need of money and certainly weren't seeking notoriety. They simply wished for the cessation of the fires and, hopefully, some explanation of how and why they occurred. They were therefore extremely interested in photographs I'd taken during the Kota Bharu episode, evidently taking some comfort in the knowledge that their ordeal was not unique.

While I can't say why it should have been centred upon, or triggered by young Thuy, I have little doubt that the Pham Quoc household, for some unknown reason, was living through a very genuine fire-poltergeist infestation.

So, as I flew home from Vietnam I could only reflect that, in the weird field of poltergeistery, as in life in general, bad things sometimes happen to good people.

Unlike the Malaysian family I'd met in Kota Bharu, and a polt-plagued Turkish family I was to meet later, the Pham Quocs didn't raise the possibility that evil spirits were starting the fires. My impression was that they felt some strange form of electricity was involved.

Angel and the fire demon

In April 2013, after reading about a Turkish family being plagued by similar outbreaks of fire, I made another on-the-spot investigation. On returning to Australia, I wrote the following report, which was published in *Fortean Times*, no. 302, June 2013.

The terror began in the town of Siirt, on the night of August 13, 2012, when a street vendor, Zeki Toprak, his wife and four children were woken by the smell of smoke and discovered a fire in their simple three-room residence.

The Toprak family. (Healy/Cropper)

Although firemen quickly extinguished the blaze, they were baffled as to how it started – because it had, most unusually, broken out on a bare ceiling, well away from readily combustible material. Power company technicians also attended and found nothing wrong with the house's wiring.

Over the course of the next few months, scores of other small fires broke out, during both day and night, on walls and ceilings, as well as on clothes, prayer mats, carpets, plastic tubs and inside closed cabinets.

Fear of frying

Terrified of being incinerated, the family moved their bedding and most precious belongings onto a balcony, where they slept for nearly two weeks – until the fires followed them outside.

Although not as frightening as the fires, plenty of other strange phenomena disturbed the tranquillity of the home. Clothes and other objects repeatedly disappeared, only to reappear in unlikely places. A washing machine also got into the act: plugging itself into a socket and beginning its cycle.

Desperate to escape the potentially lethal weirdness, the family moved to a relative's house – but the fires again followed.

Calling the clerics

Feeling, not unreasonably, that something decidedly uncanny was going on, the Topraks appealed for help to local imams, who declared the phenomena to be the work of mischievous *djinn*, and attempted to cleanse the site with prayer.

Each time the family called the clerics, however, the fires flared up even more frequently, seemingly aggravated by the rituals.

Hot-footing it

The imams having failed, Mr. Toprak appealed for help to the Siirt District Governor, Ahmet Aydın, who, accompanied by a Kanal 56 film crew, promptly visited, interviewed the family and inspected the damage. Although the *djinni* refrained from starting any major fires, a cameraman, Soyler Ozan, on leaving the residence, felt a burning sensation and found that a section of the sole of his shoe had melted.

Duly impressed, the Governor declared the problem a "transcendent (i.e. paranormal) event".

By now the story had reached the mainstream Turkish media, and dozens of reports soon appeared in regional and city newspapers, on television and radio.

Dr. Erman investigates ... "Siirt" of ...

As interest peaked, the Rector of Siirt University, Professor Murat Erman, decided to see if science could shed some light on the situation.

In late December his team, including a psychiatrist, a sociologist, a physicist and several engineers, interviewed the family, and together with the police, set up cameras to monitor key points throughout the house.

Frustratingly for the scientists, the poltergeist, *djinni* – or hoaxer – refused to perform on cue, and all the fires that occurred during the month-long investigation flared up just outside the cameras' limited fields of view.

In late February, in a three-page report that addressed only the fires and ignored the other strange aspects of the case (such as the cameraman's hot-foot), the boffins presented their predictably sceptical conclusions:

"... this commission believes that: possibility of metaphysic involvements is negligible.

Wholly comprehending the problem requires a long time observation of socio-physiologic nature of all members of the Toprak family."

Most damningly, the report stated, falsely, that the Toprak children had been caught with cigarette lighters.

Deeply insulted, and exhausted by the attention, the family packed up and moved 140 kilometres south to Cizre, hoping once again to outrun their demon.

By March 2013 they'd lived in six different residences, but each time they moved the fiery nightmare dogged their steps. In the seven months since the terror began, it was claimed, no fewer than 300 blazes had occurred.

Meet the Topraks

Just as Dr. Erman was endeavouring to stifle it, an English language report of the case arrived in my Inbox. Its similarity to the Malaysian and Vietnamese cases was so striking that I immediately decided to check it out in person.

After a 21-hour flight from Sydney to Istanbul, two connecting flights to Siirt, and a three-hour bus ride across the barren, snow-covered mountains of south-eastern Turkey, I arrived at the town of Cizre, on the Syrian border.

I was fortunate to be accompanied by two very friendly and helpful government officials, Arzu and Faik, who would act as interpreters.

Our first point of contact was the Sirnak District Governor, and, just as I walked into his office, Mr. Toprak, who I recognised from the media reports, walked out. The confounded fires, as he'd just informed the Governor, had started yet again, on March 21st, at his latest residence.

The well-spoken, intelligent man readily agreed to escort me to his new home, an unfurnished three-room, ground floor dwelling. As we sat outside on soft mats, he told how the family's reputation had preceded them to Cizre, and how, as a consequence, they'd had trouble finding a place to rent. Their first night had been spent on the street.

He was adamant that no family member was starting the fires: "We bought all our own furniture; I worked hard for it – why would we burn it?" He didn't want money or notoriety – just a peaceful place to live and work. "We always pray", he said, with evident sincerity, "that nobody else will have to experience this."

His wife and children eagerly confirmed all the facts as reported in the media, and provided interesting additional details.

Shortly before the first fire, they'd had to call a locksmith when a key inside the front door of their original house had, seemingly impossibly, turned and locked them all outside.

Mrs. Toprak described how, on another occasion, she'd set out plates for breakfast, stepped into another room, and returned moments later to find them gone. They were discovered arranged neatly in the garden. A TV remote, a mobile phone and other appliances also vanished from closed rooms and were, apparently, teleported outdoors.

As at Kota Bharu, food was often interfered with: salt mysteriously appearing in a

Washing machine destroyed by fire. (Zeki Toprak)

sugar bowl and a water bottle filling with vinegar.

Perhaps the weirdest of all the fires broke out *inside a refrigerator*: "It was empty and [when] we looked inside … there were clothes in there, burning."

Family members found and extinguished most of the fires, but, interestingly, all of the others *extinguished themselves* before major damage was done: "We sometimes smell smoke and look around and can't find anything, and later find something has been burnt."

Bad-mouthed by boffins

Mr. Toprak was still very annoyed with Dr. Erman's report, particularly his allegation that the children had been caught with cigarette lighters. The truth was somewhat different.

"One night in Siirt", he explained, "we were all sleeping in the same room because we were so scared, and all of a sudden we smelled smoke and [searched the other rooms]. We found nothing, but when we returned to our bedroom we saw our beds burning. Then I found a lighter under my pillow – but where it came from we don't know".

So the academics would never have known about the lighter if Mr. Toprak hadn't mentioned it – yet they gave a different account of its discovery and implied that the entire family were mentally disturbed hoaxers.

While I found the detail of the lighter a little disconcerting (why would the spook, apparently capable of all kinds of supernatural feats, have needed it?) this wasn't the first time I'd heard of a polt toying with one. When a colleague, Wing Commander Ken Llewelyn, was investigating Liz Fleming's polt-plagued brothel in Canberra in the 1996, he watched as a lighter sailed slowly across a room, lighting itself as it passed by (Chapter Four).

Mr. Toprak was also exasperated that the academics focused entirely on the fires and ignored the other strange phenomena: "We told them, but they didn't publish what we'd said." He had also told them the fires probably wouldn't happen for their cameras: "Because even we never see them start. We are at home always and nobody saw it in 300 times. It happens at our back, in another room; we smell it, then we realise. I think whatever happens doesn't want to be seen."

Though sceptics may scoff, it seems that refusing to perform for cameras is standard operating procedure for polts. This was certainly the case during the 1998 Humpty Doo episode where Tony Healy, myself, and several professional cameramen tried in vain to film the many objects that fell and flew all around us.

Comforted by faith – and a miracle

I was somewhat surprised to find that the family, rather than being emotional and disturbed, appeared quite calm – even somewhat serene – considering what they'd been through.

They had, they admitted, been very frightened at first, but, as no one had been even slightly injured, they'd slowly become used to living with the nuisance. They also found comfort in their religion: "Allah will protect us … and we had a miracle, that's why we are not scared."

The "miracle" occurred when they found a blanket covering their sleeping three-year-old son engulfed in flames a metre high. "We had only a cup of water to put on it, but when we took him out there was no injury to him – not even his clothes – nothing!"

Angel in the flames

Students of poltergeist lore will be completely unsurprised to learn that the fiery phenomena seem to be focused mainly on one particular family member – and that that person is an adolescent girl.

In this case it is the Topraks' eldest daughter, 11-year-old Melek, whose name translates as "Angel".

In case sceptics are tempted to assume that Melek must therefore be hoaxing the entire episode, I should mention that after the first fires, when Mr. Toprak sent his family away from the original house for safety, fires continued to occur when he was home alone.

It seems somewhat appropriate that this case should involve both an "angel" and a possible *djinni* because, according to Muslim tradition, God first created angels, then *djinn*, and only later, as an afterthought, human beings.

Melek (Angel) Toprak. (Healy/Cropper)

In any case, I found this young angel to be a polite, good-natured child, but with a sometimes intense manner and rather piercing eyes. She was certainly quite intelligent: her conversation and style of speech, according to the translators, "seemed far older than her actual years".

Books for burning

It seems that Melek's own guardian angel must have been kept very busy, these past few months, shielding her from serious harm.

One day she arrived at school to find that all of her books had moved from the top of her desk to the floor beneath. They were then scorched by an unexplained fire. Her teacher, Erhan Stars, later moved them to his own table, from which they promptly disappeared, only to be found smouldering under Melek's desk once again.

In another bizarre incident, Melek returned home with her favourite jacket, only to have it suddenly vanish. In the morning she was told that her teacher, while working after hours, had found it smouldering on a peg in her classroom.

When Mr. Stars searched all the children for matches he found none, and, as he later told a journalist, "These events have ruined the children psychologically. They don't listen, they don't pay attention. The whole school is affected."

In view of all the weirdness that whirls around her, Melek is remarkably calm and seemingly well-adjusted – quite different, it seems, from the troubled tween-agers at the centre of many other poltergeist episodes. She is no longer, she says, at all afraid: "At first I was scared, but now I've got used to it and I don't even feel surprised anymore." Everything that had happened was simply "the will of Allah". A little angel, indeed.

"Yes – just like here!"

When, after hearing their story, I told the Topraks about the remarkably similar Kota Bharu episode and showed them several pictures I'd taken there, their interest and excitement seemed entirely unfeigned. "Yes, yes", they kept exclaiming, "Just like here! Just like here!"

"Will it ever end?"

As I departed his weirdly beleaguered dwelling, Mr. Toprak asked me if the fires would ever end. I told him that while some such episodes run their course within a couple of weeks, others, like this one, last for months. All, however, eventually wind down and fade away. (I didn't add to his worries by mentioning the few cases where fiery persecutions have culminated in dwellings being razed to the ground).

Reasons to believe

During the long drive back to Siirt I concluded that the events being endured by the brave and stoical family constitute a genuine fire-poltergeist case.

That wasn't only because of the Topraks' quite evident honesty (plus the testimony of the Kanal 56 cameraman) but also because their story corresponded, in six significant ways, to events recorded during other well-attested fire-polt episodes:

- None of the fires spread to cause major damage, as would be expected from conventional blazes.
- Some broke out, improbably, on bare walls and ceilings.
- Objects inexplicably vanished and reappeared.
- Foodstuffs were interfered with.
- Religious ritual aggravated, rather than ameliorated, the situation.
- The invisible tormenter followed the family from house to house, and from town to town.

Fort's thoughts

In *Wild Talents* (1932), Charles Fort, a pioneering chronicler of the unexplained, discussed several cases where adolescent girls were at the centre of similar outbreaks. The common elements that intrigued him are very reminiscent of the Toprak case: the fires were always highly localised, the damage rarely spread, most took place during the day and they often broke out, improbably, on ceilings, floors and walls.

He speculated that the ability to spontaneously generate fire might be a latent human ability:

… we can think of a fire-inducing power appearing automatically in some human beings, at a time of its need in the development of human phenomena. So fire-geniuses appeared. By a genius I mean one who can't avoid knowledge of fire, because he can't help setting things afire.

Steven King's 1980 novel *Firestarter* featured a young girl with the ability to generate fire who was hunted by the U.S. military, eager to turn her unique abilities into a weapon.

Fort, too, toyed with the notion of units of adolescent female fire-starters being deployed on the battlefield:

Girls at the front – and they are discussing their usual not very profound subjects. The alarm – the enemy is advancing. Command to the poltergeist girls to concentrate … and under their chairs they stick their wads of chewing gum. A regiment bursts into flames, and the soldiers are torches …. The little poltergeist girls reach for their wads of chewing gum.

Genius or genie?

So, are the Topraks' fires the work of – to use Fort's term – a fire genius (Melek) or a genie (*djinni*)?

Some polt researchers suggest that all poltergeist phenomena, including fires, are generated by the externalised angst of adolescents via recurrent spontaneous psychokinesis (RSPK). Others believe disembodied spirits really are involved, at least in some cases. It is speculated that to intrude from the "Other Side" and mess with we hapless mortals, those mischievous spooks might need to draw strength from the seething emotions of natural mediums, usually adolescents like Melek.

But no less of an authority than Guy Lyon Playfair cheerfully admits that after many decades of research, he and his Society for Psychical Research colleagues are still far from understanding just what poltergeists are and why they engage in such seemingly pointless mischief.

So, in the weird field of poltergeist research, where uncertainty is the name of the game, I think it would be very rash to engrave any particular theory in stone.

Although many poltergeist episodes in my files don't involve adolescent girls, many others, including all three apparent fire-polt cases that I have investigated at first hand – in Malaysia, Vietnam and now Turkey – certainly do. Why this should be so is still anybody's guess, but I suppose we should, at least, be grateful that spontaneous blazes don't occur *every* time an anguished adolescent throws a hissy-fit – otherwise every second house in the world would be engulfed in flames!

APPENDIX B – WILD TALENTS

The following three stories feature individuals who could allegedly produce poltergeist-like effects at will. Charles Fort (1874–1932) coined a term for such weird and wonderful abilities: he called them "wild talents".

These tales, though too poorly documented to be included in the main body of the book, are so intriguing – not to say mind-blowing – that we can't bring ourselves to simply throw them into the "Too Weird" bin.

The first two appeared in *The Barrier Miner* (Broken Hill, NSW) on 17 and 24 May 1894.

Here they are, in their original form:

Our third "wild talents" story comes from a Mrs. Vandenborg, and was published in the *Western Mail* (Perth) on 24 February 1949. She was prompted to write to the paper after reading reports of the on-going poltergeist episode at Tarcutta, NSW (Chapter Three).

"Such a story as the above", commented the sceptical editor, "would have made Baron Munchausen turn green with envy."

While those three Australian stories aren't particularly well-documented, we know of a much more detailed foreign case which leaves little doubt that some individuals really are capable of inducing stone falls.

The story comes from the *Sunday Times*

> **THE STONE-THROWING SCARE.**
>
> TO THE EDITOR OF THE BARRIER MINER.
>
> Sir,—In writing this I thought I would be able to assist in throwing a little light on that mysterious case of stone-throwing near Sydney, mention of which appears in your paper now and again. While travelling through to Mount Brown with a variety show some little time back, I met my brother at the White Cliffs opal fields. He told me to be on the look-out while on the way to Mount Brown for a young fellow who was very clever—in fact, he was a mystery—in regard to stone-throwing. One night this man, my brother, and several others were sitting down together, when this young fellow asked one of them to fetch him a stone from outside; and when he received the stone he placed it on his hand or little finger, and all of a sudden they received a shower of stones on the roof. There was also a gun hanging up on the wall and some crockery on a table. The crockery was all smashed. During all this time the man never once left his seat. At several other times while in my brother's company at a certain hotel in that part he has made the bottles crack and shake on the shelf while he was on the other side of the counter. I could not find the man, as they told me he had gone towards Sydney. If you want further proof of this my brother is here at present, and I daresay there are others on the Hill and on the opal fields who can support my statement. In explanation of this mysterious affair, he says he can only do it as at certain times. My brother says he seems a steady young fellow and follows up station work: he was working with him at the time. My brother has just told me his old mate did go to Sydney or somewhere east about then.
>
> I am, &c.,
> J. J. CRITCHLEY.
> North Broken Hill.

> TO THE EDITOR OF THE BARRIER MINER.
>
> SIR,—With reference to the reports and correspondence which have appeared in your columns at various times, and especially with respect to Mr. J. J. Critchley's letter, which in the main I respectfully desire to support, I may state that a few years ago I was one of a rabbiting party on Taryung station, in New South Wales. One of the party was a perpetrator of deeds similar in their effects to the strange and mysterious stone-throwing, &c., of the present day. Scores of times I have known him to cause showers of stones of different sizes to descend from various heights. The falling rapidity of the stones was remarkable. As regards its changes, the tendency was toward a slow, waving nature to within a few feet of terra firma, from which point the rate of fall was greatly increased. I have often been in camp with him and other mates, when he would cause the cooking utensils on the cross rail to rock, shake, and drop violently. I have known the camp-oven to fall from above as if it were merely a hazel nut. He could cause a report as of firearms, and the stones in such instances would go whizzing past, closely resembling the noise of travelling bullets. One afternoon, in carrying into camp a plum pudding I had just cooked, the dish and its contents were hurled out of my hands by a big stone. When this occurred all of my mates, together with this strange performer, were seated within the tent. I may further add that he was considered to be of a quiet demeanor and steady habits. His father was in business in or near Sydney. Sydney. Sydney. Sydney.

(South Africa), 20 July 1980. We summarised it briefly in Chapter One. Here is the full text:

Don't mock witch doctors or you could find yourself being stoned by a poltergeist. That's the conclusion of tennis player Okkie Kellerman, 17, of Cape Town.

About the first week in July, he and a friend, Andre Wulfse, 17, travelled to Maritzburg for the Natal Open Tennis Championships when their train pulled into a siding near the city. On the platform they saw a strange-looking man in a white safari suit carrying what seemed to be a doctor's bag.

Okkie says: "I was suffering from a cold and decided to ask him how I could shake it off before the championships. It was all a bit of a joke, really. I started by asking him if he was a doctor. He replied that he was, but not the type I meant. He said he was a witch doctor.

"Andre and I laughed. Our impression was that witch doctors wore tribal dress, not Western clothes. He told us not to laugh at him. He said he did have a remedy that would fix my cold – that I should use Vicks. We laughed again. By that stage the train was pulling out and the witch doctor seemed upset at our attitude. He started wagging his finger at us. We left him standing at the station with his finger in the air."

The sequel began the next day after a practice session. "A small stone suddenly landed on my shoe", continues Okkie. "I thought I had kicked it up, but a few metres down the road a bigger stone came out of nowhere and landed next to me. I ducked behind a wall thinking someone was using me for target practice or something. I looked but couldn't see anyone – but I could hear more stones landing in the bushes all round me."

After a while the barrage ceased long enough for him to run to his lodgings. However, the

Flying Plates

FURTHER information has come to hand regarding the milking machine at Tarcutta which has been throwing off its plates. Seemingly it ceased its skylarks on January 22, and the whole matter has been referred to the Council for Scientific Research for investigation.

But in the meantime a Mrs. Vandenborg who lived near Tarcutta as a child has come forward with an amazing story. "Something very strange happened in Tarcutta," she says, "when I was 12. My brothers used to ride from our old homestead to visit a young housemaid living in the district, who had extraordinary powers. She would stand outside the door of her house, raise her hands and two large boulders would come flying out of the air, over the roof, and fall at her feet. There was no trick about this as it took four or five men to move the boulders. This housemaid would also cause cups, saucers and other china to fly through the air."

affair was far from over. Every time Okkie and Andre tried to leave the house "suddenly the stones would be all around us."

Matters came to a climax on the night of 11 July. Up until then the youths had been safe inside the house, but that night Okkie was woken by a stone dropping off his bed onto the floor. "Andre was sleeping in the same room but his bed was untouched. Meanwhile I was being pelted with stones. I woke Andre and together we collected the stones and put them on the dressing table. Then I got back into bed and put the pillow over my head just in case – but more stones kept on coming. I was scared out of my wits." After three hours of bombardment the lads could take no more and went to spend the night in their landlord's room.

The house-owner, Peter Dove, confirmed the events. "The rocks started flying virtually from the time Okkie and Andre arrived at the house and stopped only when they left."

APPENDIX C – WILD IDEAS

By Tony Healy

As mentioned in the introduction, there seems to be a very fine line between poltergeist episodes and "ordinary" ghostly hauntings. Colin Wilson and others have cited many cases where polt infestations morphed, over time, into "ordinary" hauntings, and vice versa. It seems to me that the polt phenomenon also occasionally morphs into, or at least has a lot in common with, several other kinds of strange phenomena.

So, as the poltergeist mystery, in isolation, seems so impenetrable, I think it might be useful if we widen our focus and consider some other (possibly) related phenomena – to have a bit of a look around "outside the box".

While some of the similarities I'll point out might seem rather slight, and some of the possible connections rather tenuous, I believe that in the weird, uncertain field of poltergeist research nothing that might be even vaguely relevant should be excluded from consideration.

Fishy falls

Rains of fishes have been reported regularly, since biblical times, all over the world – our files contain more than 70 Australian cases – and the reality of the phenomenon is beyond dispute. While sceptics suggest such falls are simply the result of tornadoes or of waterspouts coming ashore and dissipating, that "logical explanation" holds very little … ahem … water, for several reasons, including the following:
- The falls frequently occur hundreds of kilometres inland, sometimes in extremely arid locations, nowhere near large bodies of water.
- They sometimes occur repeatedly at exactly the same location a few minutes, a few days or even a few years apart. Between 1989 and 1994, for instance, fish fell on four separate occasions at the tiny settlement of Dunmarra, NT. In each instance, no tornado was reported anywhere in the vicinity. The nearest sizable body of water, Lake Woods, is 100 kilometres to the south. The homestead at Wellbourne Hills cattle station, near Oodnadatta, South Australia, has also experienced

- repeated fish falls – in 1977 and again in 1997.
- The terminal velocity of a naturally-falling fish (51 km/h) would be enough to kill it, but in most cases the creatures are found to be alive. So the fish, like many objects observed during polt events, seem to fall unnaturally slowly.
- Although most of the fish that fall are found to be alive, some are frozen solid. Even more remarkably, on rare occasions it has been claimed that the free-falling fish were found to be dried, or even rotten.
- They sometimes fall with pin-point accuracy into small, very well defined areas, as if dropped from a stable point directly above.
- In most cases they are found to be of a single species and sorted as to size. Debris, such as seaweed, that one might expect to find if a waterspout was responsible, is rarely, if ever, observed.
- Although most falls occur during heavy rain, some have been observed during fine, still, and even foggy weather. At 11.30 am on February 6, 1989, for instance, as Harold Degan was working outside at Rosewood, Queensland, more than 800 sardine-sized fish fell like hail onto his house and yard. There was no roaring tornado, no torrents of rain: just a light drizzle and a mild easterly breeze.
- Many rains of other creatures such as frogs, snakes and earthworms have been recorded, as have falls of hazelnuts, berries, grains and other organic matter – almost always sorted as to size and species.

While I don't claim that these freaky falls are exactly the same phenomenon, it is impossible not to notice their similarity, in some respects at least, to poltergeist events. I am far from the first to make that observation.[100]

Ball lightning

As pointed out earlier, several of the most remarkable Australian polt episodes occurred during periods of very stormy weather, so it worth mentioning that one particular type of lightning – "ball lightning" – sometimes displays what might be seen as poltergeist-like characteristics.

These floating balls of plasma have often been observed passing through solid walls. Oddly, some witnesses also describe what seems like playful, intelligent behaviour.

A Canberra lady told me that, during a severe storm, she watched from her sitting room as a glowing object the size of a tennis ball bounced along the ground below power lines at the base of Mount Ainslie. On reaching her back fence it jumped into the air, flew towards her plate-glass window, passed through it without leaving a mark, floated across the room, turned left and passed out of sight down a corridor.

---

100 Paul Cropper and Tony Healy, "It's Raining Sprats and Cods", *Fortean Times*, January 1998; John Michell and Robert J. M. Rickard, *Phenomena, A Book of Wonders*, pp. 12–15.

The only thing affected by the weird intruder was a radio situated in the corridor: it emitted a few wisps of smoke, then resumed normal operation.

Another witness observed a similar object floating rather playfully down a flooded gutter during a storm. Having gone some distance, it shot back upstream and repeated the process.

While flying through a storm on a commercial airliner, another man saw a glowing cricket-ball-sized object pass through the cockpit door and float slowly down the aisle of the passenger compartment. As it passed within inches of his elbow, he had ample time to observe it. It was a shiny, gun-metal grey, and *it looked solid,* yet the glow it threw off seemed to come from within. Even more weirdly, the man had the strong impression that *the object was just as aware of him as he was of it.*[101]

Spook lights

One of the most interesting aspects of the amazing Mayanup episode (Chapter Two) was the large number of flying lights, both large and small, that appeared in and around the Hack properties while the poltergeist phenomenon was in full swing and for some time afterwards.

The smaller type seem to resemble what are commonly referred to as Min Min lights – "spook lights" that are seen in various remote areas of Australia and other countries. Similar lights were reported during at least one other intense poltergeist event: the famous "Bell Witch" episode of Robertson, Tennessee.

Some people who have been close to them say that (like the "ball lightning" observed by the airline passenger) Min Mins seem to be aware they are being observed. Others say that, not unlike poltergeists, they engage in playful and tricky behaviour.

UFOs?

Some of the larger flying lights around the Mayanup farms – the dazzling, moon-sized ones that zoomed high into the sky, chased cars and even, supposedly, pulled one to a stop, might easily be classified as UFOs. As I don't consider myself an expert on the multi-faceted UFO phenomenon I won't follow that line of thought much further, beyond noting that some investigators consider UFOs to be intruders, not from outer space, but from other dimensions.

It is, in any case, worth noting that various poltergeist-like phenomena, including levitation, teleportation and weird electrical effects, are often mentioned in UFO reports.

---

101 Eyewitness testimony collected by Tony Healy during a ball lightning seminar at the Australian National University in 2003.

So much for phenomena that are merely strange. Now for a couple of things from even further out in left field:

The "Prankster" lends a hand

As mentioned briefly in Chapter One, our involvement in the 1998 Humpty Doo episode involved a remarkable coincidence: we were alerted to the story just as we were writing an article about the "Guyra Ghost", the Mayanup Poltergeist and other classic Australian cases for the British journal of strange phenomena, *Fortean Times*.

The timing couldn't have been better, and we jokingly suggested that our old mate, the "Cosmic Prankster" had come to our aid once again. On a couple of previous occasions, as we'd been delving deeply into, and preparing to write about other mysteries, Fate, Lady Luck – or the Prankster – decided to lend a hand by producing, just at the right time, a new and fascinating case of the type we needed. Other fortean researchers have noticed the same happy phenomenon. As mentioned earlier, another polt researcher, Wing Commander Ken Llewelyn, was also led to Humpty Doo by a very fortuitous coincidence.

Hairy and scary

By 1998 the two of us – Canberra-based Tony and Sydney-sider Paul – had been researching a wide variety of mysteries for more than 25 years.

Although we'd visited several supposedly haunted houses and maintained a file of poltergeist cases, the mysteries that most interested us were of a zoological nature. Sometimes individually and sometimes together, we'd visited scores of supposedly monster-haunted lakes and investigated reports of a whole range of strange, semi-legendary, apparently uncatchable creatures in several different countries and in every state and territory of Australia. It was occasionally scary, often frustrating – but always interesting and a great deal of fun.

One Australian zoological mystery that particularly interested us was the age-old legend of the huge, hairy, yeti-like yowie. Known by many other names, including doolagarl, yahoo and Hairy Man, the creatures feature strongly in Aboriginal lore and sightings have been reported by hundreds of non-Aborigines from the colonial era to the present day.

In our first book, *Out of the Shadows – Mystery Animals of Australia* [Ironbark/Pan Macmillan, 1994], we devoted a chapter to the yowie. By 1998 we'd collected 300 sighting reports, personally interviewed 120 eyewitnesses, and were working on a second book devoted entirely to the super-elusive Aussie ape-men.

Various theories have been put forward to explain, or explain away, the yowie phenomenon. Many people believe (and most eyewitnesses are convinced) that the creatures are real, flesh and blood animals, others suggest they are paranormal entities akin to ghosts and yet others think they might be intruders from another dimension. Sceptics, of course, dismiss the whole phenomenon as hoaxing, hallucination and the misidentification of common animals.

Whatever the creatures are, however, one thing is certain: they are part of a worldwide phenomenon. It seems that wherever in the world – the Americas, Russia, China, south-east Asia, Africa – there is a reasonable expanse of forest and a few stretches of rugged mountains, one will find similar age-old beliefs and modern-day reports of big, hairy, super-elusive ape-men.

The morphology and habits of these creatures, as reported by native people and contemporary eyewitnesses, is similar from country to country. The similarities between the yowie and North American sasquatch/bigfoot are particularly striking.

Katrina Tucker's sketch of the creature.

Just before we heard of the polt activity at Humpty Doo, Paul had conducted a telephone interview with Katrina Tucker, who claimed to have recently experienced a close encounter with a seven-foot-tall, screaming, stinking, ape-man on her Northern Territory mango farm. Although the site was hundreds of kilometres from the region most associated with yowies, she appeared to be a particularly calm, sensible lady and was, we soon learned, not the only person in the area to have seen such a creature.

So the coincidence was a "double-header": we learned of the Humpty Doo poltergeist episode not only while researching other Australian polt cases but also just as we were toying with the idea of flying 3000 kilometres up to the Territory to visit Katrina's farm. A glance at the map showed just how helpful the "Prankster" was being: the yowie site was only eight kilometres from the polt-plagued property – just around the corner by Northern Territory standards!

So we booked our flights and, during eight days in the NT, were able to document the polt activity and the yowie outbreak at virtually the same time.

If this was the only instance of mysterious, seemingly uncatchable ape-men appearing in close proximity to a poltergeist event it would rightly be dismissed as "just one of those things". There is, however, another case in our files that is quite unambiguously a dual yowie/poltergeist episode.

"A bloody big gorilla or somethin'"

George Nott told historian Martin McAdoo that as soon as he and his family moved into a long-abandoned homestead near Wilcannia in 1946, strange things began to happen. Huge five-toed footprints appeared in the home paddock, horses became seriously spooked and one night they heard what sounded like a man walking around in the loft. The "steps" were heavy: "dust was fallin' down onto the bed".

In the morning George "got up and looked in the ceiling, and there was no one up there; it was clean as a whistle. We couldn't make it out …whether it'd be a ghost or somethin'".

A couple of nights later, "the wife went to put the youngest child to bed … we heard a scream … raced in, and this big, hairy monster [was] goin' out the door … about six foot easy … tall, broad an' sort of brownish fur … all over 'im, an' standin' up like a man.

"The wife said she was just bending over the bed and this thing grabbed 'er by the back of the neck [and] seemed like it was tryin' to drag 'er. So … we reckoned that was the bloody tracks we'd been seein' … I [thought] it must've been a bloody big gorilla or somethin' [but] I've been readin' a bit about them lately … an' they're known as the 'Yowie'".

George Nott. (Courtesy Martin McAdoo)

The family retreated to an out-station but the hairy horror followed them: Mrs. Nott woke one night to find it standing over the bed. "She screamed and I woke up and followed it outside [where they could hear it] thumpin' on the ground as it was runnin', and it was bellerin' as it was going; just bellerin' like a bull'.

Later, one of the daughters saw it in broad daylight – 3 pm – on the verandah of the homestead, and as George was checking the grounds an object hit – "Bang! Against the inside of the window … but [there was no one] inside at all … two salt shakers that'd been on the table was layin' on the floor near the window".

Poltergeist-like effects also occurred at the out-station: every door in the residence was repeatedly found wide open after being securely fastened, and at times *so many pebbles showered onto the tin roof that they "sounded like a heavy shower of rain"*.[102]

This is the only instance I know of where a yowie event was so closely intertwined with what was clearly poltergeist phenomena. Many other yowie reports, however, tell of the creatures engaging in behaviours that are very reminiscent, at least, of polt activity.

---

102 Martin McAdoo (ed.), *"If Only I'd Listened To Grandpa" – Recollections Of The Old Days In The Australian Bush*, Lansdowne Press, Sydney, 1980.

Stone-throwing, wall-pounding

Most significantly, in many of the 300 or so yowie cases in our files the creatures are said to have thrown stones. While those missiles, like the ones projected by poltergeists, often come very close to people they almost never hit them, and when they do, the impact is light and harmless. In many cases also, the creatures are said to have repeatedly pounded, poltergeist-style, on the walls of remotely located houses. Strange electrical effects are sometimes mentioned.

Reactions of other animals

Another characteristic that yowies (and sasquatches for that matter) share with poltergeists is their ability to scare the living hell out of other animals. When the hairy ape-men are seen, horses either bolt or become utterly catatonic. Dogs, even savage guard or hunting dogs, wet themselves in fear or run for their lives.

Foul weather fiends

As mentioned earlier, some of our most remarkable poltergeist episodes – the Mayanup, Tarcutta, "Caressa" and Humpty Doo cases – were associated with heavy rain or electrical storms, so it is worth noting that some Aboriginal groups believe the hairy ape-men, too, are most active during stormy weather. Some white pioneers and modern-era bushmen have made the same connection.[103]

Disturbances to the natural environment

In some of our poltergeist cases it was suggested that the outbreak of strange activity was triggered by disturbances to the natural environment. In 1895, for instance, the hut at Six-Mile Flat, NSW, was bombarded only when a nearby ant bed was disturbed. Aborigines involved in the making of the "Spirit Stones" documentary about the Mayanup episode suggested that the *jannick* was stirred into action by an unprecedented amount of land-clearing.

It may, therefore, be worth mentioning that outbreaks of yowie activity have also been linked to land clearing, new roadwork, etc.

I don't want to labour the point much further, but, as the Australian yowie phenomenon is strikingly similar in almost every way to the North American sasquatch mystery, it is

---

103 Tony Healy and Paul Cropper, *The Yowie*, p. 15.

worth noting that the mysterious, apparently uncatchable American ape-men have also been linked, at times, to poltergeist phenomena, malfunctioning electrical equipment, stormy weather, road building and land clearing.

While the vast majority of people who have encountered yowies, yetis and sasquatches sincerely believe the hulking ape-men are flesh and blood, some eyewitnesses suspect they're a whole lot stranger than that: something paranormal.

Having studied the phenomenon for 45 years and having interviewed about 130 eyewitnesses I can state with some confidence that although the yowie *phenomenon* is real, the creatures themselves cannot be real in the usual sense of the word.

That leaves, as I see it, two possibilities: either the phenomenon is psychological/sociological in nature or the creatures are apparitions of some kind – semi-solid intruders from somewhere beyond our ken. This would fit with what an Aborigine once told me about yowies: "Oh yes, they're real, but you can't catch them", and with what a Miccosukee Indian of the Florida Everglades told me about the *yati wasagi* (sasquatch): "these things are part real and part not … [they] are from another dimension".[104]

Peeking through "window areas"

For many years ufologists have referred to localities that produce unusually large numbers of UFO reports as "window areas". Some of us who investigate a wider range of mysteries now use the term when referring to locations where people report encounters with several different types of strange phenomena.

Some of those "hot spots" produce a mind-boggling variety of reports: huge, uncatchable ape-men, equally uncatchable "black panthers", lake and river monsters, "little people", spook lights, UFOs, ghosts, poltergeist phenomena, strange electrical effects and other odd things.

As complicated as ABC

Such a wide variety of strange phenomena occurred there in 1955–57 that the Hack property at Mayanup (Chapter Two) might well be considered something of a "window area". So it is worth mentioning that as well as experiencing a veritable tornado of polt activity, plus Min Min lights, plus what might be termed UFO activity, the Hacks' farm was also visited by a large "black panther".

Of all Australian mystery animals, "black panthers" are the most commonly reported. Although they kill many other animals and sometimes leave clear, feline tracks, they appear to be invulnerable to bullets, traps and poison baits. The fact that identical,

---

104 Tony Healy, "Monster Safari", MS, Canberra, 1983, pp. 183–84 and 272.

apparently uncatchable, alien big cats (ABCs) are seen all over the United Kingdom and feature heavily in North American "window areas" strongly suggests that, rather than being real, flesh-and-blood animals, they are something way beyond our ken.[105]

One afternoon in 1995, Tom and Helen Hack's young daughters, Joanna and Emma, arrived home in a very excited state. That morning, they said, they were waiting at the crossroads for their school bus when they were frightened by a panther-sized black cat with a very long tail that was stalking towards them through the roadside trees along their grandfather Bill's boundary. To their relief, it turned and slunk across the road, disappearing into their great-uncle Doug's property[106].

In other words, the alien big cat – one of Australia's most notorious cryptids – walked from one notoriously poltergeist-haunted farm to another – across a road that featured in many of the UFO-type events. While it is true that "black panthers" have been reported (but never caught) in many other West Australian locations, the appearance of one right there – in the epicentre of Australia's most remarkable poltergeist site – should not go unremarked.

As we have seen, in the weirdest of all our Australian cases – the "Coalbaggie Bogey" episode of 1891/94 – the spook is said to have bragged that it could take the form of any animal it chose to. The "Bell Witch" said something very similar. In Muslim lore, also, it is said that the polt-like *djinn* can assume the form of various animals – including *black cats*.

Before leaving this odd topic I should mention one other thing. A pioneer of Australian cryptozoology, R. W. MacKay, was the first researcher to notice the apparent connection between yowies and the super-elusive big cats, both of which he believed were "something supernatural". In 1940 he wrote that "Whatever these animals are, they have something protecting them". It occurs to me that since the creatures have been implicated in the killing of many kangaroos, sheep and other animals, but few, if any, people, it might also be said that something is protecting *us* from *them*.

That, it could be pointed out, is another parallel with the polt phenomenon. Poltergeists have proven time and again that they can run rings around anyone who tries to photograph, in flight, the objects they throw, who tries to understand them or to pin them down in any way. So polts, it might be said, have something protecting them from us.

On the other hand polts, despite being, in many cases, downright malicious, almost never inflict serious physical injury on the people they harass. So, as with the alien big cats and the yowies, *something appears to be protecting us from them*... thank goodness.

---

105 Michael Williams and Rebecca Lang, *Australian Big Cats, An Unnatural History of Panthers*; Tony Healy and Paul Cropper, *Out of the Shadows, Mystery Animals of Australia*, pp. 55–97.
106 Tony Healy, interview with Tom and Helen Hack, July 2002.

Here be spooks

As mentioned earlier, Paul, like D. Scott Rogo and other knowledgeable researchers, favours the theory that most, if not all, poltergeist phenomena is generated unwittingly, via RSPK, by individuals – usually adolescents – at the centre of the episodes.

I, on the other hand, find it difficult to imagine how some of the more extreme phenomena could be generated, via RSPK, by any individual, adolescent or not. In the Mayanup/Pumphrey/Boyup Brook episode, for instance, the phenomena started on one property, then occurred simultaneously on two other farms 150 kilometres apart.

So I'm inclined to believe that at least some of the strange phenomena is orchestrated by disembodied entities, be they spirits of recently deceased people or something else entirely.

That's not to say that anguished adolescents or troubled adults don't play a role in the proceedings. Perhaps the spooks find it easier to come through from "the other side" by "feeding off" the seething emotions of a seriously unhappy person.

In a few of our cases it seems pretty obvious that spirits of recently deceased people *were* involved. The 1990 Alice Springs episode is the best example. After Irene Cronin and her brood were repeatedly pelted by grapefruit and oranges, neighbours told them that the former owner of the house, who'd died on its doorstep, had been extremely proud of his citrus trees.

The man was not only heard and felt, via the flying fruit, but was actually *seen*. When questioned about her apparently one-way conversations, four-year-old Bonnie Jean said she'd been talking to a "nice old man". Twenty-year-old Walter Cronin also saw him: walking from one room to another.

Although the strange vibes given off by thirteen-year-old Craig might have somehow facilitated the activity, I think it very likely that the other "old bloke", who died while knocking desperately on one of its walls, was largely responsible for the weird phenomena that afflicted the house at Barkley Avenue, San Remo, in 1986. It seems reasonable to suspect, also, that the chaos and fires at Granite Creek in 1935 were orchestrated by the restless spirit of the old Chinese leper. Jimmy Ah Quay certainly thought so: "I burn him; he burn me."

Other cases where spirits of the recently deceased were thought (for a while, at least) to be involved were the "Guyra Ghost" episode of 1921 and the 1998 Humpty Doo case.

Friendly – but clumsy?

But in all of those cases, except perhaps the Alice Springs episode, there seems to be no reason why the deceased should have been angry with the mortals who became the focus of the frightening phenomena. In most instances, indeed, one would have expected them to be very well disposed towards the people left behind. Why would they terrorise loving family and friends – as at Guyra and Humpty Doo – or Good Samaritan neighbours, as at San Remo and Cannibal Creek?

The best explanation I can think of is that it might sometimes be, for reasons unimaginable to the living, rather difficult for spirits to "fine tune" the physical effects they produce. At Guyra for instance, May Hodder, in trying to communicate with her beloved half-sister Minnie via some gentle knocks, might have inadvertently produced the barrage of elephantine thumps that shook the Bowen house to its foundations.

At San Remo, the "old bloke", while dying, promised to take care of his benefactor, Ron Berrell. But later, if he was attempting, via gentle tapping, to reassure Ron that he was hovering nearby, he somewhat overdid it – managing instead to scare the hell out of two entire families.

One incident that occurred at Humpty Doo might, possibly, illustrate the difficulty spirits have in "coming through" quite as they intend to. Although it seems that several other factors combined to generate the maelstrom of weirdness that occurred there, it is also possible – some might say likely – that the gruesome death of Trouy Raddatz, a good friend of the housemates, had at least something to do with it.

As detailed in Chapter One, Trouy was incinerated in a road accident just before the stones began to fall in and around the house. Words – "Car", "Fire" "Help" and "Troy" – that appeared inside the residence clearly referred to his death.

Trouy's friends refused to believe that he was responsible for the spooky messages, choosing instead to believe that a malicious spirit was playing upon their grief to torment them. It is interesting to note, however, that his own mother thought it possible he was indeed trying to communicate, however clumsily.

In mid-April 1998 she flew up to Darwin from her home in Canberra, and arrived at Humpty Doo while cameramen Jarrod Suttee and Danny Sim were still on the property.

As Danny looked on, the bereaved lady gathered some Scrabble tiles, dropped to her knees and spelt out a heartfelt message on the bathroom floor: "Is that you Trouy? It's Mum here, and everything's all right". No sooner had she finished when a shard of window glass fell through her hair to the floor. She wasn't harmed and, remarkably, the glass didn't shatter as it hit the tiles. Furthermore, as Mrs. Raddatz dissolved in tears she told Danny that, far from feeling like glass, the object had created the sensation of *fingers running through her hair.*

"It was", Danny said later, "an emotional moment for all of us … I was close to tears … it was impossible for someone to [have] set it up."[107]

Glowing hands

Invisible ghostly fingers are strange enough, but – whether they suggest spirits of the dead were at work or not – it is interesting that we have, in our Australian files, five reports of spectral *hands* being seen.

During the Mayanup/Pumphrey/Boyup Brook episode(s) young Tom Hack saw a

---

107   Ken Llewelyn, *Caressa*, pp. 134–35.

luminous green hand under the floorboards of the Smiths' cottage at "Keninup". Alf Krakouer at "Lynford Hill" and Harvey Dickson at "Eastington" also saw luminous hands – but in their case the hands were blue.[108]

Other phantom hands were reportedly seen during the extremely creepy "Coalbaggie Bogey" case of 1891–94 (Chapter Eleven) and during an episode at Adelong in 1889 (Case 12, Chapter Twelve).

An astral traveller's tale

People often suggest that if spirits are invisible, insubstantial entities, they shouldn't be able to move solid objects. So it is interesting to note that a man who, apparently, became adept at astral projection, claims to have produced a physical effect during one of his out-of-body experiences.

In his book *Journeys Out of the Body*, Robert Monroe tells of how, while astral travelling, he "visited" the home of a female business acquaintance, where he found her sitting with two teenage girls. In an attempt to prove his experience was real, he decided to pinch the woman, who reacted sharply. When they met later, she confirmed that she *had* been sitting with two girls and that she *had* felt a pinch and jumped up in alarm. She displayed two livid bruises on her side, just above the hip.[109]

Sacrilegious spooks

Finally, one aspect of polt behaviour that must surely be of significance is their violent reaction, noted repeatedly here and in other countries, to religious ritual.

Religious people might view reports of such behaviour as proof of the existence of God and of poltergeists' demonic nature, whereas sceptics will see them as evidence that the phenomenon is entirely subjective and imaginary – the product of credulous minds.

While some of our cases involved religious people, like the Stein family of Coalbaggie, who were devout Catholics, those at the centre of other good cases were distinctly non-religious. No one, for instance, could have mistaken the tough, tattooed housemates at Humpty Doo for meek god-botherers.

Although the Hacks – the owners of the first two properties infested by the Mayanup polt(s) – weren't particularly religious, and didn't summon priestly assistance, their Aboriginal employees did. Interestingly, the efforts made by the Aboriginal shamans to corral the *jannick* were just as counter-productive as exorcisms performed at other polt sites by Christian and (as detailed in Appendix A) Muslim priests: the stone falls simply intensified.

---

108   Helen Hack, p. 44.
109   Robert A. Monroe, *Journeys Out of the Body*, Corgi Books, London, 1974, pp. 59–62.

If, as sceptics might imagine, all polt phenomena is simply imagined by deluded religious people, then surely the exorcisms performed by their priests, shamans and imams would almost invariably work, whereas, in practice, they almost invariably fail – and usually aggravate the situation.

And if, as suggested by some researchers, all polt phenomena is unwittingly generated by troubled people via RSPK, then one might again expect the exorcisms to work, particularly in cases where the troubled individuals are devoutly religious.

Even some of us who think that disembodied spirits really are involved can't take much comfort from this aspect of polt behaviour. Does the fact that polts find religious ritual annoying mean that a god, or gods, angels, saints, heaven, hell, purgatory – any or all of those things – necessarily exist?

While I like to think "it ain't necessarily so", I must admit that as a believer in some kind of afterlife and in something like (to borrow a phrase popular with creationists) Intelligent Design, but who is otherwise rather agnostic, I don't know quite what to make of it.

As several of the world's religions claim to be the one true faith, and many preach wildly differing doctrines, they can't all be right. In fact most, if not all of them, must be wrong in much of what they preach. Many of them, also, have been at each other's throats through much of recorded history. So why on earth (or wherever they reside) should polts care about them at all, let alone hate them all equally – and go into such paroxysms of fury whenever a few prayers are bandied about?

To say it's all very weird would be something of an understatement …

BIBLIOGRAPHY

Baglio, Matt, *The Rite, The Making of a Modern Exorcist*, Simon and Schuster, UK, 2009.

Bayless, Raymond, *The Enigma of the Poltergeist*, Parker Publishing, West Nyack, N.Y., 1967.

Cowan, James, *Aborigine Dreaming – An introduction to the wisdom and thought of the Aboriginal traditions of Australia*, Thorsons/HarperCollins, 2002.

Carrington, Hereward and Fodor, Nandor, *The Story Of The Poltergeist Down The Centuries*, Rider and Company, London, 1953.

Clarkson, Michael, *The Poltergeist Phenomenon*, Career Press, New Jersey, 2011.

Close, Frank, *Neutrino*, Oxford University Press, 2010.

Colvin, Barrie, "The Acoustic Properties of Unexplained Rapping Sounds", *Journal of the Society for Psychical Research*, Vol 73.2 No. 899, April 2010.

Cropper, Paul and Healy, Tony, "It's Raining Sprats and Cods", *Fortean Times*, January 1998.

Cusack, Frank (ed.), *Australian Ghost Stories*, William Heinemann Ltd., Melbourne, London, 1967.

Dobie, J. Frank, *Tales of Old-Time Texas*, Little, Brown and Company, Boston, 1928.

Fort, Charles, *Wild Talents*, Ace Books, New York, 1932.

Hack, Helen, *The Mystery of the Mayanup Poltergeist*, Hesperian Press, Victoria Park, Western Australia, 2000.

Healy, Tony, "Monster Safari", MS, Canberra, 1983.

Healy, Tony and Cropper, Paul, *Out of the Shadows, Mystery Animals of Australia*, Pan Macmillan/Ironbark, Sydney, 1994.

Healy, Tony and Cropper, Paul, *The Yowie, In Search of Australia's Bigfoot*, Anomalist Books, San Antonio, 2006.

Lebling, Robert, *Legends of the Fire Spirits; Jinn and Genies from Arabia to Zanzibar*, Counterpoint, Berkley, California, 2010.

Llewelyn, Ken, *Caressa; From Call Girl to God's Child*, Sandstone Publishing, Leichhardt NSW, 2002.

McAdoo, Martin (ed.), *"If Only I'd Listened To Grandpa" – Recollections Of The Old Days In The Australian Bush*, Lansdowne Press, Sydney, 1980.

McDonald, Neil T., *The Belledoon Mysteries, An O'er True Story*, Wallaceburg News Book and Job Print, Ontario, 1905. (Princeton University copy, digitised by Google).

Manning, Mathew, *The Link*, Holt, Rinehart and Winston, New York, 1975.

Michell, John and Rickard, Robert J. M., *Phenomena, A Book of Wonders*, Thames and Hudson Ltd, London, 1977.

Monroe, Robert A., *Journeys Out of the Body*, Corgi Books, London, 1974.

Newsome, Colin, *Minnie Bowen – The Guyra Ghost*, self-published, Glen Innes, 1993.

Playfair, Guy Lyon, *This House is Haunted*, Souvenir Press, 1980.

Smith, Keith, *Supernatural 2*, Pan Macmillan, Melbourne, 1993.

Wallace, Lennie, *The Palmer Poltergeist*, Robyn's Nest Productions, 2004.

Williams, Michael and Lang, Rebecca, *Australian Big Cats, An Unnatural History of Panthers*, Strange Nation Publishing, Hazelbrook NSW, 2010.

Wilson, Colin, *Poltergeist! A Study in Destructive Haunting*, New English Library, London, 1981.

Wilson, Colin, *Beyond the Occult*, Caxton Editions, London, 1988.

INDEX

A

Aboriginal curse 28–29, 51, 83, 192
Aboriginal shamans ("clever men") 51, 56, 65–68, 75, 82, 192
Aborigines 27–29, 56–60, 64–75, 81–87, 108, 184, 191–192, 257, 293
Ackland, Richard 41
Adelaide, SA 173–174
Adelong, NSW 83, 164, 193
Agius, Andrew 9, 11–55
Agius, Jasmine 9, 11–55
Agius, Kirsty 9, 11–55
Ah Quay, Jimmy 109–112
Alice Springs, NT 132–135, 258
Anderson, Max 12, 16–21, 24, 40, 46, 53, 55
Astral Projection 102, 291
Australian Skeptics 7–8, 24–25
Avery, James 210
Azhar, Syed 263

B

Ball Lightning 281–282
Ballarat, VIC 179–180, 213
Balmain, NSW 239
Barnes, Joseph 183
Barnett, Rachelle 45
Barron, Colin 63
Barron, Gordon 65
Batchelor, NT 28–29, 51
Bateman, William 197–198
Bathurst, NSW 177–178
"Bell Witch" 165–166, 282
Bell-Smith, Eric 252
Belledoon Mysteries 49, 256
Bender, Professor Hans, 259
Bendigo, VIC 185
Berrell, Craig 115–121, 289
Berrell, Julie-Ann 115–116, 120
Berrell, Margaret 113–122
Berrell, Ron 113–122
Berridale, NSW 181–182
"Black Panthers" 287–288
Bigfoot/sasquatch 284, 286–287
Bingen, Germany 165–166
Bishop, Stephen 16, 21, 53
"Blue Jacket" 190–192, 257
Borden, WA 75, 83, 85, 253
Bowen, Minnie 29, 136–157, 257, 290
Bowen, William 136, 152
Boyup Brook WA 56, 69, 75–80, 83, 85, 88
Braidwood, NSW 205–206
Brady, Diana 153, 157
Breaden, WA 94, 98
Broken Hill, NSW 226–233, 277–278
Brown, Edward 96
Brown, George 128–130
Brown, Jan 128–130
Brunswick, VIC 219–220
Burke, Ian 181–184

Burnley, VIC 223

C

Cairns Historical Society 109, 112
Callaghan, Paul 117
Campling, Marilyn 117–122
Canberra, ACT 53, 101–107, 272, 281
Canberra Skeptics 7, 103
Cannibal Creek, QLD 53, 87, 108–112, 163, 258, 261
Cantwell, Eliza 130
"Caressa" 7, 39, 43, 53, 55, 101–107
Carrington, Hereward 2, 166
Carroll, Joseph 171
Cavanagh, Greg 30
Chifley, Ben 92–93
Choueifate, John 114, 116
Cizre, Turkey 163, 269–276
Clark, Dave 9, 11–55
Clarke, Dick 109–112
Clarkson, Michael 257
Clifton, QLD 242
Close, Frank 259
Coalbaggie, NSW 83, 158–166
Colvin, Barrie 258
Cooksey, Thomas 236
Cooktown, QLD 108, 111
Cooma, NSW 181–182
Cooyal, NSW 123–127, 150, 192, 199, 255
Cosgrove, John 155–156
"Cosmic Prankster" 15, 27, 102
Coulter, Jack 73–74, 88
Cowan, James 51
Creer, Captain 207–208
Cronin, Irene 132–135
Cronin, Val 132
Cronin, Walter 133–135, 289
Crossbow 175–176
Crucifix 12, 15, 32, 35, 43, 45, 49, 160

Cryptozoology 288
CSIRO 89, 92–93, 95, 97–99
Cunningham, William 223
Cusack, Frank 88, 157, 246

D

Darling Point, NSW 236–238, 261
Davey, Ben 141–142
De Souza, Father Stephen 11
Degan, Harold 281
"Dick the Sailor" 172
Dickson, George 75–84
Dickson, Harvey 75–83, 88
Dickson, Rose 79–80, 88
Djinn 4, 166, 204, 261–266, 269–275
Dobie, J. Frank 48
Donahue, Roy 91
Donahue, Veronica 96
Donaldson, Alan 69–70, 73–74, 84
Donaldson, Brian 70–71, 88
Donaldson, Ian 70–71
Douglas, Athol 72–73, 85
Dove, Peter 52, 279
Dunmarra, NT 280

E

Eades, Aden 60, 65, 75, 81, 253
Eades, Alf 66–68, 87
Eddy, Margaret 213
Eichorn, August 193–194
Electrical anomalies/storms 2, 53, 60, 87, 92, 95–97, 99, 104, 107, 127, 132, 134–135, 227, 232, 267–269, 281–282, 286
Elkin, A.P. 51
Elliot, Sam 112
Ellis, Jack 14–15, 32, 39
English, Father Tom 11–12, 15, 32, 53
English, Muriel 130
Enmore, NSW 202–204, 213

Erman, Professor Murat 270

F
Farrar, Tracy 44–45, 49
Fatili, Nur 264
Fires 2, 80, 109–112, 115, 160–161, 163, 169–170, 236–238, 261–269, 261–276
Fleming, Liz 7, 43, 101–107, 272
Fodor, Nandor 2, 166
Fort, Charles 275, 277
Fortean Times 15, 52, 55, 166, 259, 261, 269, 281

G
Gawler, SA 224–225
"Ghost break" 59–60
Ghost catching 67–68
Glen Innes, NSW 148–149
Glenbarra, NSW 214–215
Gorman, Clem 91
Gosford, NSW 28
Goulburn, NSW 171–172
Gowdie, Brendan 21–23, 37, 40, 55, 256
Graham, A. J. 187
Gray, Chester 95, 97–99, 100
"Greek curse" 52
Green, Lloyd 14
Greenland, C.A. 235
Grieves, Eva 202–204
Gulgong, NSW 199, 206
Guyra, NSW 15, 29, 105, 126, 136–157, 235, 240, 257
"Guyra Ghost Mystery" (Film) 154–155

H
Hack, Alex 61
Hack, Bill 59–64, 66, 69, 81, 84, 87
Hack, Doug 61–64, 67, 81–82, 86, 255
Hack, Emma 288
Hack, Ethel 56–65, 75–76, 81, 84, 86, 88
Hack, Helen 56, 60–65, 67, 69, 72, 75, 77–78, 81, 83, 86–88, 102, 253
Hack, Joanna 288
Hack, Julie 60
Hack, Kim 62
Hack, Marjory 81
Hack, Murray 63
Hack, Ron 58
Hack, Tom 83, 88
Hack, Wilton 87
Halliday, Alderman 177–178
Halligan, Don 63
Hamers, Monica 103, 106
Hamilton, Jimmy 23, 55
Hardy, Constable 145–148, 151
Hart, George 197
Haviland, C. 198
Hay, NSW 190–192
Hay, Alex 142, 147–148, 151
Hayward, H. 187
Hayward, Henry 216, 225
Hayward, Ken 65
Heggarty, J.B. 245–246
Herbert, George William 159, 166
Herbert, Julia 159
Hip Wah, Willie 109–112
Ho Chi Minh City 163, 266–269
Hodder, Clifford 152–153
Hodder, May 141–142, 152–153
Holtern, Max 73
Howell, Philip 174
Hugundra, NSW 181–184
Humpty Doo, NT 2, 11–55, 61, 68, 77, 83, 85, 87, 101–102, 110, 126, 156, 160, 165, 192, 199, 204, 211, 215, 255–256, 273

I
Irby, Ross 52

J

Jannick 65–69, 74–75, 82–84, 87
Jones, Joe 109–112
Jouva, Percifone 179

K

Kanaris, Maria 52
Kanaris, Stavros 52
Kellerman, Okkie 51, 278
Kennard, Russell 117–122
King, Steven 275
Kingstown, NSW 235
Kobold 163–164, 166
Koran 262, 265
Kota Bharu, 163, 261–265, 271, 274
Krakouer, Alf 83
Krakouer, Molly 64, 86
Kurri, NSW 130

L

Land clearing 87, 286
Lang, Rebecca 288, 294
Large, Mary 123–127
Launceston, TAS 168–70, 243
Lecouteux, Claude 166
Leichhardt, NSW 212
Lenton, Rob 72
Llewelyn, Ken 17, 19, 39, 53, 55, 101–107, 272, 294

M

McAdoo, Martin 285, 294
M'Grath, Terence 205
MacKay, R.W. 288
Maclean, NSW 197–201
Manning, Matthew 154, 157, 294
Mannum, SA 216, 225
Mayanup, WA 3, 7, 55–88, 126, 164, 167, 192, 206, 211, 251, 253, 255, 282
McCreery, Leila 76–78, 85, 88
McDonald, Joanne 182–183
McDonald, John 48
McDonald, Neil T. 49, 294
"Media Watch" 41
Melbourne, VIC 196, 219, 221–223
Meredith, John 56, 88
Michell, John 281, 294
Michie, Andrew 214–215
Mikhailova, Mme. 154, 157
Miller, Sammy 66–68
Millington, David 61
Min Min lights 40, 81–83, 112, 282
Mitchell, F. 235
Mitchellstown, VIC 217
Moncrieff, Frederick 196
Monroe, Robert 291, 294
Moolian, A. 155
Moors, H. J. 143
Morpeth, NSW 130
Morse, Roger 95, 97, 99
Mortdale, NSW 249–250
Mount Ainslie, ACT 281
Mumford, R. 96
Murder 130, 160, 166, 172, 217
Murdie, Alan 258–259
Murphy, Doug ("Murph") 9, 11–55
Murwillumbah, NSW 240–241

N

Narrabri, NSW 209–211
Naughton, B. 199
Navidad, Texas 48, 255
Neutrinos 259
Newcastle, NSW 128–131
Newsome, Colin 136, 154, 157, 294
Nicholson, Rona 62
Northern Territory Skeptics 38–39

Nurfatifa, Wan 263–265

O
O'Loughlin, Genny 134
Ozan, Soyler 270

P
Palmer River, QLD 108
Parabeena Creek, QLD 245–246, 257
Parker, J. 123, 127
Pauli, Wolfgang 259
Pearson, Richard 142
Peebles, Gillian 65
Penny, Cyril 69, 72–76, 83, 253
Penny, Lorna 74
Phantom cars 79
Phantom hands 83, 164, 290–291
Pine Mountain, QLD 175–176
Playfair, Guy Lyon 4–5, 276, 294
"Poltergeist Project" 259
Port Melbourne, VIC 221
Portors, Alexander 89–99
Potter, Simon 25, 38–39
Pumphrey, WA 56, 69–70, 74–76, 83–85, 88, 251, 253

Q
Quail, Greg 16–29, 46–48, 55

R
Raddatz, Trouy 13, 20, 31–32, 50, 290
Rendell, W.G. 236–238
Reynolds, Evangelina 237–238
Rickard, Bob 15, 294
Ridge, Sergeant 137, 139, 141, 144–145, 147–148
Roberts, William 226–233
Robson, Frank 2, 11–12, 14, 23, 41–47, 53–55, 110

Rogers, Charles 171–172
Rogo, D. Scott 256–257, 260
Rose, Carol 166
Rosenheim, Germany 259
Rosewood, QLD 281
Rosier, Bill 117
Round Mountain, NSW 241

S
Sambell, Chris 82
Sambell, Neil 82
San Remo, NSW 113–122, 258
Schmitt, Hugh 61
Schulz, Sissy 188–189
Sellersville, Pennsylvania 156
Sidek, Zulhanifa 262, 265
Siirt, Turkey 269–272, 274
Sim, Danny 16–19, 24, 40, 47
Smith, Gilbert 57–88
Smith, Jean 57–88
Smith, Keith 56, 88, 294
Society for Psychical Research 4, 98, 258, 276
Solomos, Herbert 236
Spook lights (see "Min Min lights")
Stanmore, NSW 200–201
Stanton, John 193
Stars, Erhan 274
Stein, Jacob 158–166
Stein, Peter 158–166
Stein, William 219
Stoney Creek, NSW 209–211
Storms/rainy weather (see "Electrical anomalies")
Styles, Brett 54, 126, 255
Suicide 183
Sulaiman, Zainab 261–265
Summerville, Jill 9, 11–55
Sunter, Inspector Slom 74

Sutch, John 185
Suttee, Jarrod 16, 24, 27, 40, 46–47
Sykes, George 113–122
Sykes, Susan 113–122

T
Tarcutta, NSW 89–100, 279
Taylor, Annette 14, 17, 53
Taylor, Tony 71
Taylor, Constable 142, 145, 147–148
Thermal imaging 21–23, 37, 256
Thomas, William 237–238
Thurston, Herbert 2
Thurston, L.C. 91
"Today Tonight" (Channel Seven, Sydney) 12, 15–29, 31, 37, 40, 46–50, 55
Toprak, Melek 269–276
Toprak, Zeki 269–276
Tucker, Katrina 284
Tuoi Tres News Agency 266

U
UFOs, 40 82–83, 282
Ugle, Alma 69, 74
Ugle, Kevin 69, 75
"Uncle Bobby" 77, 80, 87, 103

V
Viet Pham Quoc 266–269
Voss, Nikki 44–45, 49

W
Walker, H.J. 241
Wallace, Lennie 109, 112
Wallaceburg, Ontario 48–49, 256
Watsons Bay, NSW 207–208
Wauchope, Andrew 77
"Wellbourne Hills", SA 280
Whitton, J. L. 258

Wilcannia, NSW 285
Wilkinson, Laurence 89–100
Wilkinson, Robin 89–100
Willesee, Mike 117
Williams, Mike 288, 294
Williams, T. 240
Wilson, Colin 3, 5, 43, 78, 166, 260, 280, 294
"Window areas" 287–288
Winmar, Freddie 66–68
Winters, Irene 52
Witch doctor 51–52, 278–279
Wulfse, Andre 51–52, 278–279

Y
Yanyarrie, SA 187
Yowies 283–288

www.ingramcontent.com/pod-product-compliance
Lightning Source LLC
Chambersburg PA
CBHW081104080526
44587CB00021B/3448